Shakespeare's Elephant

in

Darkest England

Wes Jamroz

Troubadour Publications

Shakespeare's Elephant in Darkest England

Editing: *Dominique Hugon, Seth Rosenblum, Trudy Rosenblum*
Cover design: *Sandra Viscuso*

Montreal, QC, Canada

TroubadourPubs@aol.com
http://www.troubadourpublications

ISBN: 978-1-928060-03-1

Table of Contents

THE ELEPHANT

An elephant belonging to a travelling troupe had been stabled near a town where no elephant had ever been seen before.

The townsfolk were anxious to see the elephant. Some of the most curious among them, hearing of the hidden wonder, ran like fools to see if they could get a preview. When they arrived at the stable they found that there was no light. Their investigation therefore had to be carried out in the dark. As they did not even know the form or shape of the elephant they groped around in the darkness, gathering information by touching some parts of it. Each thought that he knew something, because he could feel a part. When they returned to their fellow-citizens, eager groups clustered around them. They asked about the form, the shape, and the nature of the elephant, and listened to all that was said.

The man whose hand reached an ear said: "It is a large, rough thing, wide and broad, like a rug". The one who had felt the trunk said: "I have the real facts about it. It is like a straight and hollow pipe, awful and destructive". The one who had felt its feet and legs said: "It is mighty and firm, like a pillar". The fourth man, who put his hand on its back, said that all the others were wrong, because the elephant was some kind of throne.

Each had felt one part out of many. None could form a complete picture; and of the part which each felt, they could only refer to it in terms of things they already knew. They were all sure that they were right; none of the other townspeople could understand what had happened and what the investigators had actually experienced. The result of the expedition was confusion.[1]

---

[1] This tale was included in Jalaluddin Rumi's "Mathnawi". The version quoted here has been adapted from Idries Shah's "Tales of the Dervishes" (Octagon Press, London, 1967).

***

Jalaluddin Rumi, a 13th century Persian poet, explains that this fable is used to illustrate the limitations of man's ordinary senses and faculties. In other words, there are certain experiences, which cannot be understood before more subtle faculties of the mind are developed:

> "The way of physical sense-perception is the way of asses. ... Besides these five physical senses there are five spiritual senses. Those latter are like gold, while these physical senses are like copper." (*Mathnawi, Book II, 48-9*)[2]

The elephant in the story symbolically represents a gamut of such subtle experiences. The main purpose of the traveling exhibition was to demonstrate to the people of the town their limitations and then help them gain access to these more subtle means of perception.

***

It was this kind of travelling troupe that arrived with its exhibition in the Darkest England of the late 16th century. The troupe brought an *elephant* from the farthest steppe of India. The elephant was inside a tent. The leader of the troupe was a young handsome boy. He was the son of a King from India. The purpose of their arrival was the same as that described by Jalaluddin Rumi: to expose man to impacts that stimulate subtle layers of the mind and give him a chance to reach toward experiences that go beyond emotional and intellectual reflexes.

Like in Rumi's fable, many curious and impatient visitors approached the "elephant", i.e., an unknown experience to them. The young Prince was standing nearby the tent and was observing

---

[2] "Shakespeare's Sequel to Rumi's Teaching", W. Jamroz (Troubadour Publications, 2015).

those who were trying to figure out what the elephant was. None of those visitors paid any attention to him. They did not realize that without the Prince's help they did not have any chance to experience the elephant. But there was one man among the visitors who noticed the boy. This man was a poet. Instead of rushing into the dark tent, the poet approached the boy. At that time, the poet did not know that the Prince's trip to England was arranged so he could meet him. The poet and the Prince became close friends. It was the Prince who told the poet that he was wasting his time and talent on useless activities and meaningless writings.

Later on, the poet described in his sonnets his encounters with the Prince. The sonnets are a record of the interactions between the Prince and the poet. In other words, there are two voices in the sonnets[3]. First we hear the Prince who appeals to the poet's conscience by pointing out how wasteful his life and his writing are. These pleas are included in the first sixteen sonnets. Then we hear the poet's reaction to the Prince's appeals. What follows are exchanges of arguments between the two men. For example, in Sonnet 2 the Prince addresses the poet thus:

"When forty Winters shall besiege thy brow,
And dig deep trenches in thy beauty's field,
Thy youth's proud livery so gazed on now,
Will be a totter'd weed of small worth held:
Then being asked, where all thy beauty lies,
Where all the treasure of thy lusty days;
To say within thine own deep sunken eyes,
Were an all-eating shame, and thriftless praise.
How much more praise deserv'd thy beauty's use,
If thou couldst answer this fair child of mine
Shall sum my count, and make my old excuse
Proving his beauty by succession thine.

---

[3] "Shakespeare's Sonnets or How heavy do I journey on the way", W. Jamroz (Troubadour Publications, 2014).

This were to be new made when thou art old,
And see thy blood warm when thou feel'st it cold."

In this Sonnet, the Prince tells the poet that he has an incredible potential for evolutionary growth. However, there is a time limit within which such progress may be realized. The Prince symbolically refers to this time limit as "forty winters". After living through forty idle seasons the poet will see wrinkles that will bruise his beautiful face, of which he is so proud now. The poet's face, says the Prince, will become like a rotten weed, with no value at all. Then, continues the Prince, the poet will be asked what happened to his beauty, and where are all the treasures of his youth. The poet will have to answer that he wasted it all on useless activities and worthless praises. In this context, beauty means the poet's inner being, which remains in its latent state. How much more valuable it would be, argues the Prince, to answer that his efforts led to a lasting testimony of the poet's proper use of his talent. The Prince concludes that it is this "child", i.e., immortal inner being, that will survive when the poet's body is dead. In other words, this inner "child" will make the poet a new man.

Sonnet 17 is the poet's first reaction to the Prince's appeals:

"Who will believe my verse in time to come,
If it were filled with your most high deserts?
Though yet heaven knows it is but as a tomb
Which hides your life, and shows not half your parts:
If I could write the beauty of your eyes,
And in fresh numbers number all your graces,
The age to come would say this Poet lies,
Such heavenly touches ne'er touched earthly faces.
So should my papers (yellowed with their age)
Be scorned, like old men of less truth than tongue,
And your true rights be termed a Poet's rage,
And stretched metre of an Antique song.

> But were some child of yours alive that time,
> You should live twice in it, and in my rhyme."

The poet intends to describe the Prince. He realizes, however, that if he describes the Prince, readers will not understand his verses. He will not be able to describe the Prince, his function, and his ability convincingly enough. If he attempts to describe the Prince and writes verses listing the Prince's wonderful attributes, the readers will accuse him of lying. They will say no human was ever so divine. The poet's verses will be scorned, like old men who talk too much without saying anything of substance; the poet's description of the Prince's role and his function will be dismissed as madness. The poet is afraid that his poems will be perceived as an exaggerated fantasy. He hopes, however, that his poems will be understood by some readers in the future. In this way, the Prince's teaching will be preserved.

It seems that the poet knew from the very beginning that it was going to take some time before his sonnets and his plays would be understood.

***

The Prince granted the poet many visits to the tent. Because of the *light* provided by the Prince, the poet was able to recognize gradually the nature of the *elephant*. Later on, the poet used Berowne, a character who appears in "Love's Labour's Lost", to spell out the nature of the search for the elephant:

> "As, painfully to pore upon a book
> To seek the light of truth; while truth the while
> Doth falsely blind the eyesight of his look:
> Light seeking light doth light of light beguile:
> So, ere you find where light in darkness lies,
> Your light grows dark by losing of your eyes.
> Study me how to please the eye indeed

By fixing it upon a fairer eye,
Who dazzling so, that eye shall be his heed
And give him light that it was blinded by.
Study is like the heaven's glorious sun
That will not be deep-search'd with saucy looks"
(*Love's Labour's Lost, I.1*)

The poet says that wisdom (*the light of truth*) is not learnt from a book, because truth is incomprehensible to the ordinary intellect (*falsely blind the eyesight of his look*). An inner eye (*light seeking light*) is needed, because the intellect is bewitched by truth (*doth light of light beguile*). So, before one finds where wisdom is hidden (*where light in darkness lies*), his inner eye has to transcend his ordinary faculties (*by losing of your eyes*). Therefore, the poet advises, one should approach wisdom by focusing his attention upon the guide (*by fixing it upon a fairer eye*). The guide is like a dazzling star, which the inner eye may recognize (*that eye shall be his heed*). Then, the guide will pass on hidden wisdom (*give him light that it was blinded by*). This study is, summarizes the poet, like looking at heaven's glorious sun, which cannot be penetrated by arrogant eyes (*will not be deep-search'd with saucy looks*).

Berowne's meditation is Shakespeare's condensed version of the story of "The Elephant in the Dark".

***

The poet dedicated his plays to the illustration of his encounters with the *elephant*, its essence and gradual development from an originally simple to a more advanced set of experiences. When the poet's plays were published, many investigators tried to explain the meaning of this latest description of the elephant. Each of them wanted to resolve the enigma of the elephant by reasoning it out. They did not realize that such an intellectual approach had no chance of success. The investigators tried to explain the curious and unknown to them phenomenon in the "darkness" of their ordinary reason and intellect. Such an approach was as fruitless as, for example, trying to explain quantum phenomena by using the laws of classical mechanics. None could form a complete picture, and of the part which each felt, they could only refer to it in terms of things they already knew. All imagined something, something that was fragmentary. Nevertheless, each of the group of investigators was sure that they were right.

The investigators assumed that it was enough to pay attention to the tent in which the supposed elephant was kept. They looked at the external form of the tent, at its colours and fabric. Indeed, on the outside walls of the tent there were images of some historical battles and other paintings showing various comic and tragic scenes. The investigators did not realize that these images were but shadows of the inner content of the tent. They assumed that everything that was there was displayed on the outside walls of the tent. "It would be foolish and against our scholarly consciousness", they said, "even to think about the existence of any sort of elephant". They did not know that there was a door that led to the inside of the tent.

- Some of the investigators decided that the nature of the elephant could be explained by applying to the images such fields of intellectual inquiry as psychology, psychoanalysis, structuralism, historicism, postcolonial theories, morality, pacifism, feminism, etc., etc. And there are more and more areas of scholarly expertise that are being continually invented and added to this list.

- Other groups claimed that the form of the elephant may be deduced from the images by using various stylometric and statistical methods. By using computers and sophisticated algorithms, they concluded that the tent was decorated by several designers. Then, they attempted to identify the designers of the tent.

- Some of the investigators believed that the details of the elephant's anatomy could only be understood by a very sophisticated use of tedious and secret codes supported by some fragmented pieces of ancient legends and mysteries.

- Some felt that the design of the tent was the mark of extraordinary human achievements, cognitively, aesthetically, and even spiritually. But its nature remained impenetrable to their minds.

- Some others implied that the elephant was constructed almost entirely out of the theological debate between various religious sects. Some among those insisted that the tent also contained a blueprint of political scheming or a sort of governmental propaganda.

- To others, none of these explanations was satisfactory enough. Therefore, they put forward a proposal that would discredit all the previously claimed characteristics of the elephant. They claimed that the elephant contained the biographical record of someone's life.

- Yet another group arrived on the scene. They claimed that all that was proposed so far was sheer nonsense. Only a displaced person, an immigrant, longing for his native land would be able to experience the depth of the elephant's feeling.

All these pronouncements encouraged many others to put forward their own ideas. They all argued vehemently that they themselves were the only ones able to grasp the true meaning of the elephant. These approaches have brought the discussion to such a level, that it encourages more and more argumentatively inclined citizens to put forward their own preferred liking and disliking of the idea of the elephant. And there is no indication that this dispute is going to be resolved soon. Such is the nature of the ordinary intellect that, if the word *elephant* is mentioned, it will simply perceive an elephant no matter what the reality of such an experience is.

***

In the meantime readers and theatre-goers have been enjoying the plays. Intuitively they have been recognizing in them some uncanny relevance to their lives. The plays have been inducing a thirst for some unknown but important knowledge. This thirst is probably as great at the present time as it has ever been.

***

For over 400 years or so, the keepers of the elephant have patiently been observing these amazing but predictable reactions. The keepers did intentionally provoke such a situation, because it was the most effective way to demonstrate the limitations of ordinary reason and intellect. They knew that it was going to take several hundred years before the human mind would be able to respond constructively to the administered impact of the *elephant*. There would be a time when man would realize that there must be other and more effective ways of approaching the elephant. At such a time all the previously unearthed facts and indications -excluding those that were simply products of imaginations driven by egoism, biased beliefs and convictions- would start to form a single and coherent image of the elephant. At such a time the keepers of the elephant would release some further hints, which would combine the realization of such limitations with the thirst for unknown knowledge. This would lead to a gradual understanding of such concepts as the evolution of the human mind, the relationship between microcosm and microcosm, and the relativity of time and existence. This realization would be a mark of the commencement of a new spiritual millennium.

INTRODUCTION

Within Shakespeare's plays a fascinating narrative is hidden[4]. This narrative consists of 37 chapters presented in Shakespeare's 37 plays. This means that all the plays are linked together. They are linked through a subtle signal superimposed on the plays' plots. Shakespeare refers to this signal as the "music that may not be heard". In order to discern Shakespeare's tale, the readers have to recognize and follow this non audible music. But this music occurs only occasionally and for very brief moments:

> "This music crept by me upon the waters,
> Allaying both their fury and my passion
> With its sweet air: thence I have follow'd it,
> Or it hath drawn me rather. But 'tis gone.
> No, it begins again."
> (*The Tempest, I.2*)

As long as the readers approach the plays with a set of preconceived ideas, favourite views or preferred personal opinions, this "music" remains imperceptible. In other words, the narrative is not perceptible to the rational mind or the speculative intellect. Or, as expressed by perceptive Lorenzo in "The Merchant of Venice":

> "But whilst this muddy vesture of decay
> Doth grossly close it in, we cannot hear it."
> (*The Merchant of Venice, V.1*)

The purpose of this sort of literary presentation is to give man a chance to reach towards experiences that go beyond the

---

[4] The narrative presented here has been extracted from the previously published four volumes of "Shakespeare for the Seeker" (W. Jamroz, Troubadour Publications). Such a compounded analysis has allowed the unveiling of another layer of Shakespeare's tale. From this perspective, like retracting the lens of a camera, it is possible to discern in the plays some new vistas, forms, and structures.

perceptions of the ordinary mind. Such a constructive impact is transmitted by embodying subtle layers of the human mind as characters in the plays. By becoming familiar with these illustrative mental relationships, man can learn things that otherwise would take years of observation or inner study. In this way, man is exposed to impacts that stimulate subtler layers of the mind. Such a function of the plays was indicated in an instruction attached to the First Folio, i.e., the first collection of Shakespeare's plays printed in 1623. The instruction said:

> "Read him, therefore, and again, and again. And if then you do not like him, surely you are in some manifest danger, not to understand him. And so we leave you to other of his Friends, whom if you need, can be your guides: if you need them not, you can lead yourself, and others. And such Readers we wish him."

By reading and re-reading the plays it is possible to gradually discern their inner content. However, the instruction implies that having "Friends" as guides would help to unlock the inner meaning of Shakespeare's plays. The custodians of the *elephant*, like the Indian Prince, are such Friends.

As Above So Below

Shakespeare's plays are designed in accordance with the formula "as above so below". In accordance with this formula, a more advanced structure serves as a template for a lower structure. The physical universe, the human body, the mind, spiritual matter, and spiritual essence consecutively represent substances in increasing degrees of refinement. The universe, with its stars, galaxies and planets is the dwelling place of material substances. The human body is the dwelling place of the mind. The mind is the dwelling place of spiritual matter and of essence. In other words, the physical universe is a reflection of the human mind. The discoveries of new galaxies are a projection of the development of higher states of mind, which prior to their activation were in their latent forms.

The development of mind is the focus of the most recent phase of human evolution. Evolution was directed and continues to be guided, encouraged or restrained into alignment with a universal plan. In accordance with this plan, humanity is evolving to a certain destiny. For the past ten thousand years or so, humanity has been given the possibility of conscious evolution. As a matter of fact, the future of humanity depends on this recent and more rarefied process. As part of the recent phase of evolution, the human organism is producing a new complex of inner faculties or -as referred to by Rumi- spiritual senses. These inner faculties are concerned with transcending time and existence. Sporadic and occasional bursts of telepathic or prophetic power are the initial markings of the working of these same faculties.

Evolution is executed through a succession of evolutionary energies, which were made available on the Earth at different times in the planetary history. For the purpose of a symbolic illustration of their effects, they may be described as a spectrum of seven sequential modes: constructive, vital, sensitive, conscious, creative, unitive, and supracognitive. These various modes of evolutionary energies were switched on in turn. Each mode of energy was higher in its developmental potential than the one before.

The switching-on of constructive energy led to the formation of the mineral world. This energy was needed for the development of man's physical body. This was followed by the activation of vital energy.

The vital energy triggered the development of man's physical senses. The main function of the physical senses was self-preservation.

The next mode of evolutionary energy, i.e., sensitive energy, allowed for the formation of the ordinary faculties of self, heart, and intellect. These faculties constitute man's ordinary, i.e., unrefined soul. Survival as well as the desire for and the pursuit of pleasure, ambitions, self-importance and greed are the attributes of the self faculty. Entertaining feelings of love and hatred, showing bravery or cowardice, forming an intention and carrying out a particular action are the characteristics of the heart faculty. Understanding and knowledge, the capacity to perceive, to recollect the things of the past and plan for the things of the future are the qualities that are attributed to the intellect faculty. In their ordinary form, the heart and the intellect are under the control of the self faculty. They are employed to satisfy man's physical survival, greed, and sensuality.

The next mode of evolutionary energies, i.e., conscious energy, led to the appearance of rational man with his intellect and reason. This energy is needed for the proper alignment (reformation) of man's ordinary faculties, i.e., when the intellect and the heart are able to subdue the self faculty. It was at this point that man was faced with his greatest challenge: conscious evolution.

The position of the ordinary faculties within the human body is precisely determined. Namely, the self faculty permeates the whole body, but is firmly rooted in the liver; the heart faculty is present throughout the whole body, but is firmly rooted in the physical heart; and the intellect faculty also pervades the entire body, but is firmly rooted in the brain. Duke Orsino, a character who appears in "Twelfth Night", refers to the liver, the heart, and the brain as "these sovereign thrones". He defines the outcome of the correct alignment of the manifest faculties as the appearance of "one self king":

"How will she love, when the rich golden shaft
Hath kill'd the flock of all affections else
That live in her; when liver, brain and heart,
These sovereign thrones, are all supplied, and fill'd
Her sweet perfections with one self king!"
(*Twelfth Night, I.1*)

The release of conscious energy was followed by the discharge of creative energy. Creative energy provided man with the possibility of the activation of subtle levels of the heart and the intellect faculties (purification). Sir John Falstaff in "Henry IV" gives a compelling description of the purification of the intellect and the heart faculties. In Falstaff's description, Shakespeare uses "sherris" (wine) to represents creative energy. The purification process is compared to the effect of sherris on man's inner being ("this little kingdom"):

"A good sherris sack hath a two-fold
operation in it. It ascends me into the brain;
dries me there all the foolish and dull and curdy
vapours which environ it; makes it apprehensive,
quick, forgetive, full of nimble fiery and
delectable shapes, which, delivered o'er to the
voice, the tongue, which is the birth, becomes

excellent wit. The second property of your
excellent sherris is, the warming of the blood;
which, before cold and settled, left the liver
white and pale, which is the badge of pusillanimity
and cowardice; but the sherris warms it and makes
it course from the inwards to the parts extreme:
it illumineth the face, which as a beacon gives
warning to all the rest of this little kingdom,
man, to arm; and then the vital commoners and
inland petty spirits muster me all to their captain,
the heart, who, great and puffed up with this
retinue, doth any deed of courage; and this valour
comes of sherris."
(*Henry IV, part 2, IV.3*)

Shakespeare indicates that through exposure of his ordinary faculties (the brain, the heart, and the liver) to creative energy (sherris), a gloomy man is made joyful, a cowardly man becomes brave, and an ignoramus turns into a clever one.

The unitive energy of love is the second highest energy available in the galaxy. This energy is needed to fuse together (unite) the purified layers of the intellect and the heart. The fused inner layers can then be transmuted into a new organ of perception. The organ of inner perception is sometimes referred to as the angelic soul. It allows man to perceive and function in accordance with the requirements of the Realm, i.e., beyond the ordinary space-time limitations. The organ of inner perception already existed in eternity and was required to be actualized in time. Though latent since man emerged from his primate ancestry, it is an organ of experience that has only intermittently been active in certain exceptional individuals. Man is due to inherit it one day as part of his total experience. Duke Senior in "As You Like It" refers to this organ as a precious jewel that is hidden in the head of an ugly and venomous toad:

"Which, like the toad, ugly and venomous,
Wears yet a precious jewel in his head."
(*As You Like It, II.1*)

Ordinary man is like an ugly toad who carries an incredible potential within itself.

The supracognitive energy is the highest energy available in the galaxy. It acts as the catalyst that is needed for the activation of this organ of inner perception. Shakespeare refers to the operation of supracognitive perception as "music that may not be heard". Here is the Clown's comment in "Othello":

"If you have any music that may not be heard, to't
again: but, as they say to hear music the general
does not greatly care."
(*Othello, III.1*)

Each new mode of evolutionary energies was made available while man was still struggling to come to terms with the previous ones. Therefore, modern man has been faced with the very difficult challenge of accommodating these evolutionary potentialities that were offered to him. Shakespeare's writings are designed in such a way as to help one overcome this challenge.

Structure of the mind

The physical universe is a reflection of the human mind. Therefore, the overall cosmic structure may be used to unfold the inner layers of the mind.

The Absolute emanates a cosmic matrix. The matrix contains a blue-print of the evolution of mankind. The matrix is like the DNA of the human mind. This matrix is to be absorbed, digested and then emulated. The elements of the matrix are encoded onto rays of creation that percolate through the various cosmic strata, until they reach the lowest level, i.e., the level of ordinary man. In this way ordinary man is provided with an evolutionary ladder. By climbing it, man may ascend from his ordinary, animal-like state, and reach toward the Absolute.

The level immediately below the Absolute is described as the Realm. The Realm is the top level of the evolutionary transmission chain. Below the Realm there is a multi-level structure, which consists of higher worlds, intermediate worlds, and the physical world. These worlds correspond to the various layers of the human mind.

Shakespeare inserted the story of Laban from the Book of Genesis to illustrate the operation of the evolutionary transmission chain. The story is quoted by Shylock in "The Merchant of Venice":

"When Laban and himself were compromised
That all the eanlings which were streak'd and pied
Should fall as Jacob's hire, the ewes, being rank,
In the end of autumn turned to the rams,
And, when the work of generation was
Between these woolly breeders in the act,
The skilful shepherd peel'd me certain wands,
And, in the doing of the deed of kind,
He stuck them up before the fulsome ewes,

Who then conceiving did in eanling time
Fall parti-colour'd lambs, and those were Jacob's."
(*The Merchant of Venice, I.3*)

In this story Jacob used partially peeled sticks, which he placed in front of breeding ewes. As a result, the ewes gave birth to partly-coloured eanlings. According to his contract with Laban, all partly coloured eanlings became Jacob's property. We may recognize that an Angel (in the original story Jacob was inspired by an Angel), Jacob, the conceiving ewes, and the eanlings represent the Realm and the three levels of the evolutionary transmission chain, i.e., the higher world, the intermediate world, and the physical world. The peeled sticks represent an evolutionary matrix that is projected from the Realm. In accordance with the Will of the Absolute, this particular matrix has to be implemented within the physical world, i.e., the level of ordinary man. The matrix (the chequered pattern on the peeled sticks) percolates from the Realm (the Angel) through the higher world (Jacob) and the intermediate world (the conceiving ewes) until it reaches the world of ordinary man (the eanlings). In this way, the Will of the Absolute may be actualized among ordinary men.

In this hierarchical structure man's ordinary faculties constitute the lowest world, i.e., the ordinary state of mind. The behaviour of an ordinary human being is driven by his survival needs and by the desires of his self faculty. Such undeveloped behaviour undermines and contaminates the proper functioning of the heart and the intellect. In such an underdeveloped stage, man is not able to make full use of life; it may be said that ordinary man is asleep.

Man may be "awakened" by making conscious efforts towards the activation of the subtle layers of the mind. In this way the ordinary faculties may be reformed and purified. This allows him to start to climb up the steps of the evolutionary ladder.

The first stage of the development corresponds to reformation, i.e., the proper alignment of the ordinary faculties. The reformation is a two-stage process. The first stage is achieved when the intellect faculty controls the heart and the self. The second stage requires that the intellect should control the heart, and the heart should rule over the self. The combination of these two forms of control leads to the appearance of the first step of the evolutionary ladder: man may enter into the intermediate world.

An ancient parable may be used to explain the function of the proper alignment of the ordinary faculties. In this parable the inner structure of the mind is compared to a chariot. A driver is seated in a chariot that is propelled by a horse[5]. The chariot represents the self faculty, i.e., the outward form which allows the driver to move toward its objective. The horse, which is the motive power that enables an intention to be actualized and a particular action to be carried out, represents the heart faculty. The driver represents the intellect faculty. It is the intellect faculty that, in a superior manner, perceives the purpose and possibility of the situation and makes it possible for the chariot to move forward and achieve its objective. One of the three, on its own, will be able to fulfill its limited function. However, the combined function of reaching its destination cannot be realized unless all three faculties are aligned in the right way. In "Julius Caesar", Shakespeare used the historical Roman triumvirate to illustrate the function of the reformed faculties. The triumvirate consisted of Caesar Octavius, Mark Antony and Lepidus. Octavius plays the role of the charioteer. His role is to prepare the needed developmental structure. Mark Antony illustrates an aspect of the heart faculty; Lepidus represents an aspect of the self faculty. The triumvirate, like the chariot, provided the basic arrangement needed for the initiation of the evolutionary process.

---

[5] This version of the parable has been adapted from Idries Shah's "Tales of the Dervishes" (Octagon Press, London, 1967).

The intellect and the heart faculties are not homogenous. They consist of a multi-layered inner structure. The inner structure may be unfolded, layer-by-layer, during the purification process. This may be compared to the splitting of atomic orbitals. In their natural form, the orbitals remain degenerate; but when exposed to a strong magnetic field, they may be split into several sub-levels.

These inner or subtle faculties are entangled. This means that they are intertwined with each other even though each of the subtle faculties may be exposed to different experiences. In this way the process may be greatly accelerated; reformation and purification may be performed in parallel. In "The Comedy of Errors", Shakespeare used the Antipholi twins to illustrate this part of the process. Antipholi, the twin brothers, represent two layers of the intellect. Here is how Egeon described the birth of the twins:

"she became
A joyful mother of two goodly sons;
And, which was strange, the one so like the other,
As could not be distinguish'd but by names."
(*"The Comedy of Errors"*, I.1)

Egeon's twins are entangled. This means that these two layers of the intellect are intertwined with each other even though they are exposed to different experiences by being placed in different locations, environments or time dimensions.

Uniting the subtle faculties leads to the formation of a new organ of supracognitive perception. The organ of supracognitive perception brings man to the Realm. It is then, as Pericles in "Pericles, Prince of Tyre", that man becomes "music's master":

"Sir, you are music's master."
(*"Pericles, Prince of Tyre"*, II.5)

In other words, such a man is able to play "music that may not be heard". In practical terms this means that man is able to retrace the various stages of the evolutionary transmission ladder and access the Realm. In this way he may overcome the limitations of time and space and acquire permanency. It may be said that at this point he acquires an angelic soul, i.e., "this fair child of mine" mentioned in Sonnet 2.

Evolutionary cosmic matrix

We may look at the Realm as a template of "heaven". This template may be acquired through the activation of higher states of mind. Shakespeare points out, however, that this evolutionary template, or cosmic matrix, is not static; the matrix is alive. The cosmic matrix changes in accordance with the evolutionary progress of the human mind. Each major spiritual breakthrough at the level of ordinary man is marked by a change in the cosmic matrix. Through such a gradual progress the evolutionary process is executed.

The different forms of cosmic matrices may be represented by geometrical diagrams. These diagrams are simplified illustrations of the inner structure of the mind. A triangle, a square, an octagon, and an enneagon are used to illustrate the sequence of the evolutionary progress. This sequence of geometrical diagrams forms the base on which Shakespeare's plays are built. At the first stage, an inner structure in the form of a triangle has to be developed. This corresponds to a chariot. Such a correctly aligned triangular structure allows for absorbing an impulse of evolutionary energy. In this way, the "chariot" may be transformed into an evolutionary triad, i.e., a carrier of evolutionary energy. For example, such a transformation is illustrated in "Antony and

Cleopatra" where the Roman triumvirate is changed into a triad consisting of Octavius, Mark Antony and Octavia. Octavia, Octavius' sister, represents an impulse of unitive energy. In Octavius' words, Octavia is "the cement of our love":

"... the piece of virtue, which is set
Betwixt us as the cement of our love,"
(*Antony and Cleopatra*, III.2)

This triad is a higher form of the Roman triumvirate.

During the following phase of the process, either the heart faculty or the intellect faculty is split into two subtle layers. Graphically, this may be presented as the transformation of a triangle into a square: a triad evolves into a spiritual quad. This new structure is capable of absorbing two impulses. In Shakespeare's illustration, a quad is represented by two couples who are married at the same time. This phase of the process is usually taking place during banishment, i.e., when a person is forced to abandon his or her ordinary environment and routine activities. For example, the final scene of "Two Gentlemen of Verona" illustrates the formation of a spiritual quad in a forest near Mantua. In this scene, Silvia with Valentine and Julia with Proteus form such a quad of the heart faculty. Here is Valentine's comment summarizing this event:

"One feast, one house, one mutual happiness."
(*Two Gentlemen of Verona*, V.4)

Afterwards, the square may be used to form an octagon. The octagon is formed through the superposition of two quads; one quad represents the spiritual heart; the other quad is the spiritual intellect. Symbolically, this is presented as four couples who are married at the same time. An example of such an inner structure is formed at the conclusion of "As You Like It". According to Hymen, such an octagonal inner structure is needed to hold "true contents":

"Here's eight that must take hands
To join in Hymen's bands,
If truth holds true contents."
(*As You Like It, V.4*)

The octagon represents "perfect balance". The formation of the octagon is the prerequisite for the appearance of a ninth point. In this way an enneagon is formed. The enneagon stands for "secret knowledge". The appearance of the enneagon marks the transmutation of the ordinary mind into the angelic soul. The correct developmental sequence requires achieving "perfect balance" (octagon) as a necessary step leading toward "secret knowledge" (enneagon). A scene with Scarus in "Antony and Cleopatra" is a reference to this particular sequence of the process. In this scene, Scarus, one of Antony's soldiers, shows him the wound that he received in the engagement. The wound is in the shape of the letter T; but then it changes its shape and becomes the letter H:

"I had a wound here that was like a T,
But now 'tis made an H."
(*Antony and Cleopatra, IV.7*)

Shakespeare uses a system of equivalence of numbers and letters. In this system, the letters "T" and "H" represent the number nine (enneagon) and the number eight (octagon), respectively. In accordance with the evolutionary process, the correct sequence requires the transition of "H" into "T". But Scarus' message indicates the reverse sequence. This scene, therefore, is a warning to Antony that, by abandoning Octavia, he has diverged from the evolutionary path. He cannot advance without working harmoniously within the triad with Octavius and Octavia, i.e., an intermediate form leading to the octagonal inner structure.

The ultimate goal of the process described in Shakespeare's plays is to arrive at a stage where an octagonal inner structure, either temporary or permanent, is formed. The sequence of the plays is arranged in such a way that there is a gradual progress towards a situation where the octagonal inner structure is formed, i.e., four couples are married at the same time.

Symbols

Shakespeare uses a wide range of symbols in his presentation of the evolutionary process. Numbers, places, names, situations and various characters are used as a symbolic illustration of the ordinary and the subtle faculties, impulses of the evolutionary energies, and the appearance of the various states of the human mind. It would be impossible to fully appreciate Shakespeare's plays without understanding these symbols.

Shakespeare's symbols, however, are neither static nor fixed. Shakespeare's symbols are like living creatures: they move, they change. Sometimes they mean something, other times they mean nothing, and later on they mean something different or even the opposite. Therefore, there is no such thing as a glossary of Shakespeare's symbols. The meaning of each symbol depends on the particular context. The same symbol may mean different things, depending on the situation in which it is applied.

Numbers

A set of numbers that are quoted by the Shepherd in "The Winter's Tale" is an example of such a dynamic application of symbols. When the Shepherd appears in the Bohemian forest, he makes the following comment:

"I would there were no age between sixteen and
three-and-twenty, or that youth would sleep out the
rest; for there is nothing in the between but
getting wenches with child, wronging the ancientry,
stealing, fighting!"
(*The Winter's Tale, III.3*)

In the context of "The Winter's Tale" the symbolic age "between sixteen and three-and-twenty" relates to the seven stages of an evolutionary cycle, i.e., from its initiation to its completion. The period between "16" and "17" represents the first stage. The seventh stage takes place between "22" and "23". Before the age of "16" nothing can be done. This is why the spiritual "winter" in "The Winter's Tale" lasts sixteen years. The age of "23" marks the completion of a particular cycle or a spiritual journey. In the following comment about his son, King Leontes, another character from the same play, refers to the completion of his own journey:

"Looking on the lines
Of my boy's face, methoughts I did recoil
Twenty-three years."
(*The Winter's Tale, I.2*)

The progress within a developmental cycle is not linear. There are some nonlinearities in the forms of "intervals" or "gaps". The intervals are indicated by the Shepherd as "nineteen and two-and-twenty":

"Would any but
these boiled brains of nineteen and two-and-twenty
hunt this weather? They have scared away two of my
best sheep, which I fear the wolf will sooner find
than the master."
(*The Winer's Tale, III.3*)

"The wolf" in this quote is equivalent to an unreformed self faculty that is driven by jealousy or revenge. It is such a "wolf" that interferes with the process and causes the gaps. The gaps are the most challenging stages of the process. "The Winter's Tale" is the third play of Shakespeare's Bohemian evolutionary branch; it corresponds to the first gap ("nineteen") within this branch. The second gap ("two-and-twenty") is illustrated in "Hamlet", i.e., the sixth play of the Bohemian branch.

Spiritual king

The universe is arranged according to a universal design that is based upon the principle of hierarchy. This hierarchy can be compared to the patterns observed in nature, among plants, animals, and planets. For example, the rose to the flowers bears the same relationship as the oak to the trees, or the honeybee to the insects, or the eagle to the birds, or the lion to the beasts, or the sun to other heavenly bodies. Among men a king is above his subjects. However, the notion of "king" is used in a different context than that ordinarily applied. Namely, a spiritually developed man is superior to other men. The developed man is just as much a separate species among the various kinds of men, as man is a separate species within other creatures. This is why a reigning king is often compared to a lion, an eagle, or the sun. In this symbolic language, the "king" represents the developed human being, while members of the royal court symbolize the various ordinary and subtle faculties. The concept of kingdom is used to illustrate the inner structure of the human mind.

The spiritual king, or the guide, is a discernible feature of Shakespeare's writings. Let's make it clear though: Shakespeare's guide is not a guru, a preacher, or a facilitator of rituals. He is a living exemplar of human perfection. The guide's function and his actions remain invisible to ordinary men. Depending on the environment in which he has to work, the guide's appearance may vary. In the plays, for example, he appears as a king, a queen, a husband, a wife, a rogue, a fool, a prince, a maiden, a nobleman, a bastard, a magician, a craftsman, a general, or a clown. In the sonnets, the guide appears as a young handsome man. Shakespeare does not identify his guides. He leaves it up to the audience to recognize the guides by their actions and their effect on those around them. For example, here is Viola's description of Feste, i.e., the character who represents a guide in "Twelfth Night":

> "This fellow is wise enough to play the fool;
> And to do that well craves a kind of wit:
> He must observe their mood on whom he jests,
> The quality of persons, and the time,
> And, like the haggard, cheque at every feather
> That comes before his eye. This is a practise
> As full of labour as a wise man's art
> For folly that he wisely shows is fit;
> But wise men, folly-fall'n, quite taint their wit."
> (*Twelfth Night, III.1*)

Viola observes that Feste is wise enough to be the *fool*, because it requires wisdom to do a fool's job. A fool acts wisely, while those who think that they are wise in reality are fools.

Evolutionary impulses

Shakespeare uses young men as a symbolic representation of latent subtle faculties. Young women represent the various impulses of evolutionary energies. The latent faculties may be activated by coming into contact with these impulses. A marriage, therefore, indicates a successful assimilation of a particular impulse. In this way an ordinary faculty is transmuted into its subtle form. Very often, however, the hero does not understand his situation. When he is approached by his woman, he does not recognize her. In the plays this is illustrated as the appearance of a beautiful woman who falls in love with a seemingly undeserving man. In each case, her love will have either reforming or purifying effects on him. By the same token, upon meeting her man, she also changes from an immature girl into a wise woman.

The women representing evolutionary impulses are perfect in their essence. However, their outer manifestation may be altered if they are placed in an inferior environment. It is the task of the guide to unveil their perfection.

Sometimes it may be necessary to split a higher impulse into its lower modes of the evolutionary spectrum. This happens when an impulse is sent from the higher world to the ordinary physical world. In this way the split modes may interact simultaneously with several faculties. Afterwards, the split modes are recombined when re-entering the higher world.

The various evolutionary energies were made available at different times. This is why there is a hierarchy among them. The more recent energies are subtler than the earlier ones. For example, unitive energy was released later and is higher in its evolutionary potential than creative energy. Therefore, a woman who represents an impulse of unitive energy will be presented as a younger or a taller woman than a woman representing a creative impulse. For example, Celia in "As You Like It" is described as "lesser" than her cousin Rosalind:

> "The lesser is his daughter
> The other is daughter to the banish'd duke."
> (*As You Like*, I.2)

Similarly, Helena in "A Midsummer Night's Dream" is taller than Hermia:

"And with her personage, her tall personage,
Her height, forsooth, she hath prevail'd with him."
(*A Midsummer Night's Dream, III.2*)

Shakespeare also uses a colour code to indicate the evolutionary functions of these various impulses. According to this colour code, *yellow* and *white* mark the impulses of creative energies designated for the heart faculty and the intellect faculty, respectively. While the colours *red* and *black* indicate the impulses of unitive energies targeted for the heart and the intellect, respectively.

The final stage of the process may be presented as the union of the four colours, i.e., *yellow, red, white,* and *black*. It is then that the organ of supracognitive perception may be activated. Symbolically, the formation of this organ is indicated by the appearance of the colour *green* ("Green indeed is the colour of lovers"). Shakespeare refers to the symbolism of the colour code in this seemingly meaningless exchange in "Love's Labour's Lost" between Don Adriano and Moth, his Page:

Don Adriano:

"Who was Samson's love, my dear Moth?"

Moth:

"A woman, master."

Don Adriano:

"Of what complexion?"

Moth:

"Of all the four, or the three, or the two, or one of the four."

Don Adriano:

"Tell me precisely of what complexion."

Moth:

"Of the sea-water green, sir."

Don Adriano:

"Is that one of the four complexions?"

Moth:

"As I have read, sir; and the best of them too."

Don Adriano:

"Green indeed is the colour of lovers."
(*Love's Labour's Lost, I.2*)

As a result of exposure to evolutionary energies, "all the four, or the three, or the two, or one of the four" subtle faculties may be activated. However, only when all the four subtle faculties are present, is there a possibility for their union, which leads to the appearance of "the best of them", i.e., the "green ... the colour of lovers". The colour green is equivalent to the appearance of a ninth point within the octagonal inner structure; it marks the formation of the enneagon. This means that the supracognitive energy, i.e., the highest energy that is available in the galaxy, is located within the human mind:

"Which, like the toad, ugly and venomous,
Wears yet a precious jewel in his head."
(*As You Like It, II.1*)

In "Two Gentlemen of Verona" Julia represents an impulse of creative energy (*yellow*); Silvia represents an impulse of unitive energy (*red*, auburn). Julia's comment about Silvia's portrait is a reference to their respective functions:

"Her hair is auburn, mine is perfect yellow."
(*Two Gentlemen of Verona, IV.4*)

Katharine in "Love's Labour's Lost" is a creative impulse coloured for the heart faculty (*yellow*, amber):

"Her amber hair"
(*Love's Labour's Lost, IV.3*)

Maria, in the same play, is described as "she in the white", i.e., an impulse of creative energy targeted for the intellect faculty (*white*). While Rosaline is an impulse of unitive energy designated for the intellect faculty (*black*):

"By heaven, thy love is black as ebony."
(*Love's Labour's Lost, IV.3*)

Similarly, the Black Lady of Shakespeare's sonnets represents an impulse of unitive energy:

"For I have sworn thee fair, and thought thee bright,
Who art as black as hell, as dark as night."
(*Sonnet 147, 13-14*)

The appearance of the Black Lady indicates experiences associated with the first manifestations of a purified intellect faculty. Such experiences are very challenging and confusing at first, because they lead to the realization of the limitation of ordinary knowledge and understanding. This is why such experiences are described as "tyrannous" and "cruel":

"Thou art as tyrannous, so as thou art,
As those whose beauties proudly make them cruel."
(*Sonnet 131, 1-2*)

The women representing evolutionary impulses are like rays projected from non-existence onto the physical world. Shakespeare emphasizes their non-earthly origin by making them half-orphans; their mothers do not appear in the plays. According to Shakespeare's code, none of the women who represent an evolutionary impulse has a living or known mother; unless her mother also represents one of the evolutionary impulses.

Through all the plays, Shakespeare tracks all impulses which, according to his presentation, have been released on the planet to develop the modern European society. Therefore, the persons representing evolutionary impulses are the key characters of Shakespeare's narrative (see Table on page 39). It is through the presence of these various modes of evolutionary energies that humankind is sustained. Otherwise, in accordance with the law of entropy, the physical world would cease to exist:

"the times should cease,
And threescore year would make the world away."
(*Sonnet 11, 7-8*)

Without evolutionary energies there would be only ignorance, destruction, and death. Time would end and the entire world would collapse within a single life time ("threescore year would make the world away").

Forests, Islands, and Imaginary Places

A court, a city, or a country is used to illustrate the ordinary state of mind.

An island represents an intermediate state.

An imaginary place signifies a higher state.

The first step towards the development of higher states is marked by Shakespeare as banishment. Usually it is the most perceptive aspect of a particular being that is banished, because he or she does not conform to the accepted norms or social etiquette. Banishment marks the initiation. During banishment, the hero ends up in a forest. It is usually there that the first encounter with evolutionary impulses takes place. For example, the Forest of Arden in "As You

Like It" or the forest near Mantua in "Two Gentlemen of Verona" represents such a transitory state. Here is Duke Senior's description of the Forest of Arden:

> "Now, my co-mates and brothers in exile,
> Hath not old custom made this life more sweet
> Than that of painted pomp? Are not these woods
> More free from peril than the envious court?
> Here feel we but the penalty of Adam,
> The seasons' difference, as the icy fang
> And churlish chiding of the winter's wind,
> Which, when it bites and blows upon my body,
> Even till I shrink with cold, I smile and say
> 'This is no flattery: these are counsellors
> That feelingly persuade me what I am'."
> (*As You Like It*, *II.1*)

A sea journey to an island signifies a transition from an ordinary state into an intermediary state. Such a journey is often associated with breaking away from the limitation of time. The islands of Mytilene in "Pericles, Prince of Tyre", Cyprus in "Othello", Sicily in "The Winter's Tale" and in "Much Ado About Nothing" illustrate intermediate states.

A journey to an imaginary place indicates a transition into a higher state. Such a journey is usually enforced by a violent sea storm. While in the higher state, a hero is outside of the limitations of time and space. Pentapolis in "Pericles, Prince of Tyre", Mauritania in "Othello", Messaline in "Twelfth Night", Prospero's Island in "The Tempest", and the Fairyland in "A Midsummer Night's Dream" represent higher states.

Key characters of Shakespeare's narrative

Play	Time	Branch	Key characters
Troilus and Cressida	13th century BC	Starting point	Helen
King Lear	9th century BC (est.)	Celtic	Cordelia
Coriolanus	5th century BC	Roman	Virgilia
Julius Caesar	44 BC	Roman	Calphurnia
Antony and Cleopatra	33 - 30 BC	Roman	Octavia, Fulvia
Titus Andronicus	4th century	Roman	Lavinia
Pericles, Prince of Tyre	From 9th century BC to 13th century (est.)	Modern cycle	Marina, Silent Lady
Cymbeline	1st, 9th, and 16th century	Celtic	Imogen
Macbeth	11th century	Celtic	-
Timon of Athens	4th – 7th century	Bohemian	Timandra
The Comedy of Errors	9th century	Bohemian	Luciana, Courtesan
The Winter's Tale	13th century	Bohemian/Italian	Perdita
Twelfth Night	15th century	Bohemian	Viola, Sebastian
Measure for Measure	16th century	Bohemian	Isabella, Mariana, Claudio, Kate
Hamlet	16th century	Bohemian	Ophelia, Laertes
All's Well That Ends Well	13th and 16th centuries	French	Mariana, Helena, Diana, Violenta
As You Like It	15th century	French	Phoebe, Audrey, Rosalind, Celia
Love's Labour's Lost	16th century	French	Rosaline, Maria, Princess, Katharine
Othello	14th century	Italian	Desdemona, Bianca
Much Ado	15th century	Italian	Innogen, Beatrice
The Merchant of Venice	16th century	Italian	Portia, Jessica
The Taming of the Shrew	16th century	Italian	Bianca, Katharina
Romeo and Juliet	16th century	Italian	Juliet, Rosaline
Two Gentlemen of Verona	16th century	Italian	Lady of Verona, Silvia, Julia
The Tempest	17th century	New cycle	Juno, Miranda, Claribel
King John	1199 - 1216	English	-
Richard II	1377 - 1399	English	-
Henry IV (part 1, 2)	1399 - 1413	English	-
Henry V	1413 - 1422	English	-
Henry VI (part 1, 2, 3)	1422 - 1471	English	-
Richard III	1483 - 1485	English	-
Henry VIII	1509 - 1533	English	-
The Merry Wives of Windsor	17th century	New cycle	Anne, Mistress Quickly, Mrs. Page, Mrs. Ford
A Midsummer Night's Dream	17th century	Conclusion	Titania, Hippolyta, Helena, Hermia

A BRIEF HISTORY OF HUMAN EVOLUTION

Shakespeare's narrative comprises a brief history of human evolution. Each of the plays illustrates an episode of the evolutionary process.

According to this narrative, in prehistoric times man was disconnected from the Realm. Symbolically this event is referred to as the Fall. Immediately after the Fall, a developmental methodology was revealed to man. Later on, however, this methodology was corrupted by partially developed men. Driven by their selfishness and sensuality, these men abused their extraordinary powers and the responsibility that they had been charged with. Instead of overseeing the evolutionary process, these ancient men focused their activities on pursuing inferior objectives. They started to act and behave as demigods and demigoddesses. They were interfering with the evolutionary process. This led to a corruption of the process. Once again, mankind was separated from the Realm. Othello refers to this situation as chaos:

"But I do love thee! and when I love thee not,
Chaos is come again."
(*Othello*, *III.3*)

It was this period of evolutionary chaos that is recorded in ancient myths, legends, and the so-called "mysteries".

Hellenic civilization

Shakespeare's narrative starts with the ancient Hellenic civilization. The play "Troilus and Cressida" illustrates the evolutionary chaos that occurred in ancient times. It provides an analysis of the circumstances that existed prior to the initiation of the process that led to the foundation of Western civilization. It is in this context that this play constitutes the starting point for all Shakespeare's plays. "Troilus and Cressida" is set during the Trojan War, i.e., in the 13th century BC (est.). Shakespeare selected an episode from this war to illustrate the nature of the corruption that led to the evolutionary disruption that affected the ancient world.

Troilus and Cressida

"Troilus and Cressida" symbolically illustrates the state of mind of the ancient world. This world is represented by Greece and Troy. Greece illustrates an ordinary state. The city of Troy is a degenerated form of an intermediate state. As a result of the break in the evolutionary transmission chain, the ancient world was cut-off from access to the flow of evolutionary energies. Prior to the break, the ancient world was exposed to conscious and creative energies. Conscious energy is needed to establish a correct inner hierarchy (reformation). Exposure to creative energy enables the recognition of the supreme priority (purification). The corruption of the ancient world disturbed these two conditions: the Greeks neglected the correct hierarchy, while the Trojans were driven by idolatry.

The correct operation of the human mind is based upon the principle of hierarchy. When this hierarchical principle is not respected, then the overall system starts to malfunction, becomes sick, and gradually degenerates. In "Troilus and Cressida" the inner structure of the mind is symbolically compared to the military hierarchy of the Greek troops. Ulysses, one of the characters that appear in the play, explains to the Greek commanders that the "neglection of degree" is the cause of their current sickness. He uses honeybees as an example:

"When that the general is not like the hive
To whom the foragers shall all repair,
What honey is expected?"
(*Troilus and Cressida, I.3*)

Then he further elaborates on the disastrous effects of non-compliance with hierarchical degrees:

"The heavens themselves, the planets and this centre
Observe degree, priority and place,
Insisture, course, proportion, season, form,
Office and custom, in all line of order;
And therefore is the glorious planet Sol
In noble eminence enthroned and sphered
Amidst the other; whose medicinable eye
Corrects the ill aspects of planets evil,
And posts, like the commandment of a king,
Sans cheque to good and bad: but when the planets
In evil mixture to disorder wander,
What plagues and what portents! what mutiny!
What raging of the sea! shaking of earth!
Commotion in the winds! frights, changes, horrors,
Divert and crack, rend and deracinate
The unity and married calm of states
Quite from their fixure! O, when degree is shaked,
Which is the ladder to all high designs,
Then enterprise is sick!"
(*Troilus and Cressida, I.3*)

After describing the importance of hierarchical degrees, Ulysses explains the mechanism of degeneration. If there is no respect for hierarchical degrees, there is misuse of "power". Misuse of "power" leads to the appearance of undisciplined "will", and then the "will" manifests itself as uncontrolled "appetite":

> "Then every thing includes itself in power,
> Power into will, will into appetite;
> And appetite, an universal wolf,
> So doubly seconded with will and power,
> Must make perforce an universal prey,
> And last eat up himself."
> (*Troilus and Cressida*, I.3)

Ulysses' speech is a symbolic description of the operation of the ordinary faculties. Namely, "power" refers to the heart faculty, "will" to the intellect faculty, and "appetite" to the self faculty. Hierarchical degrees are necessary for the proper functioning of the faculties, i.e., the intellect should control the heart, and the heart should control the self. If this inner hierarchy is corrupted, i.e., when "power" and "will" are driven by "appetite", the self faculty becomes a "universal wolf" that drives a man to his extinction.

The Trojans, on the other hand, misplaced their priority. Their misplaced priority is reflected in Hector's challenge to the Greek warriors:

> "If there be one among the fair'st of Greece
> That holds his honour higher than his ease,
> That seeks his praise more than he fears his peril,
> That knows his valour, and knows not his fear,
> That loves his mistress more than in confession,
> With truant vows to her own lips he loves,
> And dare avow her beauty and her worth
> In other arms than hers, - to him this challenge."
> (*Troilus and Cressida*, I.3)

Hector, the Trojan prince, offers to fight a Greek lord in single combat, with the honour of their respective mistresses as the issue. We may recognize in Hector's challenge the principle on which the future chivalric love courts will be formed. However, the "mistress" of the love courts was not an ordinary woman: she was a symbolic representation of the supreme priority. Hector's challenge, however, refers to ephemeral and earthly mistresses. It is this misplacement of priority, or idolatry, which is the main cause of Troy's disease. The mechanism that has led to the formation of idols is explained in the debate that takes place in Troy between King Priam and his sons. They dispute the pros and cons of continuing the war and the possibility of ending it by simply returning Helen to the Greeks. Hector argues that while the theft of Helen may have been a brave act, she cannot be worth the great and bloody price they are paying for keeping her:

> "Brother, she is not worth what she doth cost
> The holding."
> (*Troilus and Cressida*, II.2)

The Trojans, therefore, should give up Helen since she clearly lacks inherent value to be worth so much death. He declares that their attitude is "mad idolatry". At the end of the dispute, Hector yields and agrees to the continuation of the war. Therefore, even this most reasonable character, easily, but not surprisingly, capitulates at the end of the debate. Let's remember that Hector himself weighted equally the well-being of Troy and his earthly mistress. It is a symptomatic moment because it reaffirms the Trojans' idolatrous behaviour.

Helen, who represents an impulse of creative energy, was needed among the Greeks. Her presence was required to induce a certain impact on ordinary men. But the Trojans, like the mythological demigods and demigoddesses, interfered with the process. By taking her away from Greece, they seriously disturbed the process.

Thersites acts as Shakespeare's fool, i.e., the guiding aspect of the being. However, his role in this play is very much limited. The developmental stage of the ancient world has reached such a low level, that there is no chance for any constructive action. Therefore, Thersites can only comment on the situation and interpret it to the audience. This is his role in this play.

Thersites, whose language tends to be abusive and coarse, provides a bitter and scolding commentary on the leading aspects of Greece and Troy. Let's follow Thersites' description of the main characters of the play.

Here is his description of his master, Ajax, a famous Greek warrior:

> "I would thou didst itch from head to foot and I had the
> scratching of thee;
> I would make thee the loathsomest scab in Greece."
> (*Troilus and Cressida, II.1*)

In other words, there is no blockhead greater than Ajax.

Achilles, Homer's hero and the greatest Greek warrior, is presented as an unpleasant, ridiculous, and villainous figure. His conduct, similarly to that of other Greek heroes, is far from being honourable and valiant. Here are Thersites' comments about Achilles:

> "Would the fountain of your mind were clear again,
> that I might water an ass at it! I had rather be a
> tick in a sheep than such a valiant ignorance."
> (*Troilus and Cressida, III.3*)

Agamemnon is the Greek general. However, Thersites declares that:

"Here's Agamemnon, an honest fellow enough and one
that loves quails; but he has not so much brain as
earwax."
(*Troilus and Cressida, V.1*)

Nestor, noted for his bravery and speaking abilities, is called an old
mouse-eaten dry cheese:

"O' the t'other side, the policy of those crafty
swearing rascals, that stale old mouse-eaten dry
cheese, Nestor."
(*Troilus and Cressida, V.4*)

Even Ulysses, renowned for his cunning and resourcefulness, is
just a dog-fox:

"And that same dog-fox, Ulysses, is
not proved worthy a blackberry."
(*Troilus and Cressida, V.4*)

Troilus, a prince of Troy, is portrayed as an ass that is in love with
a whore:

"That that same young Trojan ass, that
loves the whore there, might send that Greekish
whore-masterly villain, with the sleeve, back to the
dissembling luxurious drab, of a sleeveless errand."
(*Troilus and Cressida, V.4*)

Finally, Thersites best summarizes the nature of the conflict
between the Trojans and the Greeks in his memorable phrase:

"All the argument is a whore and a cuckold."
(*Troilus and Cressida, II.3*)

In summary, "Troilus and Cressida" presents the famous Greek and Trojan characters as unheroic, violent, and lustful fools. The ancient world is presented as a being in which noble warriors turn out to be brutes, and beautiful women wanton and whorish.

Shakespeare in his plays uses the leading female characters to represent evolutionary impulses. Cressida and Helen represent such impulses of conscious and creative energies, respectively. The fact that Cressida and Helen are described as whores further emphasizes the consequences of the ancient world's separation from the transmission chain. The Trojans and the Greeks misused the available evolutionary energies. This is why Helen and Cressida are presented as empty shells devoid of their inherent values. These impulses could not induce impacts in accordance with their potential. If an impulse is placed in an inferior environment, it acquires a veil that masks its inner value. In such a form, it cannot correctly discharge its function. Unveiling requires quite a sophisticated procedure that is available only to a spiritual guide. But first, the overall environment would have to be correctly prepared.

The ancient world was disconnected from the chain of transmission. The transmission gap occurred between the Realm and the higher state. Secondly, the higher state was contaminated. This contamination was manifested by the interference of various demigods and demigoddesses into human affairs. It was this developmentally degenerated situation that was recorded in ancient myths and legends. The events recorded in Greek and Roman mythologies are symbolic illustrations of the consequences of the evolutionary failure.

At this point a new phase of the evolutionary process was initiated to remedy the situation. In accordance with the universal plan, the next phase of the evolutionary process was to be implemented in Western Europe.

Queen of Cartage

Despite the fact that humanity was cut-off from the evolutionary transmission chain, the overall development of the galaxy had to be kept in accordance with the universal plan. Regardless of whether or not humanity was ready for their effective assimilation, the next modes of evolutionary energies had to be released on the planet according to the original plan. Because of its corruption, Ancient Greece could not be used as an adequate "container" for the release of the next mode of evolutionary energy. A new infrastructure had to be built to serve as a substitute. At the top of the evolutionary hierarchy it was decided to found Rome as the receptacle for the future release of the second highest energy in the galaxy, i.e., the unitive energy of love. In order to discharge this function, Rome would first need to be reconnected to the evolutionary transmission chain. Secondly, it would have to assimilate the previously released conscious and creative energies. Shakespeare indicates that, because of the interference of ancient demigods and demigoddesses, the foundation of Rome was not correctly executed.

Shakespeare uses the story of Dido, the Queen of Cartage, to describe the circumstances leading to the foundation of Rome. The story of Dido is presented in a few episodes inserted in several of the plays. Let's follow Dido's story according to Shakespeare's account.

Dido was the daughter of a king of Tyre. According to Shakespeare's presentation, Tyre was an earthly anchor of the transmission chain and a receptacle of the evolutionary energies. The previously released impulse of creativity was misused by Ancient Greece. At the time of "Troilus and Cressida", this particular impulse was represented by Helen. Later on, widowed Dido symbolized a renewed form of that impulse. This particular energy was to be fully assimilated by Rome prior to the release of unitive energy.

After her husband was murdered, Dido escaped from Tyre and settled in Carthage. In only seven years after her exodus from Tyre, she built a successful kingdom under her rule. Aeneas, when escaping from Troy, was brought by a tempest to Carthage. Aeneas was one of the few Trojans who was not killed or enslaved when Troy fell. He was commanded by demigods to travel to the Apennine Peninsula to found Rome there. But the goddess Juno interfered with that plan. She arranged for Aeneas to be forced by a tempest to land in Cartage. He met Dido there. In "Titus Andronicus", Tamora gives an account of Dido's and Aeneas' encounter:

> "Let us sit down and mark their noise;
> And, after conflict such as was supposed
> The wandering prince and Dido once enjoy'd,
> When with a happy storm they were surprised
> And curtain'd with a counsel-keeping cave,
> We may, each wreathed in the other's arms,
> Our pastimes done, possess a golden slumber."
> (*Titus Andronicus, II.3*)

Juno and Venus used Cupid to stain the relationship between Dido and Aeneas with sensuality. Cupid disguised himself as Ascanius, Aeneas' son, and enchanted Dido by telling her stories about Aeneas' brave acts in Troy. This part of Dido's story is referred to by Queen Margaret in her conversation with King Henry VI:

> "The agent of thy foul inconstancy,
> To sit and witch me, as Ascanius did
> When he to madding Dido would unfold
> His father's acts commenced in burning Troy!
> Am I not witch'd like her? or thou not false like him?"
> (*Henry VI, part 2, III.2*)

Afterwards, Mercury forced Aeneas to abandon Carthage and to continue his journey. Mercury did not want Aeneas to stay in Carthage. Mercury reminded Aeneas that he was supposed to found Rome. Aeneas departed leaving Dido behind. Here is Lorenzo's comment in "The Merchant of Venice" referring to this event:

> "In such a night
> Stood Dido with a willow in her hand
> Upon the wild sea banks and waft her love
> To come again to Carthage."
> (*The Merchant of Venice, V.1*)

After Aeneas' departure, Dido could no longer bear to live. She asked her sister Anna to build a pyre under the pretence of burning all that reminded her of Aeneas. Here is Lucentio's comment in "The Taming of the Shrew" about this episode:

> "And now in plainness do confess to thee,
> That art to me as secret and as dear
> As Anna to the queen of Carthage was,
> Tranio, I burn, I pine, I perish, Tranio,
> If I achieve not this young modest girl."
> (*The Taming of the Shrew, I.1*)

Dido ascended the pyre, laid again on the couch which she had shared with Aeneas, and fell on a sword that Aeneas had given her. Here is Hermia's account of Dido's death inserted into "A Midsummer Night's Dream":

> "And by that fire which burn'd the Carthage queen,
> When the false Trojan under sail was seen."
> (*A Midsummer Night's Dream I.1*)

Finally, witty Mercutio in "Romeo and Juliet" summarizes the entire story of Dido:

"She had a better love to
be-rhyme her; Dido a dowdy; Cleopatra a gipsy;
Helen and Hero hildings and harlots; Thisbe a grey
eye or so, but not to the purpose."
(*Romeo and Juliet*, II.4)

Mercutio lists the ancient heroines who, according to Shakespeare's account, were either unable to discharge their evolutionary roles, or were interfering with the process. In this way Shakespeare points out that Dido was also one of those ancient heroines who were not able to discharge their evolutionary function correctly. This particular impulse of creative energy had to be transferred into another milieu.

Shakespeare indicates that the purpose of founding Rome was to short-circuit an evolutionary failure that occurred in antiquity. Aeneas' encounter with Dido was a preparatory stage. Carthage symbolically represented an intermediary stage of the process. On his way from corrupted Troy, Aeneas was supposed to marry Dido and stay with her as king of Carthage. At that time Aeneas was not ready yet to found Rome. It may be presumed that it was up to Ascanius, Aeneas' son, to continue his father's journey and to found Rome. Forced by the demigods, Aeneas abandoned Dido and went to Italy to make a new settlement there. In Italy he married Lavinia, a daughter of a king of the Latins. As a result of the demigods' interferences, the founding of Rome was not correctly executed. Rome's future was thus seriously compromised before it was even founded.

Celtic evolutionary branch

Because the conception of Rome was not correctly implemented, an alternative approach was needed to continue the process. Ancient Celtic Britain was chosen as an alternative milieu. As part of the contingency plan, an impulse of creative energy was transferred to pre-Roman Britain. Previously this impulse was represented by Dido. In pre-Roman Britain this impulse appears as Cordelia, the youngest daughter of King Lear. The appearance of this impulse led to the activation of the ancient Celtic evolutionary branch. The Celtic branch was intended as a backup plan for Rome. Shakespeare illustrates this branch in his Celtic trilogy, i.e., "King Lear", "Cymbeline", and "Macbeth". "King Lear" is the first play of the trilogy. It is set in 9th century BC (approx.) Britain.

King Lear

King Lear is the leading aspect of pre-Roman Britain. For whatever reason, this aspect has not been developed according to its potential. King Lear is used to absolute power and flattery. He does not respond well to being contradicted or challenged. King Lear wishes to maintain the power of a king while unburdening himself of the responsibility. This is illustrated in the opening scene where King Lear announces his plans concerning his kingdom:

> "Know that we have divided
> In three our kingdom: and 'tis our fast intent
> To shake all cares and business from our age;
> Conferring them on younger strengths, while we
> Unburthen'd crawl toward death."
> (*King Lear*, I.1)

Because Cordelia is his favourite daughter, King Lear intends to give her the largest part of the kingdom. King Lear expects that

Cordelia will comply with his wishes. He wants Cordelia to demonstrate openly and publicly her obedience to him. However, Cordelia's function is too advanced to be brought down to that of her father's egotistic wishes. Cordelia remains silent:

"I am sure, my love's
More richer than my tongue."
(*King Lear, I.1*)

When King Lear insists, Cordelia tries to explain to him:

"Good my lord,
You have begot me, bred me, loved me: I
Return those duties back as are right fit,
Obey you, love you, and most honour you.
Why have my sisters husbands, if they say
They love you all? Haply, when I shall wed,
That lord whose hand must take my plight shall carry
Half my love with him, half my care and duty:
Sure, I shall never marry like my sisters,
To love my father all."
(*King Lear, I.1*)

In her answer, Cordelia clearly indicates that her future husband would have half of her love; the other half of her love would be dedicated to her evolutionary duty. But Lear is incapable of realizing what Cordelia's role is, nor does he understand the situation and Cordelia's evolutionary function. Instead, he flies into a rage, disowns her and banishes her from Britain. By making this fundamental error, he sets in motion the tragic events that are illustrated in the play.

Cordelia, whose "love's more richer than my tongue", represents an impulse of creative energy. Yet, there is no man from Britain among those who court her. Cordelia's suitors are foreigners, i.e., the Duke of Burgundy and the King of France. Therefore, right from the beginning of the play, it is obvious that this particular impulse cannot be effectively assimilated within Britain. This means that it was to serve a different purpose. The entire play explains what this secondary purpose was and how it was accomplished.

The King of France, one of her suitors, knows what Cordelia's true role is. He has been sent to Britain to protect her. When King Lear disowns her and the Duke of Burgundy refuses to marry her, the King of France takes Cordelia away from Britain.

It should be noted that the action of "King Lear" takes place in the 9th century BC (est.). At that time France did not exist yet as a kingdom. The Frankish kingdom was established much later, i.e., in the 5th century AD. From the perspective of 9th century BC Britain, France is an entity that exists in the future. It is also important to notice that the relationship between the King of France and Cordelia is based on the code of chivalry and courtly love. This is reflected by the manner in which the King of France addresses Cordelia. The King of France addresses Cordelia as "queen of us, of ours, and our fair France":

"Fairest Cordelia, that art most rich, being poor;
Most choice, forsaken; and most loved, despised!
Thee and thy virtues here I seize upon:
Be it lawful I take up what's cast away.
Gods, gods! 'tis strange that from their cold'st neglect
My love should kindle to inflamed respect.
Thy dowerless daughter, king, thrown to my chance,
Is queen of us, of ours, and our fair France:
Not all the dukes of waterish Burgundy
Can buy this unprized precious maid of me.
Bid them farewell, Cordelia, though unkind:
Thou losest here, a better where to find."
(King Lear, I.1)

The King of France is a Knight of Chivalry. The Chivalric orders were established in 11th century France. This indicates that the King of France represents an aspect sent from a higher state, which operates outside the limitations of conventional time. The King was sent to Britain to protect Cordelia. The presence of "France" in 9th century BC Britain is an example of an evolutionary intervention, whereby an event within the ordinary state is induced from a higher state.

So, what is the role of Cordelia within King Lear's Britain?

Evolutionary gains may be obtained only within an intentionally created environment of friction. Such an approach may appear to be strange and contrary to ordinary human judgment. However, such an approach is allowed by the measure of freewill that man has and its consequences may not be annulled by evolutionary forces, no matter how much is at stake. All that may be done is to arrange situations that will provide additional opportunities for man to choose differently.

Such a situation is illustrated in "King Lear". Although Cordelia's death at the end of the play marked the withdrawal of this particular impulse, some constructive gains were realized within the being of Britain. Namely, the most destructive aspects of Britain were eliminated and only the constructive aspects remained on the scene at the end of the play. Among them is Edgar, a noble and honourable young man. At that time, there was no opportunity for Edgar and Cordelia to meet together. Instead, the presence of Cordelia was used to cleanse Britain from its most destabilizing aspects and prepare this being for an event which was going to be actualized sometime in the future. This particular event took place nine centuries later. It is illustrated by Shakespeare in "Cymbeline", i.e., the second play of the Celtic trilogy. First, however, let's follow the events that shaped the Roman evolutionary branch. It is there that the impulse of creative energy was transferred from Britain.

Roman evolutionary branch

After its withdrawal from Britain, the impulse of creative energy was placed within the newly founded Rome. Despite the fact that Rome was not correctly prepared for an effective assimilation of this energy, such a transfer was required by the overall evolutionary plan. There was still a chance that, through incredible efforts and determination, Rome could overcome the upcoming challenges.

The effect of creative energy on Rome is described by Shakespeare in his Roman tetralogy, i.e., "Coriolanus", "Julius Caesar", "Antony and Cleopatra" and "Titus Andronicus". In its first manifestation within Rome, the impulse of creative energy is represented by Virgilia, a character that appears in "Coriolanus".

Coriolanus

"Coriolanus" is the first play of Shakespeare's Roman tetralogy. The play is set in 5th century BC Rome. At that time Rome was in transition from a previous tyrannical monarchy into a republic, which was to be an intermediary stage toward the future Empire. Shakespeare selected this particular historical time to describe a period when man was capable of no more than minimal consciousness, yet was confronted with creativity. It is in this sense that "Coriolanus" provides a reference play for the more advanced evolutionary stages that are described in the following plays of the Roman tetralogy. This is one reason why "Coriolanus" is written in such a way as to present Rome as a relatively simplistic and unsophisticated being. The characters that appear in "Coriolanus" have not been exposed to higher evolutionary energies yet, therefore they are purposely presented as inwardly one-dimensional and unrefined.

It may further help to follow Shakespeare's narrative to notice that bread (grains, corn), gold, and wine are used as symbols to mark the effect of the most recent modes of evolutionary energies. All three of these substances are obtained through processes which require a consecutively more refined extraction. Grains are harvested; gold is extracted from the ore; wine is a product of fermentation. In this symbolic presentation bread, gold, and wine represent the effect of conscious, creative and unitive energies, respectively.

The opening scene of the play describes riots on the streets of Rome. The Republic of Rome is faced with a shortage of corn. The riots started after stores of corn were withheld from ordinary citizens. In this way Shakespeare points out that 5th century BC Rome was not capable of using conscious energy correctly. Conscious energy was needed to form an adequate hierarchical inner structure. Without such a structure, Rome was not ready for the next phase of the evolutionary process.

This is further explained by Menenius, a Roman patrician, in his parable about the stomach. Menenius explains to the plebeians the importance of a correct hierarchical structure for the proper functioning of the city. In Menenius' parable, the stomach describes its function in the following way:

> "I receive the general food at first,
> Which you do live upon; and fit it is,
> Because I am the store-house and the shop
> Of the whole body: but, if you do remember,
> I send it through the rivers of your blood,
> Even to the court, the heart, to the seat o' the brain;
> And, through the cranks and offices of man,
> The strongest nerves and small inferior veins
> From me receive that natural competency

Whereby they live.
(*Coriolanus, I.1*)

Menenius explains that the Roman Senate, like the stomach, serves as a storehouse and a collecting-place for nutrients and then dispenses those nutrients throughout the rest of the body. Then he spells out what the role of the plebeians is:

"You, the great toe of this assembly."
(*Coriolanus, I.1*)

The stomach's parable is used here to illustrate the current evolutionary state of Rome. Rome is capable of no more than minimal consciousness, yet it is confronted with creativity. In order to benefit fully from this new kind of evolutionary "food", a properly functioning digestive system needs to be developed. As long as Rome is incapable of properly distributing and digesting "corn" it will suffer from a developmental indigestion which will disturb its correct growth.

The impulse of creative energy is symbolically illustrated by Virgilia. Virgilia is the most gentle of all the characters. She is the current projection of Cordelia. Like Cordelia whose "love's more richer than my tongue", Virgilia distinguishes herself by being ... eloquently silent. In this way Shakespeare indicates that at the time of "Coriolanus" this impulse was made available to Rome, but was not yet fully assimilated. This impulse was implanted within Rome before the city was properly prepared for it. This resulted in the development of an outgrown heart faculty. The heart faculty is represented by Caius Martius, Virgilia's husband. Caius Martius is a brave general, fearsome in battle, and extremely honourable. However, he is overly proud, inflexible, and stubborn. These features, combined with a fierce contempt for the plebeians make him an incongruent aspect of Rome. Despite his unquestionable military skills and abilities there is no place for him among the Romans. In fact there is no adequate environment or mechanism to properly harness the skills that have been endowed in this particular aspect of Rome. One may suppose that Caius Marius was prematurely exposed to the creative energy. This led to his deformed growth. Menenius compares Caius Martius to a cumbersome dragon evolved from an ordinary man:

"There is differency between a grub and a butterfly;
yet your butterfly was a grub. This Marcius is grown
from man to dragon: he has wings; he's more than a
creeping thing."
(*Coriolanus, V.4*)

The current situation of Rome is further explained by the stomach's parable. In this parable, the other members of the body rebel against the stomach. The being cannot function efficiently with such a governing arrangement. Rome may be described as an upside down city:

"That is the way to lay the city flat;
To bring the roof to the foundation,
And bury all, which yet distinctly ranges,
In heaps and piles of ruin."
(*Coriolanus, III.1*)

The shortages of corn are an indication that the previously released conscious energy was not correctly assimilated. There is no indication that the Rome of "Coriolanus" would be able to make any evolutionary progress. Yet, some five centuries later, Rome became the centre of an empire stretching from Britain to North Africa and from Spain to Persia. This would indicate that something significant took place in Rome between the 5th and the 1st centuries BC. This "something" greatly enhanced the evolutionary potential of Rome.

It may be presumed that sometime between the 5th century and the 1st century BC Rome was exposed to a significant evolutionary event. Shakespeare would not allude to such a possibility without explaining it in greater detail. We find those details described in "Julius Caesar".

Julius Caesar

"Julius Caesar" is the second play of the Roman tetralogy. Shakespeare uses the historical figure of Julius Caesar to symbolically illustrate a spiritual guide. Julius Caesar is charged with the incredibly difficult task of facilitating the utilization of the newly released unitive energy of love. Despite the fact that Rome is not ready, the cosmic plan required the release of unitive energy on the planet at that time. Julius Caesar directs this particular phase of the evolutionary process.

Rome can benefit from the presence of this spiritual king only if the Romans are capable of recognizing his role and his function. However, the Romans are not capable of comprehending the need for such a king. Based on their experiences from the past, they associate the concept of "king" with its ordinary and corrupted form. For them, "king" means tyranny, therefore a king is the enemy of the people. The king should not be allowed to exercise power; quite the contrary, he should be eliminated in order to preserve the welfare of the Republic.

It should be emphasized that Caesar never explicitly says that he is the king. Quite the contrary, he refuses the crown in a dramatic public display. Moreover, on several occasions Caesar makes sure that his companions realize that he is a mortal creature. At the same time, however, Caesar says things that point out that he is special and superior to other mortals. In his own words he refers to himself as "the northern star":

"But I am constant as the northern star,
Of whose true-fix'd and resting quality
There is no fellow in the firmament.
The skies are painted with unnumber'd sparks,
They are all fire and every one doth shine,
But there's but one in all doth hold his place:
So in the world; 'tis furnish'd well with men,
And men are flesh and blood, and apprehensive;
Yet in the number I do know but one
That unassailable holds on his rank,
Unshaked of motion."
(*Julius Caesar, III.1*)

Shakespeare, by comparing Caesar to the northern star, clearly defines his position within the spiritual hierarchy. The northern star is unique in its fixedness. It is the only star that never changes its position in the sky. It is the star by which sailors have navigated since ancient times; it is the star that guides them in their voyages. Such a description corresponds to a highly developed man.

The current state of Rome is such that it is incapable of absorbing the newly released impulse of evolutionary energy. Such incapacity is further indicated in the episode in which Caesar asks some priests to carry out an animal sacrifice to find out what the current state of Rome is. The priests perform the sacrifice and they find out that:

"Plucking the entrails of an offering forth,
They could not find a heart within the beast."
(*Julius Caesar, II.2*)

In other words, Rome is like a beast without a spiritual "heart". Rome's inner structure has not been correctly developed yet. There is no adequate container to hold the newly released spiritual charge.

Calphurnia, Julius Caesar's wife represents the current manifestation of creative energy. She is a spiritual heir of Virgilia from "Coriolanus". The appearance of Julius Caesar allowed for the assimilation of creativity. In this way the process was greatly accelerated. Shakespeare has inserted an episode with Calphurnia that further clarifies the spiritual state of Rome. In this episode, Caesar asks Mark Antony to "touch" Calphurnia when running in the race:

> "Forget not, in your speed, Antonius,
> To touch Calpurnia; for our elders say,
> The barren, touched in this holy chase,
> Shake off their sterile curse."
> (*Julius Caesar, I.2*)

The term "barren" in the quote does not apply to Calphurnia. "The barren" means the Roman spiritual heart. Antony represents an aspect of this faculty. He is the current manifestation of that aspect that was represented by Caius Martius in "Coriolanus". Caesar points out that Antony might be awakened through a "touch" of creativity. While taking part in "this holy chase", Antony might be able to "shake off their sterile curse" of the Roman heart by absorbing creative energy. This episode explains the function of the spiritual triad which, later on, was brought to Europe by the Troubadours. The Roman triad consists of Julius Caesar, Antony, and Calphurnia, i.e., a guide, a disciple, and an impulse of evolutionary energy, respectively. However, Calphurnia is not a maid, but a married woman. Therefore, this impulse is out of Antony's reach. Such a ménage à trois symbolizes a sterile triad; it represents a certain potential. By properly serving the king and through the "touch" of the lady, the disciple may remove his sterility. And this is the current function of this particular form of the Roman triad.

Rome, however, rejected the presence of the spiritual king. This particular Roman triad was destroyed. This is illustrated by the assassination of Julius Caesar. Such a rejection is allowed by the measure of freewill that Rome has. Nevertheless, this rejection disturbed the overall cosmic plan. This was the reason why Rome was plagued with violent weather and a variety of bad omens and portents, the walking dead, and lions stalking through the city. Horatio in "Hamlet" gives a vivid description of this very night:

"In the most high and palmy state of Rome,
A little ere the mightiest Julius fell,
The graves stood tenantless and the sheeted dead
Did squeak and gibber in the Roman streets:
As stars with trains of fire and dews of blood,
Disasters in the sun; and the moist star
Upon whose influence Neptune's empire stands
Was sick almost to doomsday with eclipse."
(*Hamlet, I.1*)

In Antony's words, it was the fall that affected all:

"great Caesar fell.
O, what a fall was there, my countrymen!
Then I, and you, and all of us fell down."
(*Julius Caesar, III.2*)

By rejecting the spiritual king, Rome demonstrated that it was not ready for the assimilation of unitive energy. The process had to be delayed.

The unitive energy was released on the planet, but mankind was not able to benefit from it. The impulse of unitive energy had to remain dormant. Shakespeare used Octavia to symbolically represent this impulse. Octavia is the sister of Octavius, the adopted son of Julius Caesar. Octavia appears in "Antony and Cleopatra", i.e., in the third play of Shakespeare's Roman tetralogy.

Antony and Cleopatra

A proper inner hierarchy was needed before Rome could be ready to absorb the available evolutionary energies. A proper hierarchy means the proper alignment of the ordinary faculties, i.e., where the intellect controls the heart and the heart rules over the self faculty. Shakespeare used the historical triumvirate to illustrate the operation of a reformed inner being. The triumvirate, like the ancient chariot, provides the basic arrangement needed for the effective assimilation of an evolutionary impulse.

Octavius is Julius Caesar's adopted son and his spiritual successor. He arrives on the scene immediately after Caesar's assassination. His role is to prepare the developmental structure that will allow for a delayed assimilation of unitive energy. Upon his arrival in Rome, Octavius forms a triumvirate with Antony and Lepidus. Octavius plays the role of the charioteer. Lepidus represents an aspect of the self faculty. Antony represents an aspect of the heart faculty. Through Calphurnia's "touch", Antony was prepared for exposure to creativity. At the time of "Antony and Cleopatra", Antony had absorbed an initial impact of creativity. In the play this is marked by his marriage with Fulvia. Fulvia represents the current manifestation of creative energy. Such a transition from the correctly aligned "chariot" (Octavius, Antony, Lepidus) into a triad (Octavius, Antony, Fulvia) corresponds to an initiation. Graphically, this is represented by a six pointed star formed by the superposition of two equilateral triangles. This is why the six pointed star may be used to represent an "opening", i.e., a spiritual initiation.

Antony, however, is still affected by the spiritual inadequacies of Rome. He does not understand the overall function and his role within the triumvirate. He attempts to control Octavius and in so doing corrupts the proper operation of the evolutionary triad. Instead of working together with Octavius, he leaves Fulvia and goes to Egypt to spend time with Cleopatra. Antony's attraction to

Cleopatra diminishes the effect of creativity. In the play this is symbolically marked by the death of Fulvia. Antony's behaviour is a sign of the reoccurrence of the tendencies that appeared at the time of "Coriolanus". At that time this sort of inadequacy was manifested by the erratic behaviour of Caius Martius.

There was still a chance to advance the process. Rome could have overcome its previous errors by forming an active triad capable of absorbing an impulse of unitive energy, i.e., a higher mode of evolutionary spectrum. Such an active triad could have been formed by bringing together Octavius, Antony, and Octavia. Octavius initiates and directs the preparation for such a triad. This step of the process requires Antony to marry Octavia. The marriage of Antony and Octavia is followed by a wine drinking party. Wine is used to symbolize the effect of unitive energy. The effect of "wine" is a test of Antony's ability to effectively absorb the unitive energy.

Antony is having difficulties with the effect of "wine". When Octavius interrupts the wine drinking festivities to remind Antony that there is more serious business to be done, Antony's answer is a most telling description of his inner state:

> "be a child o'th' time."
> (*Antony and Cleopatra, II.7*)

Antony tries to persuade Octavius to forget his duty and he urges his men to drink until they reach complete lethargy:

> "Come, let's all take hands,
> Till that the conquering wine hath steep'd our sense
> In soft and delicate Lethe."
> (*Antony and Cleopatra, II.7*)

In this particular context, "soft and delicate Lethe" indicates spiritual intoxication. The main purpose of the availability of such experience is not enjoyment but gaining capacity for carrying on additional responsibilities. However, Antony prefers to enjoy the moment. He neglects his duties in order to enjoy his "drunkenness". His tendency to live for the moment, with little regard for the overall process, is one of the factors of his failure. After the party, Antony abandons Octavia and returns to Egypt. At this point the Roman triad collapses. The impulse of unitive energy is withdrawn from Rome. After the withdrawal of unitive energy, Rome's evolutionary function is nullified. Rome is left to its disintegration.

Rome was not able to discharge its intended function. The outcome of Rome's failure is summarized by Shakespeare in "Titus Andronicus", the last play of the Roman tetralogy.

Titus Andronicus

Rome in the 4th century AD, i.e., at the time of "Titus Andronicus", was pretty much in a degenerated state. The leading aspects of this being were either ignorant, corrupted or under the influence of destructive elements. The modus operandi of Rome was cruelty and revenge.

"Titus Andronicus" is by far Shakespeare's bloodiest play. It has even been suggested by a group of scholars that, due to the "un-Shakespearean barbarity" of the play, Shakespeare did not write it at all. By now, we may realize that Shakespeare's plays depict a series of events that reflect the evolutionary process. Therefore, their meaning cannot be unfolded by using such conventional moral or psychological norms. Ordinary social, emotional or intellectual criteria do not apply to the interpretation of the evolutionary process.

The cruelty of the destructive forces corresponds to the spiritual state of the particular being. The more degenerate a being the crueller are the forces that are attached to it. At the time of "Coriolanus", it was Brutus, a tribune, who led the plebeians to revolt against Coriolanus. Then it was Cassius in "Julius Caesar", who was the leader of Caesar's assassins. In "Antony and Cleopatra", Cleopatra played the destructive role. Now it is Aaron, who represents the destructive agent that is attached to Rome. However, there is no comparison between the degree of cruelty exercised by Aaron and the behaviour of his predecessors. Shakespeare emphasizes this point by purposely making the play his bloodiest: "Titus Andronicus" is a play with 14 killings, 6 severed members, 1 rape, 1 live burial and 1 case of cannibalism.

It should be noted though, that Aaron committed his greatest misdeeds just before he was buried chest-deep and left to die of thirst and starvation. He managed to save his new born child in exchange for disclosing to Lucius all the horrors that he had committed. In this way Aaron was able to preserve his roots within Rome. By preserving the life of his child, Aaron re-implanted on the European continent a seed of destruction. This seed will grow to its malignant form. Its fruit will reappear at the inception of the most recent evolutionary cycle.

At the time of "Titus Andronicus", Lavinia represents the impulse of creative energy that has been embedded within Rome. In accordance with the developmental methodology, Rome has been exposed to or coated with creative energy several times. This particular impulse of creative energy was previously represented by Virgilia in "Coriolanus", Calphurnia in "Julius Caesar", and Fulvia in "Antony and Cleopatra". Yet, this impulse has not been fully assimilated. It has not had a chance to fulfill its developmental potential within the Roman evolutionary branch. At the end of "Titus Andronicus", it is deactivated. This is symbolically illustrated as Lavinia's brutal rape followed by her death. Afterwards, this particular impulse was withdrawn from the ordinary state. It was transferred onto the intermediate state of Mytilene, which was activated at that time. The period that followed the events described in "Titus Andronicus" is known in the history of Europe as the Dark Ages. This was a period of disorder among events, confusion among men, processes without design, humanity without direction.

"Titus Andronicus" concludes the Roman Plays. By describing the Roman cycle in four plays, Shakespeare points out that the cycle did not come to its completion. The Roman cycle was terminated at the 4th stage. This means that Rome was not able to develop enough inner strength to bring itself onto the next evolutionary stage. Shakespeare traces this incapacity back to the time of the founding of Rome. The main reason for this failure was the fact that the founding of Rome was not correctly implemented.

We may notice that the evolutionary state of Rome at the time of "Titus Andronicus" is similar to that of Greece described in "Troilus and Cressida". "Titus Andronicus" illustrates the state of Rome at the time of its collapse which led to the Dark Ages in Europe. "Troilus and Cressida" illustrates the state of collapsing Greece, i.e., the pre-Roman civilization. The collapse led to the Greek Dark Ages. Both civilizations are examples of unfulfilled evolutionary potentials that were separated by a spiritual millennium. However, there were substantial qualitative differences between the Greek and the Roman civilizations. Namely, before its collapse Rome assimilated conscious energy. Rome, however, was not able to come to terms with creativity. On the other hand, a partial assimilation of creative energy was accomplished by Greece. This is significant, because pre-Roman Greece was able to accommodate a higher mode of evolutionary impulse, while Rome stumbled at an earlier stage. This anomaly within the evolutionary process was also recorded on the level of ordinary men. Namely, the historical signature of Greece was the development of creative arts such as drama, music, philosophy and mathematics. Rome's signature was the development of a basic infrastructure, i.e., a code of law, public works and an Empire-wide chain of roads. This anomaly reconfirms that Rome fell short of its evolutionary potential: Rome collapsed before it reached its intended evolutionary expectation.

Shakespeare indicates that prior to Rome's failure, a rescue was already initiated in another place on the planet. This rescue was part of a complex operation that led to the European Renaissance. The details of this operation are described in "Pericles, Prince of Tire".

Pericles' mission

The origin of the evolutionary corruption was related to an event that took place in ancient times. Therefore, the correction of something already actualized in time could be accomplished only by an agency which was not only outside time but also outside existence. This would imply that the corrective action was initiated at the level of the Realm. The details of the rescue are illustrated in "Pericles, Prince of Tyre". The play provides compelling insights into the overall implementation of the evolutionary process. The play presents events taking place in ancient Britain, ancient Rome, Byzantium and medieval France as seen from the Realm, i.e., from the evolutionary command post. This means that the episodes described by Shakespeare in the Celtic trilogy, the Roman tetralogy, the Bohemian hexalogy and the French trilogy - are earthly projections of events taking place on higher levels of the evolutionary ladder.

A message was sent from the Realm. It was perceived by Pericles, Prince of Tyre, in the 7th century AD, i.e., when Europe was experiencing her Dark Ages. After receiving the message, Pericles, whose name in Greek means "Surrounded by Glory", embarked on his mission.

Pericles' mission is presented as a journey whose various stages are symbolically illustrated as a series of places located en route from the Levant to Europe, i.e., Tyre, Antioch, Tarsus, Ephesus, and Mytilene. These places represent various links of the evolutionary transmission chain. Antioch and Tarsus are degenerated remnants of the previous transmission chain; Antioch represents a corrupted higher state and Tarsus is a deteriorated intermediate state. Mytilene is a newly activated intermediate state. Ephesus serves as the temporary anchor of a new chain of transmission, i.e., a spiritual power house.

The time-span of Pericles' journey encompasses two historical millennia between the 9th century BC and the 13th century AD (approx.). Shakespeare implemented several chronological gaps to accommodate such a long time span. He used Gower as Chorus to fill-in the time gaps between the various stages of Pericles' journey:

"From bourn to bourn, region to region.
By you being pardon'd, we commit no crime
To use one language in each several clime
Where our scenes seem to live. I do beseech you
To learn of me, who stand i' the gaps to teach you,
The stages of our story."
(*Pericles, IV.4*)

Pericles' journey takes place in several time dimensions. These various time dimensions are indicated by "dumb shows", i.e., short acts of dramatic mime. Each dumb show marks one of the moments when Pericles exits or re-enters the different worlds by breaking away from the ordinary (historical) time dimension.

Pericles starts his journey from the city of Tyre, i.e., the city of Dido. The name of Tyre means "Rock". In this way Shakespeare indicates that the city of Tyre represents an earthly anchor of the chain of transmission, i.e., a permanent power house. Pericles' role is that of a receptor for the evolutionary energies ("Surrounded by Glory") that he has received from the Rock. Coincidentally, Tyre was the legendary birthplace of Europa, a Phoenician woman of high lineage, from whom the name of the continent of Europe has ultimately been taken. In other words, Pericles' journey is an allegorical illustration of the various stages of the evolution of Europe.

Let's follow the various stages of Pericles' journey.

Greek connection

At the beginning, Pericles travels through time into the past. The city of Antioch is his first stop. He arrives in Antioch at the time of the reign of King Antiochus. The character of Antiochus refers to the historical Antiochus III the Great, who died in the 2nd century BC. This corresponds to the end of the Hellenic civilization. Antioch represents a degenerated higher state. Antioch's evolutionary stage is determined by the creative energy that was previously released there. It was this creative energy that had led to the founding of Ancient Greece.

At the beginning of his mission, Pericles is charged with the task of forming an evolutionary triad that would allow for the reactivation of creative energy. For such a triad to be formed, Pericles would have to marry Antiochus' daughter Hesperides. Hesperides represents the ancient impulse of creativity. She is the current manifestation of Helen of Troy; she encompasses the experiences that Helen was previously exposed to. When Pericles arrives in Antioch he realizes that Hesperides, like Helen, is devoid of spiritual essence. The process has been corrupted. This corruption is symbolically described as Antiochus' incestuous relationship with his daughter. Pericles compares Antiochus and Hesperides to poisonous snakes:

"And both like serpents are, who though they feed
On sweetest flowers, yet they poison breed."
(*Pericles, I.1*)

Driven by his selfishness and sensual desires, Antiochus has abused the responsibility that he was charged with. In the manner of the mythical demigods and demigoddesses Antiochus selfishly misuses his privileged position and in this way prevents the continuation of the evolutionary process. Such a corruption of priority and responsibility corresponds to idolatry and spiritual usury, respectively. The damage is quite severe because it occurred at the level of a higher world. It is important to point out that this particular corruption originated in ancient times:

> "But custom what they did begin
> Was with long use account no sin."
> (*Pericles, I. Prologue*)

The transmission chain had been broken a long time ago. As a result of the break, lower links of the chain of transmission were also disconnected from the Realm. It is this period of idolatry and spiritual usury in the higher world that is recorded in ancient myths and legends.

Pericles realizes that his mission has to be modified. His current task is to restore the entire transmission chain. He compares his role to the tops of trees which protect the roots on which they depend:

> "Who am no more but as the tops of trees,
> Which fence the roots they grow by and defend them."
> (*Pericles, I.2*)

A rescue action has to be implemented. However, because Antiochus is a very powerful monarch, Pericles cannot challenge him directly:

> "The great Antiochus,
> 'Gainst whom I am too little to contend,
> Since he's so great can make his will his act."
> (*Pericles, I.2*)

Pericles has to apply a different strategy.

Roman connection

Pericles realizes that the corruption of Antioch has affected the next link, i.e., the intermediate state of the transmission chain. Tarsus represents this intermediate state. When Antioch was disconnected from the transmission chain, Tarsus was also cut off from access to evolutionary energies. As a result of the break, the previously released conscious energy was exhausted. Shakespeare uses "corn" to mark the symbolic presence of conscious energy, i.e., an earlier evolutionary impulse. This is why the effect of the break is illustrated as Tarsus being besieged by famine. Tarsus has to be rescued from this famine before it can serve as an active link of the transmission. Pericles' sea journey to Tarsus is the continuation of his allegorical travel through time further into the past. When Pericles arrives in Tarsus, Cleon is the governor of the city. Pericles revives the city by providing it with corn which he has brought from Tyre. Tarsus regains its previous function within the transmission chain: it is reactivated as an intermediate state.

The change within the intermediate state has an effect on the world of the ancient demigods and demigoddesses. Shakespeare's long narrative poem "Venus and Adonis" illustrates the effect of the re-injection of consciousness onto the degenerate higher world, i.e., the world of ancient demigods and demigoddesses. In "Venus and Adonis", this effect is marked by Adonis' sudden loss of interest in Venus, Goddess of sensual love. Adonis becomes conscious that there is another and more potent kind of love than the ordinary sensuality represented by Venus. Against Venus' warning, Adonis abandons her and goes to hunt a Boar. In this poem the Boar represents Mars, Venus' jealous consort. Unlike Pericles who knew that he was "too little to contend" with Antiochus, Adonis challenges Mars directly. Adonis is not properly prepared for such a challenge: he is killed. There is no place for consciousness among the ancient demigods and demigoddesses.

Pericles' arrival in Tarsus was projected onto the ordinary world at the time of the founding of Rome in the 9th century BC. Pericles's arrival and the following events taking place in Tarsus were projected onto Rome. These events are illustrated in the Roman tetralogy. Let's recall that Rome was supposed to short circuit the transmission gap that was caused by the deterioration of the Greek civilization. As the first step, it was necessary to ensure that Rome was provided with a sufficient amount of the basic energy needed for its inner infrastructure. The energy of consciousness ("corn") serves this purpose.

Shakespeare dedicated his second narrative poem "The Rape of Lucrece" to illustrate how Rome was affected by its exposure to this evolutionary commodity. In this context, "The Rape of Lucrece" is a sequel to "Venus and Adonis". It takes place in 5th century BC Rome, i.e., after Pericles's arrival in Tarsus but prior to the events described in "Coriolanus", the first play of the Roman tetralogy.

The action of "The Rape of Lucrece" takes place during the siege of Ardea. The Roman commanders decide to take a break from the battle and go spy on their wives. They find out that all their wives are having fun in a variety of lustful ways, except for Lucrece, Collatine's wife. She alone carries herself in a chaste and virtuous manner. Prince Tarquin becomes possessed with an uncontrollable lust for her. At night Prince Tarquin breaks into Lucrece's bedroom and rapes her. After revealing Tarquin's crime, Lucrece stabs herself. This incites a revolt against King Tarquin's family. The Tarquins family is expelled from Rome; Rome becomes a republic. In this narrative Lucrece represents an impulse of the conscious energy projected from Tarsus to Rome. The death of Lucrece marks the withdrawal of this energy from Rome. This explains why Rome was experiencing the shortage of "corn" described in the opening scene of "Coriolanus". At that time

Rome, like Adonis within the corrupted world of mythical demigods, was not properly prepared for such an encounter.

After the restoration of Tarsus, Pericles must continue his journey. Now, however, the next steps of his mission become more sophisticated. Pericles has to enter a higher state on the evolutionary ladder so he can be exposed to the entire spectrum of evolutionary energies. Pericles' traveling route is directed by the forces of the Realm. Neptune and Diana represent non-corrupted agents of the Realm. In other words, Pericles is under Neptune's and Diana's guidance. By the force of Neptune, Pericles' ship is wrecked. Pericles is tossed upon the coast of Pentapolis. According to Shakespeare's symbols, Pentapolis is an imaginary place that represents a higher world. Pericles' arrival in Pentapolis establishes a link between Pentapolis and Tarsus.

French connection

As a symbolic representation of the higher world, Pentapolis exists beyond the limitations of time and space. Simonides, the king of Pentapolis, and Thaisa, his daughter, represent two elements of the evolutionary triad that presently are available within the higher world. Thaisa was born in Pentapolis. She represents a dormant impulse of the highest, i.e., supracognitive energy. This means that she encompasses the entire spectrum of the evolutionary energies available in the galaxy.

While in Pentapolis, Pericles takes part in a jousting tournament which is organized to celebrate Thaisa's birthday. At this point an additional piece of information will help us understand the nature of Pericles' experiences. The first jousting guidelines were written in 1066 in France. This particular historical time corresponds to the appearance of the Troubadours, the creation of the love courts and the chivalric orders in the South of France. In other words, Pericles is teleported to Pentapolis which represents a certain evolutionary potential that already existed in eternity and was needed to be actualized in the physical world. Pericles' teleportation corresponds to an evolutionary intervention that is implemented outside of the limitation of time in order to short circuit a fault in the planetary past.

Pericles' overall intention is to be of service to the restoration of the evolutionary transmission chain. While in Pentapolis, Pericles recognizes the objective that will allow him to realize his intention. His objective is symbolically represented by Thaisa. By being married to Thaisa, Pericles may gain access to the entire spectrum of energies and be able to fulfil his mission.

Pentapolis means "five cities" and symbolically encompasses the remaining five stages of Pericles' journey. The challenges of these upcoming stages are represented by five knights with whom Pericles must fight in the tournament. Each of the knights is associated with one of the five cities, i.e., Tarsus, Antioch, Tyre, Mytilene, and Ephesus. The stages are shown to Pericles in reverse chronological order, i.e., starting with the last and the final stage that is symbolically illustrated by the first knight. In this way he is prepared for his upcoming challenges.

Pericles wins the tournament. Pericles and Thaisa are married. By marrying Thaisa, Pericles completes the higher evolutionary triad. The triad consists of King Simonides, Thaisa, and Pericles. The formation of a new triad that is in harmony with the design of the "heavenly spheres" may be compared to an instrument that can generate the "music of the spheres", i.e., "music that may not be heard". It is this music that "would draw heaven down, and all the gods, to hearken". In other words, Pericles' experience in

Pentapolis makes him "music's master". This is emphasized by King Simonides' comment on the music played by Pericles:

"I am beholding to you
For your sweet music this last night: I do
Protest my ears were never better fed
With such delightful pleasing harmony."

"Sir, you are music's master."
(*Pericles, II.5*)

Shakespeare consistently uses such music in his plays to mark the manifestations of supracognitive energy.

By marrying Thaisa, Pericles has attuned himself to the design of the "heavenly spheres". Through this experience he has been exposed to the entire spectrum of evolutionary energies. This experience will percolate through the levels of the transmission chain all the way down to ordinary man. We will find an echo of this event in the Celtic, French, Italian, and Bohemian plays. It will be symbolically manifested by the appearance of a beautiful and wise woman who falls in love with a seemingly undeserving man. In each case, her love will have a transmuting effect on her partner. Very often, however, he will not understand his situation. Their encounters will be driven by the currently operating cosmic matrix. This is why their adventures may appear absurd or ridiculous. Nevertheless, they are very accurate representations of experiences associated with the evolutionary growth of man.

The formation of the new triad is a significant moment in the evolution of European man. Prior to the arrival of Pericles in Pentapolis, the evolutionary state of European man was represented by the Chivalric Knights courting Thaisa. This situation would later be reflected in the symbolism of the ménage à trois of the Troubadours, the love courts, and the chivalric orders. Like Thaisa of Pentapolis, the "mistress" of the Troubadours was praised and worshiped by the Chivalric Knights. However, she was for them essentially unattainable. After Pericles' arrival in Pentapolis, the overall situation is changed. King Simonides dismisses his Knights. There is no need for them in Pentapolis any longer. Their function in Pentapolis has been completed. Now their experiences are needed on the level of ordinary man:

> "Knights, from my daughter this I let you know,
> That for this twelvemonth she'll not undertake
> A married life."
> (*Pericles, II.5*)

"That for this twelvemonth" refers to the time needed for the chivalric sequence to percolate down along the transmission chain to reach the level of ordinary man. Historically, the period of "twelvemonth" corresponds to the twelve centuries. Now it is possible to realize that the ménage à trois of the Troubadours represented a certain potentiality; it was a preparatory stage. At the time of their appearance in Europe, European man was not ready yet for the actualization of this particular potentiality.

Pentapolis, existing in the higher world, serves as a template for the lower levels. The relationship between King Simonides and Thaisa represents the optimal pattern that was needed at the lower levels. The pattern is illustrated by Simonides' attitude towards Thaisa's decision to marry Pericles, "the stranger knight":

> "She tells me here, she'd wed the stranger knight,
> Or never more to view nor day nor light.
> 'Tis well, mistress; your choice agrees with mine;
> I like that well: nay, how absolute she's in't,
> Not minding whether I dislike or no!
> Well, I do commend her choice;
> And will no longer have it be delay'd."
> (*Pericles, II.5*)

The presence of the Chivalric Knights in Pentapolis was projected through Tarsus to King Lear's Britain. It was manifested by the appearance of the King of France in 9th century BC Britain. He was one of the Knights who were courting Thaisa of Pentapolis. The King of France arrived in Britain to protect Cordelia and, if necessary, remove her from Britain. Later on, Cordelia insisted on returning to Britain to help her father:

> "O dear father,
> It is thy business that I go about;
> Therefore great France
> My mourning and important tears hath pitied.
> No blown ambition doth our arms incite."
> (*King Lear, IV.4*)

At that time the Roman project had already been instigated. Cordelia's fate was determined: the charge that she represented was to be transferred from Britain to Rome. This is why the King of France could not be involved in Britain's affairs any longer. He left Britain just before the decisive battle at the end of "King Lear". He had to attend to more urgent matters. The death of Cordelia marked the removal of this particular impulse of creativity from Britain. After Cordelia's death, it was transferred to Rome. As indicated earlier, this impulse appeared as Virgilia at the time of "Coriolanus" in the 5th century BC.

***

At the time when Pericles becomes a music master, a new transmission chain is activated. The previously corrupted links are eliminated. A message arrives in Pentapolis announcing that Antiochus and his daughter are dead. They were shrivelled up by "a fire from heaven" while riding in a chariot. Antiochus misused the chariot, i.e., the developmental triad that he was charged with. This was marked within the ordinary world as the collapse of the ancient Greek civilization. The new triad formed in Pentapolis is the replacement of Antiochus' corrupted chariot. At this moment the ancient world of demigods and demigoddesses is also greatly diminished. The Boar of "Venus and Adonis" and his accomplices are no longer the driving forces within the higher world. Yet, some traces of this ancient corruption will remain and interfere with the future stages of the process.

After the death of Antiochus, Pericles' state is changed from Prince into King. Pericles becomes King of Tyre. Through his experiences in Pentapolis, Pericles was prepared for his role as a spiritual king. This event was projected down onto the ordinary world as the appearance of Julius Caesar in 1st century BC Rome.

Inception of unitive energy

Now Pericles has to retrace the stages of his journey, which were shown to him during the jousting tournament. Pericles leaves Pentapolis and starts his descent back to Tyre. This time he is travelling back into the future. During his sea trip, Thaisa gives birth to Marina. Marina is born in the transition zone between Pentapolis and Tarsus, i.e., between the higher and intermediate worlds. She represents a seed of unitive energy that encompasses latent modes of all previously released energies, except the highest one. At this time, however, the higher triad is temporarily disassembled. Thaisa dies while giving birth. The higher triad was formed, but its operation had to be interrupted. It had to be interrupted, because at this particular time, ordinary man was not yet ready for such an experience. This non-readiness of ordinary man is illustrated by the assassination of Julius Caesar in Rome. The assassination of Julius Caesar is the cause of Thaisa's death. The circumstances that led to the assassination are described in "Julius Caesar".

Although the entire spectrum of evolutionary energies was activated within the higher world, it could not yet be transmitted onto the level of ordinary man. Thaisa and Pericles had to be separated at the moment of their re-entry into the intermediate world. The higher modes of the evolutionary spectrum had to be protected and hidden from ordinary man until the earthly environment was correctly prepared for their assimilation.

Thaisa's body is tossed off the ship in a wooden casket. The casket washes up on shore near the residence of Lord Cerimon in Ephesus. Cerimon revives Thaisa. Thaisa becomes a high priestess in the temple of Diana in Ephesus. In this way the impulse of supracognitive energy is transferred to Ephesus and temporarily put under Diana's protection. Thaisa's resurrection in Ephesus was projected onto Rome as the arrival of Octavius, Caesar's adopted son. Octavius formed a triumvirate to prepare Rome for the assimilation of the postponed release of unitive energy. The birth of Marina triggered the appearance of an impulse of unitive energy in Rome. Octavia, Octavius' sister, was the first earthly manifestation of unitive energy.

After Thaisa's death at sea, a storm forces Pericles to land in Tarsus, i.e., the newly reactivated intermediate state. Pericles leaves Marina in the care of Cleon and his wife Dionyza. In this way a seed of unitive energy is entrusted to Tarsus. Dionyza promises to take as good care of Marina as of her own daughter.

Pericles departs from Tarsus and sails to Tyre. Pericles may only restart his journey once the impulse of unitive energy becomes active, i.e., when Marina is ready to get married. In the meantime Dionyza falls prey to jealousy and envy when she realizes that her daughter is not as beautiful as Marina. Hence Dionyza plots to kill Marina. Dionyza's jealousy interferes with the process. By rejecting Marina, the city of Tarsus cuts itself off from the chain of transmission. Once again, Tarsus becomes spiritually corrupt. Later on, as a result of this rejection, Cleon of Tarsus and his family are killed in their palace. The intended murder of Marina by Dionyza is replayed in Rome as Mark Antony's rejection of Octavia. The outcome of this rejection by Rome is illustrated in "Titus Andronicus". These events led to the collapse of the Roman evolutionary branch: Europe entered into the Dark Ages.

Celtic connection

Rome was incapable of fulfilling its evolutionary function and this failure necessitated another adjustment to the evolutionary plan. Once again, the Celtic branch was used for this purpose. Let's recall that Celtic Britain had been prepared for this task through the events described in "King Lear".

After Mark Antony's rejection of Octavia, the impulse of unitive energy was transferred to 1st century Britain. The details of the Celtic intervention are described in "Cymbeline", the second play of Shakespeare's Celtic trilogy.

Cymbeline

"Cymbeline" is the sequel to "King Lear". Therefore, it is not surprising that the plot of the play bears a striking resemblance to "King Lear". Imogen is the daughter of Cymbeline, the King of 1st century Britain. The relationship between King Cymbeline and Imogen parallels that of King Lear and Cordelia.

Imogen represents the impulse of unitive energy that was transferred from Rome. She is the current projection of Octavia.

Imogen goes against her father's wishes and marries a young man of meagre means named Posthumus Leonatus. Posthumus is a Roman who was brought up at Cymbeline's court. The marriage infuriates King Cymbeline because he had arranged for Imogen to marry his uncouth stepson Cloten. Cloten is the son of Cymbeline's second wife. As a punishment, Posthumus is sent into exile in Italy.

From the perspective of the Realm, there is no such thing as past, present and future. The past, present and future appear when some events within the Realm are projected onto our ordinary space-time split perception. At the level of the Realm it is possible to access the future in order to implement an effective strategy in the present. In "Cymbeline", Shakespeare illustrates another example of such a past-present-future intervention. He sends Posthumus from 1st century Britain via 13th century France to 16th century Renaissance Rome. On his way back from Rome to Britain, Posthumus makes a brief stop in 9th century Wales.

When Posthumus is at Philario's house in Rome, he encounters an Italian named Iachimo. Iachimo argues that all women are naturally unchaste, and he provokes Posthumus into making a wager that he will be able to seduce Imogen, Posthumus' wife. This is similar to the situation of Prince Tarquin and Collatine described in "The Rape of Lucrece". However, the outcome is very different. It is different because now the overall process is directed by the Realm through the newly formed transmission chain (at this time, Pericles has already arrived in Pentapolis). Posthumus' seemingly unhappy events serve a constructive purpose. They are administered as medicine for a specific illness; the dose is controlled and adjusted accordingly. Previously, the actions of the demigods and demigoddesses kept humanity in a sort of vicious circle; a cure was impossible.

Posthumus accepts the wager. Iachimo travels to Cymbeline's court, but he fails in his attempt to seduce Imogen. Iachimo is more cunning than Prince Tarquin was. He is not driven by lust; he does not ravish Imogen. His aim is to disgrace her. Therefore, he resorts to trickery. He hides in a large chest and has it sent to Imogen's bedchamber. At night, he slips out and steals a bracelet that Posthumus once gave her. Iachimo returns to Rome, and, displaying the stolen bracelet and an intimate knowledge of the details of Imogen's bedchamber, convinces Posthumus that he won the bet. Posthumus, furious at being betrayed by his wife, sends a letter to Britain ordering his servant Pisanio to murder Imogen. But Pisanio knows that Imogen is innocent. Pisanio reports to Posthumus that he has killed his wife. At the same time, Pisanio convinces Imogen to disguise herself as a boy and go search for her husband. Imogen follows Pisanio's advice. But she becomes lost in the wilds of Wales. In the meantime, Octavius' army has invaded Britain seeking the restoration of a certain tribute that Britain had ceased to pay to Rome. The disguised Imogen hires herself out to them as a page. At that time, Posthumus and Iachimo are traveling with the Roman army. During a battle in Wales, Posthumus switches to the garb of a peasant and fights valiantly for Britain. The Romans are defeated. After the battle, Posthumus switches back to his Roman attire. He is taken prisoner by Cymbeline's soldiers. That night, the god Jupiter arrives in the prison and informs the interceding spirits of Posthumus' dead ancestors that he is taking care of their descendant. The next day, Cymbeline calls the prisoners before him, and the confusion is sorted out. Posthumus and Imogen are reunited.

As illustrated in the prison scene, the Celtic intervention is executed by Jupiter. Jupiter, like Neptune and Diana in the case of Pericles, represents the non-corrupted agents of the Realm. Jupiter arrives and announces that:

"Our Jovial star reign'd at his birth, and in
Our temple was he married."
(*Cymbeline, V.4*)

"Our Jovial star reign'd at his birth" refers to the birth of
Posthumus. Posthumus was born when his father, Sicilius, was
fighting together with the Britons against the Romans at the time
of Julius Caesar. Posthumus' future function is to be a receptor of
unitive energy. This is significant because it points out that the
Celtic evolutionary intervention was instigated prior to Julius
Caesar's assassination. Posthumus' birth was arranged to balance
out the *future* failure of Rome. This is why Jupiter's intervention
was needed. At the moment of Julius Caesar's assassination, the
transfer of unitive energy from Rome to Britain was already
arranged. This is why, in his last words, Julius Caesar stated that he
was "unassailable". At the time of his assassination, he knew that
his function would be fulfilled; the transfer of the impulse of
unitive energy was already secured ("Our Jovial star reign'd at his
birth and in our temple was he married.").

Although Imogen and Posthumus are reunited at the end of the
play, their marriage could not be prolonged. Despite his
experiences in France and Italy, Posthumus is not quite ready for
Imogen. This is illustrated in the final scene where he is not able to
perceive Imogen's inner beauty. When Imogen is still disguised as a
page, Posthumus does not recognize her:

Imogen:

"Peace, my lord; hear, hear-"

Posthumus:

"Shall's have a play of this? Thou scornful page,
There lie thy part."

Striking her: she falls

This is why Imogen has to be transferred to another place. The transfer of Imogen is indicated in Jupiter's oracle that Posthumus found in the prison. When Jupiter departed, Posthumus found on the ground beside him a richly decorated book:

> "A book? O rare one!
> Be not, as is our fangled world, a garment
> Nobler than that it covers: let thy effects
> So follow, to be most unlike our courtiers,
> As good as promise."
> (*Cymbeline, V.4*)

Posthumus' words "Be not, as is our fangled world, a garment nobler than that it covers" is a reference to the Book of Kells. This book appeared in the 9th century. This indicates that the scene in the prison applies to 9th century Wales. This richly decorated book contained the oracle along with an allegorical summary of Posthumus' experiences:

> "When as a lion's whelp shall, to himself unknown,
> without seeking find, and be embraced by a piece of
> tender air; and when from a stately cedar shall be
> lopped branches, which, being dead many years,
> shall after revive, be jointed to the old stock and
> freshly grow; then shall Posthumus end his miseries,
> Britain be fortunate and flourish in peace and plenty."
> (*Cymbeline, V.4*)"

The oracle applies to Posthumus and to the overall evolutionary process implemented in Western Europe. The evolutionary transmission chain is compared to a "stately cedar", while its broken branches may be described as "lopped branches". "A lion's whelp" indicates a receptor of evolutionary energy. At the moment when a man is exposed to an impulse of unitive energy, he may be described as "embraced by a piece of tender air". According to Jupiter's oracle, at that time the Celtic branch was "being dead many years". This means that the evolutionary impulse of unitive energy had been withdrawn from Britain. What remained within the 9th century Celtic branch was a record of the events associated with the release of unitive energy and a projection of the future outcome. "Britain be fortunate and flourish in peace and plenty" applies to the final chapter of Shakespeare's narrative.

Imogen was transferred back onto the Italian Peninsula, i.e., the place of the first appearance of this particular impulse. The important thing is that this impulse remained within the ordinary world.

The question may be asked: what the purpose of such a sophisticated intervention was. Obviously, Posthumus did not learn much from his adventures in 13th century France and 16th century Italy. The answer to this question is provided in the remaining plays. The details are explained in the discussion of "The Merchant of Venice".

Shakespeare's plays are a compelling illustration of how freewill and causality are accommodated within the universal design. Namely, causality at the level of ordinary man is the field of operation for the Will of the Realm. The Realm transmits its Will through the transmission chain. Any adjustment to the evolutionary plan is manifested on the level of ordinary man as a series of intertwined opportunities that appear in different places and at different times. For example, in accordance with the Will of the Realm, the timing of the release of unitive energy on the earth was dictated by the evolutionary needs of the galaxy. Therefore, the conditions on the earth had to be correctly prepared if the event was to fulfil the galactic need. Julius Caesar's Rome was not able to fulfil this evolutionary requirement. All that could be done was to provide other opportunities so man might make his choices. Each of these opportunities was providing man with a new chance to make a constructive choice. It took a series of such challenging situations before man was able to comply with the galactic need. According to Shakespeare's presentation, it took some fourteen centuries before the unitive energy could be assimilated within the ordinary world.

Macbeth

The removal of Imogen from Britain had a dramatic effect on the Celtic branch. The consequences of the removal are illustrated in "Macbeth", i.e., the concluding play of the Celtic trilogy. It is the story of Scottish general Macbeth. The play is set in 11th century Scotland. The most noticeable feature of Scotland is the absence of an impulse of unitive energy. "Macbeth" is a play that illustrates what happens in the absence of an active evolutionary charge.

At the beginning of the play Macbeth and his friend Banquo succeed in defending Scotland against rebels and against the invasion of Sweno, a Norwegian king. Afterwards, Macbeth and Banquo encounter three witches. The witches prophesy that Macbeth will become thane of Cawdor and then king of Scotland. The witches also prophesy that Banquo will never be king himself but will beget a line of kings. Macbeth and Banquo are sceptical about the prophecy. Then they meet some of King Duncan's men who had come to tell Macbeth that he has indeed been named thane of Cawdor. Macbeth is awestruck by the possibility that the second part of the witches' prophecy might also be true. When Lady Macbeth learns from her husband about the witches' prophecy, she wants Macbeth to become king. She manages to override her husband's objections and persuades him to kill King Duncan. Macbeth murders Duncan and seizes the throne for himself.

The witches represent destructive forces. Their appearance is a further mark of the absence of an evolutionary charge. Where there is no evolutionary charge, the destructive forces have more space to exercise their damaging influence. The witches choose Macbeth as their target. The spectators can see clearly how Macbeth was influenced by their messages. It is obvious that the witches' messages are constructed in such a way that they would affect the hearer according to the hearer's inner state. It is in this manner that prophecies may become self-fulfilling.

On the other hand, the witches' prophecies have to be based on a template that consists of an accurate presentation of future events. The witches' means are limited to a marginal degree of deceptive emphasis and biased presentation. According to the formula, "like attracts like", the witches are not perfect in their actions either. Hecate, the goddess of witchcraft, is upset at them because they have not consulted with her before their first encounter with Macbeth. She is angry because the witches invested their charms in a rather weak aspect of Scotland. From Hecate's perspective, Macbeth is not vicious enough; he is not able to serve evil efficiently enough. Macbeth is only after his own personal greed and simplistic wants. Macbeth can be easily corrupted. However, he is not truly a villain to the extent that, for example, Aaron was in "Titus Andronicus". Macbeth does not represent the same degree of viciousness and determination. As a matter of fact, he is rather weak and shaky in handling himself. Macbeth's "loves for his own ends, not for you" may spoil Hecate's overall objective. Therefore, she tells the witches that she will arrange for Macbeth to come back to them looking for further prophesy. And when he comes, they must summon visions and spirits whose messages will enhance Macbeth's viciousness by filling him with a false sense of security and drawing him into a stronger determination towards their wicked quest:

"As by the strength of their illusion
Shall draw him on to his confusion:
He shall spurn fate, scorn death, and bear

He hopes 'bove wisdom, grace and fear:
And you all know, security
Is mortals' chiefest enemy.
(*Macbeth, III.5*)

Because "security is mortals' chiefest enemy", Macbeth falls into the witches' trap. He chooses a path that leads him to his destruction.

Banquo represents the most conscious aspect of Scotland. Banquo's perception is demonstrated right at the beginning of the play, when he and Macbeth encounter the witches. The witches promise Banquo that his descendants will inherit the Scottish throne. Unlike Macbeth, Banquo does not translate the witches' prophecy into action. He does not allow himself to fall into the witches' trap. He tries to explain to Macbeth:

"And oftentimes, to win us to our harm,
The instruments of darkness tell us truths,
Win us with honest trifles, to betray's
In deepest consequence."
(*Macbeth, I.3*)

Banquo, however, is incapable of influencing Macbeth.

Fearful of the witches' prophecy that Banquo's heirs will inherit the throne, Macbeth hires murderers to kill Banquo and his son Fleance. He designs the killing scenario and, in disguise, joins the killers. Banquo is killed but Fleance escapes.

Hecate uses the Ghost of Banquo to prompt Macbeth's return to the witches. During their second encounter with Macbeth, the witches show him a procession of crowned kings. Banquo's ghost walks at the end of the line. Here is Macbeth's reaction to this vision:

"Thou art too like the spirit of Banquo: down!
Thy crown does sear mine eye-balls. And thy hair,
Thou other gold-bound brow, is like the first.
A third is like the former. Filthy hags!
Why do you show me this? A fourth! Start, eyes!
What, will the line stretch out to the crack of doom?
Another yet! A seventh! I'll see no more:
And yet the eighth appears, who bears a glass
Which shows me many more; and some I see
That two-fold balls and treble scepters carry:
Horrible sight! Now, I see, 'tis true;
For the blood-bolter'd Banquo smiles upon me,
And points at them for his."
(*Macbeth, IV.1*)

The procession of the kings may be interpreted as a confirmation of the witches' previous prediction that Banquo's heirs will be the future kings. At this point it should be noted that King James I, Shakespeare's patron, claimed descent from the historical character of Banquo. King James I was separated from the historical Banquo by nine generations. It might be assumed that Shakespeare used this scene to flatter the King. But such an interpretation is exactly what the witches wanted Macbeth and the audience to believe in. One has to be careful not to take the witches' prophesies at face value. Let's remember Banquo's warning, "the instruments of darkness ... win us with honest trifles, to betray's in deepest consequence". Shakespeare's plays may seem to flatter the audience too, but only if the audience's self conceit allows them to do so.

It is important to notice that Macbeth was not overpowered by Fleance or any of Banquo's heirs. Malcolm, the elder son of Duncan and his heirs formed the line of Scottish kings. Malcolm was not a relative of Banquo. As a matter of fact, Macbeth was related to Malcolm; he was his cousin. This means that the kings in the witches' procession were not Banquo's descendants.

Macbeth was eliminated with the help of King Edward of England. Without the involvement of England, it would have been impossible to restore inner balance to Scotland. Shakespeare describes King Edward as a miracle maker and a natural healer. This is illustrated in a scene where Macduff, a Scottish nobleman talks with Malcolm. This scene takes place outside of King Edward's palace in England. A doctor appears briefly and says that a "crew of wretched souls" is waiting for King Edward so they may be cured:

"Ay, sir; there are a crew of wretched souls
That stay his cure: their malady convinces
The great assay of art; but at his touch-
Such sanctity hath heaven given his hand-
They presently amend."
(*Macbeth, IV.3*)

When the doctor leaves, Macduff asks Malcolm:

"What's the disease he means?"

Malcolm explains that King Edward has a miraculous power to cure a disease "called the evil":

" 'Tis call'd the evil:
A most miraculous work in this good king;
Which often, since my here-remain in England,
I have seen him do. How he solicits heaven,
Himself best knows: but strangely-visited people,
All swoln and ulcerous, pitiful to the eye,
The mere despair of surgery, he cures,
Hanging a golden stamp about their necks,
Put on with holy prayers: and 'tis spoken,
To the succeeding royalty he leaves
The healing benediction. With this strange virtue,
He hath a heavenly gift of prophecy,

And sundry blessings hang about his throne,
That speak him full of grace."
(*Macbeth, IV.3*)

Shakespeare used the historical figure of King Edward the Confessor to illustrate the working of natural protection mechanisms. Such mechanisms may be activated when the evolutionary process reaches a critical stage and there is a risk of extinction of a particular being. Such mechanisms may prevent a total fiasco. However, they are not capable of bringing a being into a higher stage of development.

In "Macbeth", King Edwards provided such a protective measure after the evolutionary charge had been removed from the Celtic branch. The protective measure was in the form of "ten thousand English soldiers" sent to Scotland. It was this remedy that allowed a cure for Scotland from its evil disease. At this point Scotland was saved, but the Celtic evolutionary branch was terminated. Instead, the future stages of the evolutionary process were invested in England. Malcolm's comment, "to the succeeding royalty he leaves the healing benediction" alludes to such a transfer into the future line of the English kings. In this context, the procession of the kings in the witches' prophesy is a symbolic illustration of a link that preserved the evolutionary process in that geographical region. Namely, the seven kings who form the procession parallel the seven evolutionary stages that are described by Shakespeare in the History Plays.

The seven stages are symbolically represented by the seven English kings, i.e., King John, Richard II, Henry IV, Henry V, Henry VI, Richard III, and Henry VIII. The eighth king corresponds to Queen Elizabeth I. The "benediction" that was passed to the succeeding royalty is symbolically indicated by Edward the Confessor's crown. King Edward's crown is referred to in "Henry

VIII", the last History Play. Anne Boleyn, the mother of Elizabeth I, inherited this crown:

> "Edward Confessor's crown,
> The rod, and bird of peace, and all such emblems
> Laid nobly on her."
> (*Henry VIII, IV.1*)

After Elizabeth I a new line of kings appeared. The kings in this new line are shown in the witches' procession as the reflections in a mirror that is held by the eighth king. Indeed, the first king of this new line will appear at the time of "The Merry Wives of Windsor".

Byzantine connection

After the failures of the Roman and the Celtic branches, the next evolutionary effort was once again focused on Greece. This effort led to the formation of Byzantium in the 4th century AD. Byzantium served as the next evolutionary option that was offered to mankind after the Roman and the Celtic failures.

Let's go back to Pericles' journey. Dionyza's attempt to kill Marina was thwarted by pirates. The pirates took Marina to Mytilene where they sold her into prostitution. Upon Marina's arrival, Mytilene is activated as a temporary intermediate state. Mytilene becomes the current replacement for the dysfunctional Tarsus.

Mytilene is used to re-activate the evolutionary process in Greece. Mytilene is presented as a brothel; a place where "love" is misused and treated as a commodity. This indicates that the city is infected by traces of the ancient impurities. First, therefore, Mytilene has to be cleansed of these impurities. Mytilene may be cleansed by exposure to creative energy, i.e., a lower mode of the evolutionary spectrum. A similar approach was used to awaken Rome's sterile heart at the time of "Julius Caesar".

Marina suggests to the brothel that there is a better way for them to profit from her presence. Namely, she offers to teach the young ladies of Mytilene how to "sing, weave, sew, and dance". The brothel agrees to her proposal. The brothel rents her out as a tutor to respectable young ladies in Mytilene. In this way Marina is able to exercise her influence over the city. Soon she becomes famous for music and other arts. At the same time an impulse of creativity is brought to Mytilene from Rome. In Rome, this impulse was represented by Lavinia. Lavinia becomes one of the ladies working with Marina in Mytilene.

Mytilene's response to its exposure to creativity marks the constructive assimilation of this particular energy. It is the first time that creative energy is correctly used on the intermediate state. Symbolically, this is illustrated as a change from treating Marina as a prostitute to employing her as a courtesan. From this point on, Shakespeare will use the courtesans to indicate impulses of creative energy.

Lysimachus, the governor of Mytilene, meets Marina in the brothel. He instantly recognizes her unusual qualities and her effect on those around her. He falls in love with her. It is then that Pericles' ship arrives in Mytilene. Lysimachus brings Marina to Pericles. He hopes that she may be able to restore Pericles' dumbness:

"Our vessel is of Tyre, in it the king;
A man who for this three months hath not spoken."
(*Pericles*, *V.1*)

Pericles and Marina are reunited. The "three months" during which Pericles "hath not spoken" are equivalent to three historical centuries. This means that Pericles' arrival in Mytilene corresponds to the historical 4th century. The events that were taking place in Mytilene were projected down onto Byzantium. This particular phase of the process is illustrated by Shakespeare in "Timon of Athens".

Timon of Athens

Neither Rome nor the Celtic evolutionary branch could provide the proper vehicle for the continuation of the evolutionary process in Europe. Instead, the modern European civilization was born in Athens.

The seed of modern Europe was planted at the time of Pericles' arrival in Mytilene. This event was projected onto 4th century Athens and was recorded as the founding of the Byzantine Empire. During the Middle Ages, the Byzantine Empire was the continuation of the Roman Empire. It is also referred to as the Eastern Roman Empire. For some time, the Balkan Peninsula and Sicily belonged to Byzantium. When the Western Roman Empire collapsed, Byzantium continued to thrive, existing for more than a thousand years. During most of its existence, this empire was the most powerful economic, cultural, and military force in Europe.

The Byzantine option was realized through a second exposure of this geographical region to creative energy. "Timon of Athens" illustrates the circumstances that led to the founding of Byzantium. "Timon of Athens" is the first play of Shakespeare's Bohemian hexalogy.

Timon is a wealthy Athenian who enjoys giving gold to his friends. But he doesn't give his presents out of a desire for return. He tells the Athenians that friendship means giving, without expecting something in return. Among his friends are a whole lot of people who stick around to try to benefit from his company. The

Athenians are amazed that Timon continues to be so generous, as it seems to them that he must have some magical power to possess such an unending bounty.

The play implies that Athens is linked to Mytilene. Mytilene's link with Athens is indicated by the Fool. The Fool's mistress runs a brothel. Here is his explanation:

> "I think no usurer but has a fool to his servant: my
> mistress is one, and I am her fool. When men come
> to borrow of your masters, they approach sadly, and
> go away merry; but they enter my mistress' house
> merrily, and go away sadly: the reason of this?"
> (*Timon of Athens, II.2*)

The Fool refers to the Athenians as usurers and to the Mytilenians as bawds. He explains that a visit to a usurer gives customers satisfaction from a fictitious gain. This is why those who visit a usurer "go away merry" because they are convinced that they have gained something. The Fool's description of "his mistress' house" is a reference to the brothel in Mytilene where Marina was brought by the pirates. It was there that men were entering the brothel merrily, but after encountering Marina and realizing their own miserable state, were going away sadly. (At the time of the Fool's appearance in Athens, Marina *is* still in Mytilene's brothel.)

The symbolic representation of Mytilene-Athens is a reflection of the inner structure of the ancient world as illustrated by Troy-Greece in "Troilus and Cressida". The intermediate state of Mytilene, like Troy, is infected by idolatry (or "whorishness"). The ordinary state of Athens, like ancient Greece, is corrupted. But there is a significant difference. Namely, Mytilene, unlike Troy, has been connected to the evolutionary transmission chain.

Marina's presence allowed Mytilene to assimilate creative energy. This creative energy was to be projected down to Athens. Timon is a custodian of the process. His role is to prepare the Athenians to exposure to creativity. The effect of creative energy is symbolically indicated by the presence of "gold" and it is this "gold" that is within Timon's possession. Timon freely gives "gold" to anyone who comes to him. He does not expect anything in return. "None can truly say he gives, if he receives" underlines the modus operandi of an interaction with evolutionary energy. Those who have "received" it should also exercise this form of "giving". In other words, Timon teaches the Athenians true generosity. Generosity is needed for an effective assimilation of creative energy. Those who are breaking the rule are called "usurers".

Yet, the city of Athens is not able to respond correctly to the impact of Timon's gifts. When time comes for "giving", the Athenians prove to be ordinary usurers. At this point Timon receives instructions from Mytilene. The instructions are delivered by the Page of the Fool's mistress. After receiving the instructions, Timon leaves the city and goes to a forest. Timon's arrival in the forest corresponds in time to the moment of the reunion between Pericles and Marina. Immediately after the reunion, Pericles falls asleep on his ship which is anchored in the harbour in Mytilene. From an historical perspective, Pericles' sleep lasted three hundred years, i.e., from the 4th century to the 7th century. Pericles' sleep marks a "forceful occasion", which provides a window of opportunity for Athens to build a permanent link with Mytilene. This link is needed to connect Athens to the transmission chain. Timon's role is to maximize on the opportunity that was offered to Athens.

While in the forest, Timon finds a cache of gold. It is then that he describes the gold's function:

> "What is here?
> Gold? yellow, glittering, precious gold? No, gods,
> I am no idle votarist: roots, you clear heavens!

Thus much of this will make black white, foul fair,
Wrong right, base noble, old young, coward valiant."
(*Timon of Athens, IV.3*)

The effect of "gold" is such that it makes "black white, foul fair, wrong right, base noble, old young, coward valiant".

While in the forest, Timon starts to distribute "gold" in a more selective manner. Only those who have managed to find him in the forest may receive it. However, those who have arrived there but are still looking for "usury" are sent away. Timon diagnoses and decides what remedy should be applied to those who have managed to find him in the forest. Among those who meet Timon in the forest are two prostitutes, Phrynia and Timandra. The appearance of Phrynia and Timandra is another feature that Athens inherited from Ancient Greece. We may recognize in Timandra and Phrynia the whorish heroines Helen and Cressida from "Troilus and Cressida".

Timon also encounters his steward Flavius. Flavius is the only Athenian who was able to correctly discharge his service. Therefore, he can be entrusted with a more demanding function. Timon gives him gold on the condition that he will keep it, but never give it to anyone, even the skinniest beggar. Flavius' new role is that of *shepherd* of the "gold".

The city as a whole is not capable of benefiting from this opportunity. In the end, there is only one possible way that might help the Athenians to save themselves from the coming catastrophe. This is their last chance. Timon tells the Athenians of a tree near his cave that he will soon cut down. Timon says that anyone, who wants to avoid the upcoming disaster, should come to the tree and "hang himself":

"I have a tree, which grows here in my close,
That mine own use invites me to cut down,

And shortly must I fell it: tell my friends,
Tell Athens, in the sequence of degree
From high to low throughout, that whoso please
To stop affliction, let him take his haste,
Come hither, ere my tree hath felt the axe,
And hang himself."
(*Timon of Athens, V.1*)

In this quote Timon spells out a possible solution for the Athenians: they could save themselves by giving up their selfish wants. This sort of giving up means "dying" to one's earthly desires, or "hanging" oneself on the tree. If they did attempt to hang themselves, the tree would fall and under it they would find Timon's "gold". This is the meaning of "man has to die before dying". However, there is a time limit for such an action: it will have to be performed before Timon cuts down the tree. The tree symbolically represents the temporary link to Mytilene. The time limit for the activation of the permanent link is set by Pericles' sleep. It will expire at the moment of Pericles' awakening.

Timon's message is incomprehensible to the Athenians at their current developmental stage. They are not capable of benefiting from Timon's teaching. Therefore, the "gold" must be preserved for some future time. Timon dies. He leaves his epitaph in which he says that he will preserve his treasure in "his everlasting mansion". This "everlasting mansion" is a reference to the place where his gold will be transferred. Timon's death marks the deactivation of Mytilene. It corresponds to Pericles and Marina leaving Mytilene and going to Ephesus.

Timon's presence gave Athens a chance to form a permanent link with the intermediate state. Athens missed this great opportunity. Despite this, the process had to be advanced and moved forward. From Athens the process continues westward. The next stage encompasses the region on the west cost of the Balkan Peninsula.

Shakespeare refers to that area as "Bohemia". It is there that Timon's gold will be transferred. The activities taking place in that area are illustrated in the Bohemian plays. It is in this context that "Timon of Athens" may be considered the first Bohemian play.

A new transmission chain

The reunion of Pericles and Marina takes place in Mytilene. At this very moment Pericles hears the music of the spheres:

> "The music of the spheres! List, my Marina."

> "Most heavenly music!
> It nips me unto listening, and thick slumber
> Hangs upon mine eyes: let me rest."
> (*Pericles, V.1*)

Immediately after hearing "the music of the spheres" Pericles falls asleep. It is then that the goddess Diana appears in his dream and commands him to go to her temple in Ephesus and reveal his story. This episode takes place on the day of Neptune's festival. It symbolically confirms that Neptune and Diana, i.e., the agents of the Realm, are involved in the process. When Pericles wakes up, he goes to Ephesus where he is reunited with Thaisa. The reunion with Thaisa takes place within the ordinary world. This brings Pericles back to the beginning of his journey: the reunion takes place in the 7th century.

Thaisa informs Pericles that Simonides, her father, has died. Pericles becomes Simonides' successor. Pericles announces that they will celebrate the marriage of Lysimachus and Marina in Pentapolis:

"This prince, the fair-betrothed of your daughter,
Shall marry her at Pentapolis."
(*Pericles, V.3*)

At this point a new structure of the transmission chain is completed. It contains Diana, Neptune, Thaisa, Pericles, Marina, Lysimachus and the "silent" Lady, who appears in the final scene. The silent Lady is one of Shakespeare's so-called ghost characters. These characters are mentioned in the stage directions, although they neither say nor do anything. Shakespeare uses these ghost characters to indicate links to his other plays. The silent Lady of Ephesus is one of the courtesans trained by Marina in Mytilene. She accompanied Marina during her reunion with Pericles (Marina's "companion maid"). The silent Lady represents an impulse of creative energy. The presence of the Lady is needed to form the lowest link of the transmission chain. This lowest link of the transmission chain is open; it has an empty spot. This means that the lowest link is accessible to those gathered in the temple in Ephesus and who were able to learn from Pericles' story. They may fill-in the empty spot. In this way they may be spiritually lifted all the way up to the Realm. It is the first time that modern man is provided with such an access.

In this newly formed transmission chain the creative energy (the silent Lady) provides a link between the ordinary state and the intermediate state; the unitive energy (Marina) links the intermediate state with the higher state; the supracognitive energy (Thaisa) provides a link to the Realm. When the lowest link will be completed, i.e., when there will be a suitable partner for the silent Lady, then the overall structure will form a new template; it will consist of four couples. This new template will take the shape of an ascending octagon that expands from the ordinary state via the intermediate and higher states all the way up to the Realm. This octagonal structure is like a ladder that provides man with an access to the Realm. It is a new form of the evolutionary template. This means that after Pericles' return to Pentapolis, the evolutionary template was changed from a triangle into an octagon.

The newly restored chain enabled the transmission of the entire spectrum of evolutionary energies. The spectrum now included the supracognitive energy, the highest energy available in the galaxy. This was the most significant event in the evolutionary history of mankind. The conscious energy was made available to ordinary men. However, neither supracognitive, unitive, nor creative energy was released to humanity at large[6].

At the end of Pericles' mission, the entire spectrum was made available to a select group of people. This group is symbolically represented by those who were present at Diana's temple in Ephesus at the time of Pericles' reunion with Thaisa. They witnessed Pericles' account of his experiences; they were exposed to the impact of the octagon. In this way they were linked to the transmission chain. Since then, this group of people, and their successors, have been acting as the custodians and the guides of the evolutionary process. Their role is to act at critical stages of the process, contriving results necessary to keep the whole evolution of the planet in step with events in the galaxy. Since that time, these custodians have supervised and directed evolutionary interventions or initiations of new phases of the evolutionary process. Some of the guides, characterized by their extraordinary perception and skills, appear in Shakespeare's plays.

***

"Pericles, Prince of Tyre" provides a key to the design on which Shakespeare's plays are based. For obvious reasons, this key was not left in the door: "Pericles, Prince of Tyre" was the only one of Shakespeare's plays that was not included in the 1623 First Folio,

---

[6] The characters representing impulses of unitive and creative energies are listed in Table on page 39.

i.e., the first collection of Shakespeare's plays. However, the "key" was very well preserved. The printing rights to the play were in the hands of the same shop that printed the First Folio.

MODERN EVOLUTIONARY CYCLE

Pericles retraces his steps and returns to Pentapolis. Upon his return to Pentapolis, the descending-ascending loop is closed. His mission has been completed. A major milestone of human evolution has been achieved. This milestone is referred to as the first spiritual millennium of the modern world. It is marked by a change of the cosmic matrix: the evolutionary template is changed from a triangle into an octagon. Chivalric Pentapolis is transformed into Mauritania.

It is obvious that the Greek and the Roman fiascos delayed the evolution of the planet. Therefore, it was necessary to implement a strategy which would allow it to catch up with the overall galactic plan. After the re-activation of the transmission chain, the custodians gained access to an advanced developmental methodology. The previous methodology was based on a sequential approach, i.e., assimilation of a lower impulse was the first step and was followed by exposure to a higher mode of evolutionary energy. Now however, access to the entire spectrum of developmental energies and the catalytic presence of supracognitive energy provide the possibility of a more effective approach. In this approach several impulses may be used at the same time. A simultaneous exposure to several evolutionary impulses enables the accelerated formation of an octagonal inner structure. Such a structure, in its simplified form, may be formed within the ordinary state. The activation of an octagon produces a "wave" that spreads and affects its immediate environment. Shakespeare uses the term "glory" to describe this effect. And he compares it to "a circle in the water" that spreads out over time:

> "Glory is like a circle in the water,
> Which never ceaseth to enlarge itself

Till by broad spreading it disperse to nought."
(*Henry VI, part 1, I.2*)

After some time, such a wave disperses "to nought". However, if there are two or more waves spreading from different places, then they may meet at a particular point and overlap. If their timing and amplitudes are correctly aligned, there is a possibility for their constructive superposition. As a result, the overall effect would be enhanced and prolonged; a permanent higher state may be activated.

It was such a strategy that was implemented in Western Europe. The decision was made to form two octagonal structures in two different geographical areas. One octagon was to be placed in Italy; the second in England. The "wave field" generated by these two octagons would cover the entire area of Western Europe. It was this wave field that would bring Europe out of her Dark Ages. In order to execute this phase of the process, two new transmission channels were needed. These two channels were activated from two new intermediate states, Cyprus and Sicily.

After the death of Timon of Athens, Mytilene was deactivated and split into two new intermediate states. These new states were represented by two islands, Cyprus and Sicily. These two islands started to serve as two parallel intermediate states. They were activated directly from Mauritania. They became parts of the new evolutionary grid. It was through them that the evolutionary charges were transmitted. The charges contained evolutionary impulses that were sufficient for the formation of two octagonal structures.

The Cypriot projection aimed at the activation of an inner octagonal structure within the being of England. This channel led from Cyprus via Moorish Spain to the South of France and England. The Cypriot charge contained the entire charge needed for the formation of an octagon. It included the four evolutionary impulses, i.e., *yellow*, *red*, *black*, and *white*. The impulse of creative energy (*yellow*) was previously released within the Celtic and Roman branches. As described in "King Lear", at the time of its first release in Britain, this impulse was under the protection of the Chivalric Knights. At the time of "Titus Andronicus", it was represented by Lavinia. After the collapse of the Roman branch, it was transferred from Rome to Mytilene. After the deactivation of Mytilene, this impulse of creative energy was placed in Cyprus. This impulse together with the remaining impulses needed for the formation of the octagon, i.e., *black*, *red*, and *white*, were to be transmitted from Cyprus via Moorish Spain to France and then to England.

The Sicilian link was designed to activate an octagonal inner structure in Italy. This channel was supposed to transmit the evolutionary charge from Sicily via the West coast of the Balkan Peninsula to northern Italy. The Sicilian projection included the impulse of unitive energy that was previously activated within the Celtic branch. At the time of "Cymbeline" this impulse (*red*) was represented by Imogen. Before the collapse of the Celtic branch, this impulse was removed from the Celtic branch and was placed in northern Italy. The charge invested in the Sicilian link consisted of the remaining impulses needed for the formation of an octagonal inner structure, i.e., *black*, *white* and *yellow*. These impulses were to be transmitted from Sicily via the Balkan Peninsula to Italy.

As stated above, in order to implement the next milestone of human evolution, two active octagonal inner structures, one in England and the other in Italy, were required. The remaining plays are a record of the efforts invested in this evolutionary milestone. In the ordinary world, this milestone would be manifested as the appearance of the European Renaissance.

Sicilian link

After the completion of Pericles' mission, the next step of the process required building an infrastructure which would allow the transmission of the needed evolutionary charge from Sicily via the Balkans to Italy. Such an infrastructure may be compared to an electricity distribution grid. Electrical energy is transmitted from a power plant to distribution stations via high voltage transmission lines. High voltage is then gradually reduced by passing through a number of intermediate substations before being fed into houses. A house's main electrical panel is the lowest substation in the transmission grid that is needed to provide a house with electrical power.

"The Comedy of Errors" describes how the Sicilian link was used to form a new evolutionary distribution grid in Europe.

The Comedy of Errors

The city of Syracuse located on the Island of Sicily was selected as an outpost for the transmission of evolutionary energies to Italy. The city of Epidamnum, which is located on the West coast of the Balkan Peninsula, was the first place linked to the Sicilian outpost. It was the place where Timon's "gold" was transferred from Athens. The Balkan Peninsula was to serve as a step leading to Italy. According to Shakespeare's presentation, this area was at one time part of Bohemia. In ancient times this region was known as Illyria.

The link between Sicily and Bohemia is formed through a transmission triad. In "The Comedy of Errors" the triad is described as consisting of Emilia, her husband Egeon, and Egeon's agent. Emilia is a custodian of the transmission. Emilia has access to the entire evolutionary spectrum and is able to exercise her supracognitive perception. Her role is to establish a new transmission link. Emilia and Egeon reside in Syracuse; Egeon's agent lives in Epidamnum.

Egeon of Syracuse has made his "wealth" during frequent trips to Epidamnum:

"Our wealth increased
By prosperous voyages I often made
To Epidamnum."
(*The Comedy of Errors, I.1*)

Egeon's "wealth" was Timon's "gold" that was transferred from Athens to the Balkan Peninsula. When Egeon's agent died, Egeon had to leave Syracuse and travel to Epidamnum. A new triad had to be formed to sustain and expand the evolutionary process. Emilia, who was pregnant, followed her husband to Epidamnum.

Shakespeare gives a compelling description of the advanced methodology that was made available to the custodians after the restoration of the transmission chain. The process is accelerated through a simultaneous activation of two triads. The preparation for the triads is marked by two sets of twins born in Epidamnum. Egeon and Emilia's twins are named Antipholi. The other set of twins named Dromios, are Antopoli's servants. It helps to understand the allegorical meaning of "The Comedy of Errors" to realize that Emilia's twins represent two aspects of the intellectual faculty; their servants symbolize the self faculty. Presently these two aspects of the intellect are still in their dormant states. They will become functional once the boys reach maturity.

Emilia's twins are entangled. This means that these two aspects are intertwined with each other even though they may be at different locations, in different environments, or placed in different time dimensions. The entanglement enables for simultaneous exposure to reforming and purifying energies.

After the birth of the boys, Emilia insists on going back to Syracuse. The ship carrying Egeon, Emilia and the two sets of twins is broken apart by a storm. It is then that Emilia forms the two triads:

> "My wife, more careful for the latter-born,
> Had fasten'd him unto a small spare mast,
> Such as seafaring men provide for storms;
> To him one of the other twins was bound,
> Whilst I had been like heedful of the other:
> The children thus disposed, my wife and I,
> Fixing our eyes on whom our care was fix'd,
> Fasten'd ourselves at either end the mast."
> (*The Comedy of Errors, I.1*)

This quote gives a precise description of the newly formed triads. By referring to "the latter-born" Egeon emphasizes a qualitative difference between the triads. This difference determines their evolutionary functions, i.e., the "latter-born" is designated for a higher evolutionary energy. Although the expression "Fixing our eyes on whom our care was fix'd" may seem to be ambivalent, its meaning is further clarified in the final scene of the play. Namely, the Syracusian Dromio clearly indicates that "the latter-born" applies to the Syracusian triad:

> "Not I, sir; you are my elder."
> (*The Comedy of Errors, V.1*)

Thus, Egeon, the younger Antipholus, and his servant Dromio form the higher triad. Emilia, the elder Antipholus and the other Dromio form the lower triad. These triads will serve as the basic infrastructure of the new evolutionary grid.

During the storm, the mast is split in half and its two parts are projected towards different destinations. The sailors from Epidaurus rescue Egeon, his younger son and his servant, Dromio.

Egeon is able to return to Syracuse. This triad is put temporarily in a standby position until the time is ripe for the next step in the process.

Emilia, together with the elder Antipholus and the other Dromio, is rescued by men from Epidamnum. However, some pirates reroute their traveling path and separate Emilia from her elder son and his servant. The elder Antipholus and his Dromio end up in the service of the Duke of Ephesus. Emilia goes to the abbey of Diana in Ephesus.

Diana's sanctuary and her devotees' role is to protect and preserve the evolutionary energies until the environment is ready for their assimilation. This part of the process follows the pattern described in "Pericles, Prince of Tyre". The separation of Egeon and Emilia, like that of Pericles and Thaisa, represents a period of protection.

The next step requires the activation of the triads by their exposure to reforming and purifying energies. In other words, each of these two "chariots" has to be transformed from a sterile into an active triad (This corresponds to the transformation that Octavius attempted to implement in Rome). This step of the process must be completed in a temporary powerhouse, represented here by Diana's abbey in Ephesus. The play describes the twins' journey to Diana's abbey.

The adventures of Antipholi describe two parallel processes, reformation and purification. The reformation process is illustrated by the experiences of the Ephesian (elder) brother. The adventures of the Syracusian (younger) brother describe the purification process.

The reformation is realized through exposure to conscious energy. Adriana, the wife of the Ephesian Antipholus, represents this previously released energy. After the reunion of Pericles and Thaisa, this energy was made available to ordinary men. For some time, therefore, the Ephesian Antipholus has been exposed to conscious energy. In accordance with the entanglement principle, the Syracusian brother has been affected by the experiences of his twin brother in Ephesus. When the Syracusian brother reaches the age of eighteen years, he feels compelled to look for his lost brother. His sea-journey marks the inception of the purification process.

The Syracusian brother travels on the sea for "seven short years" before his arrival in Ephesus. These "seven short years" apply to the time dimension of the transitory zone between Syracuse and Ephesus, i.e., between an intermediate state and an ordinary state. The "seven short years" are equivalent to his brother's seven days in Ephesus. It was during "this week" that his elder brother, Antipholus of Ephesus, felt distraught and troubled and as a result, started to meet with a courtesan. This change was noticed by Adriana, his wife:

> "This week he hath been heavy, sour, sad,
> And much different from the man he was."
> (*The Comedy of Errors, III.1*)

The purification process is accomplished by exposure to creative energy. The play indicates that, at this time, the centre in Ephesus released two impulses of creative energy. In preparation for the formation of the Italian octagon, the creative energy provided by the centre consisted of two impulses, i.e., *white* and *yellow*. The impulse designated for the Italian intellect (*white*) is represented by Luciana, Adriana's sister. The impulse targeted for the Italian heart (*yellow*) is represented by the Courtesan of Ephesus. These two impulses were made available in Ephesus.

The final stage of the purification process is realized when Antipholus of Syracuse meets Luciana. After meeting Luciana, the Syracusian Antipholus seems to be showered with gold. First, he is given a bag of gold; then he is presented with a golden chain. When the Syracusian Antipholus is exposed to creative energy, the Ephesian Antipholus is also affected by the experience of his brother. At this very moment he is having lunch with the Courtesan.

It should be emphasized that it is not an ordinary attraction that brought the Ephesian Antipholus into the company of the Courtesan. The Courtesan is the current projection of the silent Lady who accompanied Marina in the final scene of "Pericles, Prince of Tyre". Her appearance is a preparation for the future stages of the Italian branch. The present role of the Courtesan is to assist the process by preparing the Ephesian Antipholus for reunion with his brother. Here is the Ephesian Antipholus' comment about her:

"I know a wench of excellent discourse,
Pretty and witty; wild, and yet, too, gentle:
There will we dine. This woman that I mean,
My wife - but, I protest, without desert -
Hath oftentimes upbraided me withal."
(The Comedy of Errors, III.1)

As in the conclusion of "Pericles, Prince of Tyre", the completion of the process takes place in Diana's abbey in Ephesus. It is there that the twins are reunited. Emilia's presence provides the catalyst for the completion of this particular developmental stage. It is then that the two chariots are transformed into two fertile triads. The lower triad consists of Egeon, Adriana, and Antipholus of Ephesus. Emilia, Luciana, and Antipholus of Syracuse form the higher triad. Through Emilia, the higher triad is linked to the Realm. They all constitute a new link in the transmission chain.

The newly formed link was used to move the process to Bohemia. It was this link that was needed to project the evolutionary energies from Sicily via Bohemia to Italy. The next stage of the process is illustrated in "The Winter's Tale". "The Winter's Tale" is set in the 13th century.

The Winter's Tale

At the conclusion of "The Comedy of Errors", a new link within the evolutionary transmission chain containing two triads was formed. The higher triad was placed in Sicily. The lower triad was moved to Bohemia. Now, this link is to be used to transmit the evolutionary charge from Sicily via Bohemia on the Balkan Peninsula to the Italian Peninsula.

Through exposure to the evolutionary energies in Ephesus, both Antipholi gained spiritual "nobility". In "The Winter's Tale" the Antipholi twins reappear as Leontes, King of Sicily and Polixenes, King of Bohemia. The "twinn'd" kings are the spiritual descendants of the Antipholi:

> "We were as twinn'd lambs that did frisk i' the sun,
> And bleat the one at the other."
> (*The Winter's Tale, I.2*)

Sicily represents the new intermediate state. Bohemia represents an ordinary state. Although the triads are physically in different locations, the entanglement between them has been preserved and maintained. Here is Lord Camillo's comment about the strong link between these two triads:

> "They were trained together in their childhoods; and
> there rooted betwixt them then such an affection,
> which cannot choose but branch now. Since their
> more mature dignities and royal necessities made
> separation of their society, their encounters,
> though not personal, have been royally attorneyed

with interchange of gifts, letters, loving
embassies; that they have seemed to be together,
though absent, shook hands, as over a vast, and
embraced, as it were, from the ends of opposed
winds. The heavens continue their loves!"
(*The Winter's Tale, I.1*)

The Sicilian triad consists of King Leontes, his wife Hermione, and their son Mamillius. Hermione is a custodian of the transmission chain. She is the inheritor of Emilia's mandate. She provides a link to the Realm. Therefore, she is able to exercise her supracognitive perception. Her role is to direct the implementation of the next steps of the process. The presence of Hermione means that Antipholus of Syracuse did not marry Luciana. Luciana and the Courtesan remained in Ephesus. As in the case of Antony and Fulvia, Antipholus' encounter with Luciana was a preparatory step. After the reunion of the twins at the time of "The Comedy of Errors", he was put on an accelerated developmental path; he married Hermione.

Mamillius, the son of the Sicilian King, represents an aspect of the spiritual heart. At the beginning of the play, this aspect is still dormant. This means that the Sicilian link is without a spiritual heart. An inner structure without a spiritual heart may be compared to a lame person who needs crutches to perform his basic functions. The current state of Sicily represents such a spiritually lame being. Here is Lord Camillo's comment about the hopes that the presence of Mamillius will "physics the subject" by rectifying their lameness and making "old hearts fresh":

"I very well agree with you in the hopes of him: it
is a gallant child; one that indeed physics the
subject, makes old hearts fresh: they that went on
crutches ere he was born desire yet their life to

see him a man."
(*The Winter's Tale, I.1*)

In other words, "The Winter's Tale" illustrates an attempt at awakening the spiritual heart within the Sicilian link. The spiritual heart is needed to form the Italian octagon. "The Winter's Tale" is the first play of Shakespeare's Italian plays.

Hermione prepares the conditions that would allow the formation of the Italian octagon. Let's recall, that the previously released impulse of unitive energy (*red*) remains dormant in Italy. This impulse is there in standby mode since its removal from the Celtic branch. Mamillius is the intended partner for this impulse. Mamillius, however, intuitively perceives that he will not be able to fulfil his evolutionary function. This is reflected by his "sad tale's best for winter", in which he foretells his death:

"There was a man -"

"Dwelt by a churchyard."
(*The Winter's Tale, II.1*)

This unfinished sad tale is a reference to the future situation when his father, King Leontes, will be dwelling by a graveyard, mourning Mamillius' death.

At the beginning of the play Hermione is pregnant. Hermione's daughter to-be-born and the dormant lady (*red*) in Italy constitute the complementary impulses to Luciana (*white*) and the Courtesan of Ephesus (*yellow*). Together they provide the complete evolutionary charge needed for the formation of an octagon in Italy. This means that Hermione's daughter is coloured for an aspect of the intellect (*black*).

Florizel is the son of Polixenes and he represents an aspect of the intellect. In accordance with Hermione's plan, Florizel of Bohemia is the intended husband for her daughter. At the beginning of the play, King Polixenes is visiting Sicily. The presence of King Polixenes in Sicily is needed to entangle this impulse of evolutionary energy with Bohemia. This is why Hermione insists that Polixenes cannot leave before the birth of her daughter. She offers Polixenes a no-choice option by bidding him to stay in Sicily either as a prisoner or as her guest. Later on Hermione explains to her husband, King Leontes, that her "purpose" of insisting on Polixenes' extended stay in Sicily is as important as was their marriage:

> "I have spoke to the purpose twice:
> The one for ever earn'd a royal husband;
> The other for some while a friend."
> (*The Winter's Tale, I.2*)

Hermione's attitude is an example of acting in accordance with the supreme priority. Her acts are driven entirely by "the purpose". She puts the same value on the two intermediate steps leading to "the purpose," i.e., earning "a royal husband" and "for some while a friend". Let's recall that Cordelia in "King Lear" also intended to follow the same approach, i.e., half her love for her husband, and the other half for her evolutionary duty:

> "Haply, when I shall wed,
> That lord whose hand must take my plight shall carry
> Half my love with him, half my care and duty."
> (*King Lear, I.1*)

The main difficulty that Hermione has to overcome is her husband's ignorance. King Leontes is unable to comprehend the true nature of Hermione's purpose. For whatever reason, he has not been correctly developed. He was not able to benefit from the accelerated path. If Leontes had been correctly developed, he would have understood the importance of "the purpose" and he would have contributed to it with joy. But in this case, his non-readiness manifests as jealousy and this jealousy interferes with the process:

> "Too hot, too hot!
> To mingle friendship far is mingling bloods.
> I have tremor cordis on me: my heart dances;
> But not for joy; not joy."
> (*The Winter's Tale, I.2*)

Driven by his ignorance and jealousy, Leontes publicly accuses his wife of infidelity and declares that the child she is bearing must be illegitimate. He sends a request to the Oracle of Delphi for a verdict. He is sure that the oracle will confirm his suspicions. Then he throws Hermione into prison. While in prison, Hermione gives birth to a baby girl. Leontes orders Lord Antigonus to take the bastard child and abandon it in some desolate place.

Because of being born in the inferior environment of the prison, the girl's evolutionary function could not be fully manifested. Her function has been degraded. Instead of unitive energy (*black*), the baby represents an impulse of creative energy (*white*). This seriously affects the future of the Italian branch. Without the *black* impulse, it will not be possible to form an octagonal inner structure.

Apollo's temple in Delphi provides a link to the Realm. Apollo delivers the oracle that reflects the "Will" of the Realm:

> "Hermione is chaste;
> Polixenes blameless; Camillo a true subject; Leontes
> a jealous tyrant; his innocent babe truly begotten;
> and the king shall live without an heir, if that
> which is lost be not found."
> (*The Winter's Tale, III.2*)

Leontes, however, ignores the oracle's message. His disregard of the oracle results in the disconnection of Sicily from the transmission chain. The break does not allow for the continuation of the process. The link with the higher state is cut off. This may be compared to blowing the fuses of a main electrical circuit. At this very moment, a servant informs Leontes that Mamillius has died. Mamillius will not be able to meet his lady: the Italian impulse of unitive energy cannot be re-activated. Mamillius is removed because his evolutionary function could not be fulfilled within the current environment of Sicily.

Hermione understands that the current situation does not allow for the continuation of the process. Because of the break in the link with the higher state, the process is interrupted. Hermione realizes that she must withdraw herself from the present situation and be absent until a time when the overall circumstances will be correctly realigned. Hermione swoons and Paulina reports that the Queen has died. Hermione's death represents her temporary absence and her withdrawal marks a temporary switching off of the process. This corresponds to the arrival of a spiritual "winter". Sicily is disconnected from the process. As a result, Luciana (*white*) and the Courtesan (*yellow*) are stuck in Ephesus.

Because of the insufficiency of the Sicilian court, another venue is required where the process may be continued. Such a venue has been prepared previously. Namely, it is the forest that was activated at the time of "Timon of Athens". Let's recall that Timon built "his everlasting mansion" in a forest near Athens where he hid his gold. In his epitaph, however, Timon advised the Athenians not to stay by his grave near Athens, but to pass by and move forward:

"Pass by and curse thy fill, but pass and stay not here thy gait."
(*Timon of Athens, V.4*)

Timon's epitaph indicated that his "gold" would be available at another place and time. As indicated in the discussion of "The Comedy of Errors", Timon's "gold" was transferred to Epidamnum onto the Balkan Peninsula. Shakespeare refers to that area as Bohemia. This is why Hermione appears to Antigonus in a dream and bids him to name her daughter Perdita and leave her in a remote place in Bohemia. In this way the newborn girl is delivered to the Bohemian forest. Immediately afterwards, Antigonus is killed by a bear and the ship that brought him to Bohemia is destroyed by a tempest: the link between Sicily and Bohemia is also severed. The impulse represented by Perdita is removed from Sicily and placed in the Bohemian forest. Italy does not have access to creative energy. Thus, the possibility for accelerated progress could not be brought to fruition.

The appearance of Perdita in the Bohemian forest fulfils Timon's prediction. The Shepherd and his son Clown live in the Bohemian forest. The Shepherd is the current projection of Flavius, Timon's faithful steward. The Shepherd finds Hermione's abandoned child. Here is Clown's remark to his father about this event:

> "You're a made old man: if the sins of your youth
> are forgiven you, you're well to live. Gold! all gold!"
> (*The Winter's Tale, III.3*)

Gold is a mark of the presence of creative energy. In other words, the Shepherd finds Timon's "gold". He raises Perdita as his daughter.

The Bohemian forest was an oppressive and chilly wilderness when Antigonus landed there. Sixteen years later the forest is a different place. Perdita has matured and her maturity is manifested by the arrival of spring. Perdita's evolutionary potential has been awakened. It is then that Florizel meets Perdita. Florizel is attracted by Perdita's beauty and he falls in love with her.

King Polixenes becomes suspicious of Florizel's frequent disappearances from the court. He decides to disguise himself so he may spy on his son. He attends a sheep shearing at the

Shepherd's cottage. When he sees Perdita he thinks that she is "too noble for this place":

"This is the prettiest low-born lass that ever
Ran on the green-sward: nothing she does or seems
But smacks of something greater than herself,
Too noble for this place."
(*The Winter's Tale, IV.4*)

Polixenes was not present at Perdita's birth, therefore he is incapable of recognizing her. When he realizes that Florizel and Perdita are about to be betrothed, he tears off his disguise and interrupts the ceremony. He orders his son never to see Perdita again.

Florizel and Perdita decide to escape from Bohemia. They board a ship and go to Sicily. The Shepherd and his son Clown join them on their voyage. In Sicily, Florizel tells King Leontes that he is on a diplomatic mission from his father. He pretends that he is coming from Libya, where he married an African princess:

"Good my lord,
She came from Libya."
(*The Winter's Tale, V.1*)

Indeed, Perdita's current function corresponds to that of Dido, who lived in North Africa. At this point it is important to remember that Florizel is destined for unitive energy (*black*). Therefore, there is an evolutionary mismatch between him and Perdita. This means that he cannot be married to Perdita.

Leontes welcomes the son of his old friend warmly. But Florizel's cover is blown when Polixenes, too, arrives in Sicily. It is then that the Shepherd tells everyone his story of how Perdita was found. Leontes realizes that Perdita is his daughter. Everyone rejoices at the happy reunion of family and friends. The entire company then goes to a country house, where a statue of Hermione has recently been finished. The sight of his wife's statue makes Leontes distraught. Then, to everyone's amazement, the statue becomes animated and Hermione is restored to life.

As a reward for his service, the Shepherd and his son are granted nobility. Here is the Shepherd's comment to his son:

> "Come, boy; I am past more children, but thy sons and
> daughters will be all gentlemen born."
> (*The Winter's Tale*, *V.2*)

Granting nobility to the Shepherd and his son was needed to open up a new venue for the continuation of the process. (In the context of Shakespeare's plays, "nobility" means capacity to play an active role in the evolutionary process.) Clown's "sons and daughters" will become substitutes for the royals. They will play the role that Mamillius could not fulfil.

After the break in the transmission chain, the Kingdom of Sicily was reduced to an ordinary state. Symbolically, this may be indicated by shifting the action from an island to the continent. The Kingdom of Sicily was comprised of the Island of Sicily and Naples on the southern part of the Italian Peninsula. Historically, the evolutionary break that occurred in Sicily was manifested by the split of the Kingdom of Sicily and the formation of the Kingdom of Naples. This means that this particular experience was transferred from the Kingdom of Sicily to the ordinary state of the Kingdom of Naples. It is there that, later on, Perdita and Mamillius will be able to discharge their originally intended roles. They will remain in Naples until the time of "The Tempest".

The Sicilian break occurred at the level between the higher and the intermediate states. This is why, at the conclusion of the play, Bohemia and Sicily remain disconnected from the Realm. This disconnection jeopardizes the sustainability of Sicily and prevents the continuation of the process within the Italian branch. By granting nobility to the Shepherd, Shakespeare indicates that Bohemia will serve as a backup for the Italian branch. However, the link between the higher state and Bohemia needs to be re-established first, before the process can be advanced there. Only then will the audience be able to meet Clown's "sons and daughters" as referred to by the Shepherd.

Othello

Upon Pericles' return to Pentapolis, the overall cosmic matrix was changed and Mauritania started to function as the higher state. Mauritania is linked to two intermediate states, i.e., Cyprus and Sicily. Let's recall that these two links were formed as the new transmission channels. As described in "The Winter's Tale", the link between Sicily and the higher state was cut-off. Without this link it was impossible to continue the transmission of evolutionary energies through the Sicilian channel. In order to continue and advance the evolutionary process in Italy, the link between Sicily and the higher state had to be re-established. In order to do this, Cyprus, which was the only available link to Mauritania, had to be used.

The situation of Sicily is very similar to that encountered by Pericles in Tarsus. At that time, Tarsus representing an intermediate state was disconnected from the transmission chain. We may expect that the remedy needed for fixing the transmission chain would be based on those previous experiences. Following Pericles' example, the restoration of the transmission chain would require a fully developed man to make a journey, all the way to the higher state. Such a man would have to be an experienced traveller who had returned from "the undiscovered country", i.e., had made such a journey previously. He would be a "music master", i.e., he would be able to exercise his supracognitive skills. This time the higher state is represented by Mauritania. This is why the guide would have to be of Mauritanian origin; he would be a Moor.

The repair of the link between Sicily and the higher state required an impulse of unitive energy. At the time of "The Winter's Tale" this impulse of unitive energy was already present within the ordinary state. This means that the Moor would have to bring this impulse with him all the way up to Mauritania. First of all, such an impulse would have to be found and re-activated. The impulse of unitive energy would be represented by a young beautiful woman.

In the analysis of "Cymbeline" it is indicated that the previously activated impulse of unitive energy was removed from the Celtic branch and embedded somewhere in northern Italy. Historically, such a location would have to be linked to Cyprus. The city of Venice located in northern Italy fits such a profile. This implies that the corrective action would be initiated in Venice.

The execution of the corrective action needed for the repair of the Sicilian link is described in "Othello". Othello, the Moor, is charged with this incredibly difficult task. To complete it, Othello must retrace Pericles' steps. First he must find and woo Desdemona. Desdemona represents the impulse of unitive energy (*red*). She is the current projection of Imogen from "Cymbeline". Afterwards, Othello and Desdemona have to travel together from Venice to Cyprus and then to Mauritania.

The later stage of their journey requires passing through the transition from the intermediate to the higher state. As shown by Thaisa's experience, such a transition requires one to "die before dying". It is only after "dying" to their earthly attachments that Othello and Desdemona can reach Mauritania. Later on, the impulse of unitive energy will have to be sent back to Venice via Sicily. In this way the Sicilian link may be re-activated.

The play illustrates how Othello was able to achieve his goal. While in Venice, Othello gathers a group of disciples who have recognized him as their guide. Among Othello's disciples are Iago, Cassio and Roderigo. Iago is the most advanced of Othello's disciples. Iago is capable of seeing and understanding things that are hidden to the other disciples and knows what they do not know.

Nevertheless it was Cassio, "a great arithmetician" with no military experience, who was promoted by Othello to be second in command. Iago could not be promoted because, despite his skills, he is entirely driven by his selfish tendencies. It is then that Iago decides that he is developed enough to be his own master and he is going to prove it. In other words, Iago's ambition to be his own master is the real driving force behind his actions. Iago is an example of a "fallen" disciple. His main and only objective is to disturb the developmental process that is implemented by Othello. Iago's actions are simplistic, naïve, and even ridiculous. Nevertheless they seem to be quite effective.

We may notice that the Iago-type of villains appear in Shakespeare's plays each time there is a break in the transmission chain. Iago appears in Venice after the break in the Sicilian link. Edmund's schemes could work only once Cordelia was removed from Britain at the time of "King Lear". Aaron was able to exercise his villainy at the time of the collapse of the Roman evolutionary branch in "Titus Andronicus". Macbeth appeared after the impulse of unitive energy was removed from the Celtic branch. As soon as the transmission chain is fixed, these most vicious villains are turned into little *Iagos*, e.g., Edmund becomes Iachimo (Little Iago) in "Cymbeline"; Iago reappears as Don John in "Much Ado About Nothing"; Aaron resurfaces as Caliban in "The Tempest".

Of course Othello is aware of Iago's objective and skills. Therefore, Othello adapts his approach in such a way that he uses Iago's motivations in his implementation plan. In this way he is able to discharge his function in accordance with his own objective.

As the first stage of their journey, Othello and Desdemona have to travel to Cyprus. Cyprus is an island that represents the currently operating intermediate state. In Cyprus the Venetians encounter Bianca. Bianca represents an impulse of creative energy (*yellow*). Bianca is the current projection of the impulse that previously appeared in "King Lear" as Cordelia and then in the Roman plays as Virgilia, Calphurnia, Fulvia, and Lavinia. After her brutal treatment at the time of "Titus Andronicus", Lavinia was withdrawn from Rome and was placed in Mytilene. She became one of Marina's pupils. After the deactivation of Mytilene, she was transferred to Cyprus.

Shakespeare emphasizes the difficulties associated with the previous attempts at assimilation of this particular energy by having Bianca appear as a courtesan. Let's recall that Cyprus was used to transmit the Chivalric sequence to the South of France. This impulse of creative energy (*yellow*) was part of the evolutionary charge that was to be projected via France to England. This means that Bianca is designated for the English branch.

It should also be noted that Othello has control over natural forces. This is illustrated when the Turkish fleet is completely destroyed by a tempest. Othello was able to invoke the help of a "foul and violent tempest" and in this way he protected Cyprus from the Turkish assault.

We should also notice that around Othello the Moor, there is an atmosphere of authentic nobility and greatness. Othello, like Julius Caesar, often refers to himself in the third person. All those around him respect him. For example, Othello is able to avert an imminent street fight with a single sentence:

"Keep up your bright swords, for the dew will rust them."
(*Othello*, I.2)

It is not a coincidence that Othello reminds us of Julius Caesar. The readers will recall that the assassination of Julius Caesar symbolically represented the rejection of unitive energy by Rome. At that time Rome was incapable of making constructive use of unitive energy, therefore the process had to be postponed. It took some 1,500 years before the next opportunity occurred in that geographical area. This next opportunity is marked by the arrival of Othello in Venice. In other words, Othello's role is the same as Julius Caesar's, but on a higher turn of the evolutionary spiral. This time the developmental methodology includes measures preventing the situations that led to Rome's failure.

Othello employs Iago to create situations that are part of his own strategy. As a matter of fact, Iago's actions follow Othello's teaching repertoire. Of course, all of these are lost on Iago. He is so full of himself and so engaged in his scheming that he, and the audience, do not register what Othello is really doing.

Objects bearing certain symbolic designs are capable of being spiritually charged. These objects may be "typed" for a specific person. They can be used as an instrument of both influence and assessment of the person acted upon. Bestowing such an object may indicate the selection of a guide's deputy in a given territory.

In "Othello", an embroidered handkerchief "spotted with strawberries" represents such a charged object. At the beginning of the play, Desdemona is the holder of the handkerchief. However, after Desdemona and Othello's departure to Mauritania, Cassio is to be Othello's deputy in Cyprus. At one point, therefore, it is necessary for Othello to transfer the handkerchief to Cassio. Othello has to arrange the transfer in such a way that it would be imperceptible to Cassio and Desdemona. Othello employs Iago to execute the transfer. Iago, who is driven by a completely different motivation, helps Othello place the handkerchief in Cassio's lodging. It is quite telling that, later on, the handkerchief in Cassio's room is supposed to be Iago's most damning proof of Desdemona's infidelity. Right after the transfer Cassio is promoted to the position of deputy-governor of Cyprus. It helps to grasp the following sequence of events to note that it was Othello himself who requested Cassio's promotion by sending a letter from Cyprus to the Venetian Senate.

Othello's biggest challenge is to prepare Desdemona for her transition to the higher state. Mauritania represents the higher state that operates outside of ordinary existence. Such a transition from the intermediate to the higher state is symbolically illustrated as "death" followed by "rebirth". In "Othello", this transition is symbolically illustrated as Othello's "killing" Desdemona's earthly attachments. Of course, such a transition does not have anything to do with physical death. The readers may recall that Thaisa in "Pericles, Prince of Tyre" went through a similar transition.

In order to continue their journey to Mauritania, Desdemona would have to trust and be obedient to Othello. While in Cyprus Desdemona is not fully "obedient" yet. Desdemona demonstrates her disobedience by trying to interfere with Othello's teaching of Cassio. Later on Desdemona's disobedience is further illustrated in the following exchange between her and Othello:

Othello:

"What, not a whore?"

Desdemona:

"No, as I shall be saved."

(*Othello*, *IV.2*)

It may help to understand this exchange to recall a similar exchange between Petruchio and Katharina in "The Taming of the Shrew".

Quoted below is Katharina's obedient response to Petruchio when he insists that the sun is really the moon:

"Then, God be bless'd, it is the blessed sun:
But sun it is not, when you say it is not;
And the moon changes even as your mind.
What you will have it named, even that it is;
And so it shall be so for Katharina."
(*The Taming of the Shrew*, IV.5)

Desdemona has not arrived yet at this degree of obedience. Another obstacle that prevents Desdemona from continuing her journey is her attachment to Othello. This is emphasized in this exchange between Desdemona and Othello. Desdemona says that her only sins:

"They are loves I bear to you."

And Othello answers:

"Ay, and for that thou diest."
(*Othello*, V.2)

Such attachment to Othello is a kind of idolatry. Desdemona does not understand Othello's function. This is why Othello insists that she is a "whore". Her attachment to Othello has to die before Desdemona may enter into the final stage of her journey. This is the meaning of "to die before dying".

Othello clearly indicates that his "killing" of Desdemona has nothing to do with physical harm; there is neither shedding of blood nor wounding:

"Yet I'll not shed her blood;
Nor scar that whiter skin of hers than snow,
And smooth as monumental alabaster.

Yet she must die, else she'll betray more men."
(*Othello, V.2*)

Desdemona has to "kill" her attachments to worldly matters. Otherwise, she will not be able to discharge her evolutionary function properly. And this, as illustrated in the Roman and Celtic plays, would "betray more men". Othello, however, cannot disclose to Desdemona his real purpose in "killing" her:

"It is the cause, it is the cause, my soul,
Let me not name it to you, you chaste stars!
It is the cause."
(*Othello, V.2*)

Otherwise, Desdemona would not be able to correctly experience this particular "exercise". In his confrontation with Desdemona in their bedchamber, Othello accuses her of giving the handkerchief to Cassio:

"By heaven, I saw my handkerchief in's hand."
(*Othello, V.2*)

and that Cassio has used her "unlawfully":

"He hath confess'd."

"That he hath used thee."
(*Othello, V.2*)

Of course Desdemona knows that she neither gave the handkerchief to Cassio nor slept with him. If she had enough trust in Othello, she would know that he would not lie to her. Therefore, she should realize that there must be another meaning to Othello's claims. Let's recall that Desdemona allowed herself to be used "unlawfully" by interfering with Othello's dealing with Cassio. Now Othello informs her that Cassio is safe and protected: the "magic" handkerchief is in Cassio's hands ("I saw my handkerchief in's hand"). Desdemona's protestations, therefore, are a sign that she does not trust Othello. If she had comprehended his function, she would be able to understand Othello's message. Desdemona's attachments to worldly matters are further manifested by her fears:

> "And yet I fear you; for you are fatal then
> When your eyes roll so: why I should fear I know not,
> Since guiltiness I know not; but yet I feel I fear."
> (*Othello, V.2*)

She could "sacrifice" her fears by putting herself willingly into Othello's hands. Because she is not able to do so, Othello has to "murder" her fears. This is why Othello says that instead of "a sacrifice", Desdemona has to experience "a murder":

> "And makest me call what I intend to do
> A murder, which I thought a sacrifice."
> (*Othello, V.2*)

It is only when Desdemona passes through this very difficult transition, i.e., when she "dies before dying", that is she able to fully comprehend Othello's actions. Then she realizes that it was not necessary for her to be "murdered":

> "O, falsely, falsely murder'd!"
> (*Othello, V.2*)

Only by "dying" was she able to see and get rid of her own shortcomings. This is why her death is "guiltless":

> "A guiltless death I die."

When Emilia asks her:

> "Who hath done this deed?"

"Dead" Desdemona explains:

"Nobody; I myself. Farewell
Commend me to my kind lord: O, farewell!
(*Othello*, *V*.*2*)

Desdemona's inner beauty may be fully manifested only when she reaches the higher state, i.e., Mauritania. Only then may her marriage be consummated. This is why the marriage between Othello and Desdemona could not be consummated before her "death". Here is Othello's comment about "dead" Desdemona:

"Now, how dost thou look now? O ill-starr'd wench!
Pale as thy smock! when we shall meet at compt,
This look of thine will hurl my soul from heaven,
And fiends will snatch at it. Cold, cold, my girl!
Even like thy chastity."
(*Othello*, *V*.*2*)

Othello says that Desdemona died not only faithful to him ("Even like thy chastity") but also as "Cold, cold, my girl!" In other words, Othello discloses that he knows that Desdemona "died" a virgin. The spiritual marriage could not be consummated, because Desdemona was not yet ready for it.

At the moment of Desdemona's transition to Mauritania the link to the higher state is re-established. Othello's mission is nearly accomplished. Now Othello also has to "die" to be reunited with Desdemona. Othello hints at this part of his journey when he says that:

"For, in my sense, 'tis happiness to die."
(*Othello*, *V*.*2*)

Before he "departs", Othello makes sure that Iago's nature and his wickedness have been fully exposed. Such exposure, or rebuke, is a sort of spiritual immunization against future encounters with this sort of villain.

Upon Othello's and Desdemona' arrival in the higher state, Mauritania is transformed into Messaline. This is similar to the transformation of the higher state into Mauritania upon Pericles' return to Pentapolis. After Pentapolis and Mauritania, Messaline constitutes the third consecutive higher state referred to in Shakespeare's plays.

To continue Othello's ascending-descending loop, the process moves from Messaline to Sicily. In this way Sicily may be reconnected to the transmission chain. This stage of the journey is illustrated in "Much Ado About Nothing".

Much Ado About Nothing

This play is the sequel to "The Winter's Tale" and "Othello". This is why its main characters resemble the ones who appeared in those two plays.

The action takes place in Messina, a coastal city in Sicily. Messina is a renewed state, which at the time of "The Winter's Tale" was represented by the Kingdom of Sicily. The Sicilian experiences are represented by Leonato and his brother Antonio. We may recognize in Leonato, the governor of Messina, Leontes, the King of Sicily. Leontes' brother, Antonio is a reflection of Polixenes.

Innogen, Leonato's wife, is another of Shakespeare's ghost characters. She is mentioned in the stage directions, but she does not do nor say anything. Her name, Innogen, further emphasizes the connection to the previous manifestation of this particular impulse of unitive energy. Her function corresponds to that of Imogen at the time of "Cymbeline" and Desdemona in "Othello". Innogen's appearance in Messina is of great importance. Her presence is a confirmation that Desdemona has been "reborn" in

Mauritania. The link between the higher state and Sicily has been re-established.

The evolutionary charge that is currently embedded within Messina consists of two impulses that are designated for the heart faculty. The first impulse is represented by Hero, "Leonato's short daughter". "Short" refers to conscious energy. Emilia, Iago's wife who was Desdemona's waiting-gentlewoman, represented this impulse at the time of "Othello". At that time, this particular impulse was completely subdued by Iago.

Beatrice, Hero's cousin, represents an impulse of creative energy (*yellow*). Beatrice is the current projection of Bianca, who appeared previously in "Othello". She has also been transferred from Cyprus. At that time Bianca was in love with disdainful Cassio. In her conversation with Don Pedro, Beatrice makes a reference to that encounter:

Don Pedro:

"Come, lady, come; you have lost the heart of
Signior Benedick."

Beatrice:

"Indeed, my lord, he lent it me awhile; and I gave
him use for it, a double heart for his single one:
marry, once before he won it of me with false dice,
therefore your grace may well say I have lost it."
(*Much Ado About Nothing, II.1*)

Beatrice's presence in Messina is also of great importance. This impulse (*yellow*) is needed for the continuation of the process within the Cypriot link. In the meantime, she may act as a substitute for the Courtesan, who is still trapped in Ephesus.

As always, the process has to be directed by a spiritual guide. Don Pedro of Aragon is the spiritual guide who directs the current phase of the process. Don Pedro, meaning "the Rock", is a successor to Othello, the Moor. Historically, the lords of Aragon were directly descended from the Moorish kings of Granada.

The experiences from Cyprus are represented by Claudio and Benedick. Claudio may be described as immature and lacking sincerity. In this respect, Claudio is a reflection of the foolish Roderigo in "Othello". Benedick is the current projection of Cassio. Claudio and Benedick are Don Pedro's disciples. Before their arrival in Messina, Claudio and Benedick were fighting in wars. In Shakespeare's symbolic language, the initial preparatory phase is called "wars". The impact of the "wars" is clearly illustrated by the effect of Hero on Claudio. Here is Claudio's comment about it:

"When you went onward on this ended action,
I look'd upon her with a soldier's eye,
That liked, but had a rougher task in hand
Than to drive liking to the name of love:
But now I am return'd and that war-thoughts
Have left their places vacant, in their rooms
Come thronging soft and delicate desires,
All prompting me how fair young Hero is,
Saying, I liked her ere I went to wars."
(*Much Ado About Nothing*, I.1)

At the beginning of the play, Claudio is not ready yet for Hero. This is why Don Pedro has to control and modulate the initial impact. He refers to his role as teaching:

"My love is thine to teach: teach it but how,
And thou shalt see how apt it is to learn
Any hard lesson that may do thee good."
(*Much Ado About Nothing*, II.1)

However, his teaching takes a strange form. He offers to woo Hero on Claudio's behalf. Such an approach to "wooing" may appear strange if considered within an ordinary social milieu. Let's remember that Shakespeare's plays are an illustration of a process that is beyond and above ordinary rational and emotional reflexes. So, it should not be a surprise that Don Pedro's approach is misunderstood. Namely, Hero's father is informed by Antonio that:

> "the prince discovered to Claudio that he loved my
> niece your daughter and meant to acknowledge it
> this night in a dance"
> (*Much Ado About Nothing, II.1*)

This is why Benedick accuses Don Pedro of stealing Claudio's beloved:

> "you, who, as I take it, have stolen his birds' nest."
> (*Much Ado About Nothing, II.1*)

This seemingly confused situation is needed so Don Pedro may inform Benedick, and the audience, what the purpose of his acts is. Don Pedro tells Benedick that:

> "I will but teach them to sing, and restore them to
> the owner."
> (*Much Ado About Nothing, II.1*)

Don Pedro's aim is to fine tune this particular aspect of the heart so that it would be in harmony with its corresponding energy ("teach them to sing"). But Claudio is incapable of trusting his guide. This lack of trust makes Claudio an easy target for Don John. Don John is the villain of the play; he is the current projection of Iago. Don John easily convinces Claudio that Don Pedro woos Hero for himself.

Don Pedro's strategy is very similar to that implemented by Othello. Like Othello with Iago, Don Pedro uses Don John as an instrument in the process. Don Pedro gives Don John enough breathing space so Don John, driven by an entirely different aim, arranges the needed developmental situation: Hero is accused of disloyalty. Don Pedro incurs blame by confirming that Hero has been unfaithful:

"What should I speak?
I stand dishonour'd, that have gone about
To link my dear friend to a common stale."
(*Much Ado About Nothing, IV.1*)

It is then that Hero is "stolen" from Claudio. This happens when Hero, like Desdemona, "dies to live". As a result, Claudio is exposed to a series of reforming experiences such as shame, grief, and repentance. It is then that Claudio is forced to sing "songs of woe, round about her tomb":

"Pardon, goddess of the night,
Those that slew thy virgin knight;
For the which, with songs of woe,
Round about her tomb they go."
(*Much Ado About Nothing, V.3*)

Such an experience has a constructive effect on Claudio: at the end of the play Claudio and Hero are reunited.

In parallel, Don Pedro initiates a set of experiences that aim at the assimilation of creative energy. This part of the process is symbolically illustrated as Don Pedro triggering affection between Benedick and Beatrice:

"I will in the interim undertake one of
Hercules' labours; which is, to bring Signior
Benedick and the Lady Beatrice into a mountain of

affection the one with the other."
(*Much Ado About Nothing, II.1*)

The process may be completed only when Benedick is able to put his love for Beatrice above his friendship with Don Pedro. This happens when Benedick tells Don Pedro that he abandons his company. In other words, Claudio's and Hero's experiences are also part of Don Pedro's working on Benedick.

Don Pedro needs an "invisible" assistant in order to implement his plan. The function of the assistant is to control the timing of the unmasking of Don John's actions. This difficult role is delegated to Dogberry, the seemingly ignorant and silly Master Constable. First, Dogberry has to arrange the interception of Borachio and Conrad. He arranges this by concluding, his otherwise confusing briefing to the watchmen, with a very specific and surprisingly clear instruction:

> "One word more, honest neighbours. I pray you watch
> about Signior Leonato's door; for the wedding being
> there to-morrow, there is a great coil to-night."
> (*Much Ado About Nothing, III.3*)

Then Dogberry must make sure that the message about Don John's plot is not delivered to Leonato prior to the planned marriage of Claudio and Hero. During his encounter with Leonato, Dogberry does not allow Verges, his partner, to spell out any details about Borachio's misdeeds. Dogberry does this by interrupting Verges' testimony:

> "A good old man, sir; he will be talking: as they
> say, when the age is in, the wit is out: God help
> us! it is a world to see. Well said, i'faith,
> neighbour Verges: well, God's a good man; an two men
> ride of a horse, one must ride behind. An honest
> soul, i' faith, sir; by my troth he is, as ever

broke bread."
(*Much Ado About Nothing, III.5*)

The message could not be delivered at this time, because it would disturb the build-up of this very carefully designed developmental situation. Finally, Dogberry has to make sure that Borachio's misdeeds are disclosed only after Benedick's constructive change. This is why Dogberry arrives with Borachio in tow after Benedick has left the company of Don Pedro.

Dogberry's incoherent behaviour exasperates Conrad who calls him "an ass". It seems that Shakespeare draws the audience's attention to the fact that Dogberry is a special kind of *ass*:

"But, masters, remember that I am an ass;
though it be not written down,
yet forget not that I am an ass."
(*Much Ado About Nothing, IV.2*)

Indeed, later on, the readers will meet another *ass* who will play a similar role.

Messina of Sicily has been re-linked to the higher state. Now it may operate again as an active intermediate state. Through this link it is possible to project Messina's experience down onto the ordinary state of Italy. The remaining Italian plays illustrate the next steps of the process implemented in Italy.

First, however, let's take a look at the parallel activities that are being implemented in Bohemia.

Bohemian intervention

The break in the Sicilian link required an adjustment to the overall strategy. Initially, Bohemia was to be used to activate the process on the Italian Peninsula but because of the break with Sicily, Bohemia could not fulfil this role. Instead, the Italian branch was activated directly through Messina. In order to continue the process in Italy, it was necessary to access the impulses of creative energy which were still in Ephesus. At the same time, there were problems occurring within the Cypriot link: the situation in Moorish Spain had disturbed the development of the leading aspect of the intellect for the English branch. And to make things even worse, some events that were taking place in Central Europe drastically deteriorated the overall situation. In other words, a corrective action was needed to preserve the process. Such a corrective action required the involvement of the Realm.

One of the objectives of the Bohemian intervention was to transfer the impulses of creativity (*yellow* and *white*) from Ephesus via Bohemia to Italy. These impulses were needed for the formation of the Italian octagon. First, however, the overall environment of Bohemia had to be correctly prepared. In accordance with an advanced methodology, the environment may be correctly prepared by exposing it to a modulated impulse of unitive energy. However, the two previously released impulses of unitive energy (*red*) were already engaged; one for the repair of the Sicilian link (Desdemona in "Othello"); the other one in France to fix the Cypriot link (Helena in "All's Well That End Well"). In this context it is interesting to observe how economical the Bohemian corrective action was: all the concerns mentioned above were addressed with a single action. Namely, an evolutionary impulse of unitive energy is sent directly from the Realm to Bohemia. This impulse enabled (i) the preparation of the environment for the assimilation of creative energy; (ii) the formation of a temporal octagonal inner structure in Bohemia that might counterbalance the destructive tendencies in Central Europe, and (iii) the development of a leading aspect of the intellect for the English branch. All these activities had to be coordinated with the events taking place within the Sicilian and Cypriot links.

The details of the first stage of the Bohemian corrective action are illustrated in "Twelfth Night".

Twelfth Night

"Twelfth Night" is the Bohemian sequel to "The Winter's Tale". The action is set in Illyria after the completion of Othello's mission, i.e., in the 15th century. Illyria refers to an ancient region on the western coast of the Balkan Peninsula, covering parts of modern Albania, Croatia and Montenegro. At the time of "The Winter's Tale", this part of the Balkans belonged to Bohemia. The inner structure of Illyria as presented in "Twelfth Night" corresponds to that developed at the time of "The Winter's Tale".

At the conclusion of "The Winter's Tale" the Shepherd and his son were granted nobility. This is an important pointer, indicating that the transmission channel had been switched from the royal families to a select group of nobles. For whatever reason, the royal channel proved to be ineffective. At that time, such a switch was implemented within the Cypriot link.

The Shepherd predicted that his grandsons and granddaughters would play active roles in the process. Consequently, the presence of "sister and brother" is a characteristic feature of the Bohemian plays. Olivia and her brother are descendants of the Shepherd. They represent two aspects of the heart. Olivia's brother, however, has died recently. This is a projection of the situation encountered previously in Sicily at the time of Mamillius' death. This means that now Olivia, a woman, represents an aspect of the heart. This is the first time that a woman represents an aspect of the heart faculty. This is a symbolic indication of an attempt at reinforcing the feminine element within the stream of European life.

Florizel, a Bohemian Prince, became the leading aspect of Bohemia at the conclusion of "The Winter's Tale". Now, it is Duke Orsino who represents the leading aspect of the intellect faculty. In this role, he encompasses the previous experiences of Florizel.

The next step of the process requires Olivia and Orsino to be exposed to unitive energy.

An impulse of unitive energy is sent from the Realm via Messaline to Illyria. In accordance with Shakespeare's symbolic presentation, the imaginary place of Messaline represents a higher state. The name of Messaline is invented from two words, Messina and Mytilene. Messina and Mytilene are two previous intermediate states within the Sicilian link. Mytilene was used to activate the Bohemian branch at the time of "Timon of Athens". Messina of Sicily was used to reactivate the Italian branch at the time of "Much Ado About Nothing". In this way Shakespeare indicates that Messaline represents the currently operating higher state, with which the Bohemian and Italian branches are entangled. This means that a "customized" impulse of unitive energy was sent directly from the higher state to the ordinary state; this transmission has bypassed the intermediate state. In order to implement such an approach, the so-called "rapid technique" has to be applied. The rapid technique is a term that describes an accelerated process when an individual or a group of people are exposed to an evolutionary impulse without the completion of preparatory training. The implementation of the rapid technique involves a certain risk. This further emphasizes the urgency of the overall situation in this particular geographical region.

An evolutionary charge travelling from the higher state into the ordinary world is like a beam of light passing from air into a glass prism. Like glass, the ordinary world is "denser" than the higher state. When entering the ordinary state, this evolutionary beam is split into a spectrum of impulses, in the same way that light is split into various colours. While entering Illyria, the evolutionary beam sent from Messaline is split into two impulses, *black* and *red*. These two impulses are represented by the twins Viola and Sebastian:

"One face, one voice, one habit, and two persons,
A natural perspective, that is and is not!"
(*Twelfth Night, V.1*)

Viola's and Sebastian's transition from Messaline to Illyria is induced by a violent sea storm. Let's recall that Thaisa in "Pericles, Prince of Tyre" went through a similar transition. Similar to Thaisa's exclamation, "what world is this?" Viola expresses her surprise when she finds herself in an unknown "country":

"What country, friends, is this?"
(*Twelfth Night, I.2*)

Upon their arrival in Illyria, Viola and Sebastian are separated, because each of them has to play a different role. The evolutionary charge sent from Messaline has been customized in such a way as to be compatible with the inner structure of Illyria: Viola is targeted for Orsino, Sebastian for Olivia. This means that these impulses have been specifically tailored for Bohemia. These two impulses are incompatible with the other branches; they cannot be used outside of the Bohemian branch.

Viola (*black*) and Sebastian (*red*) are complementary to Luciana (*white*) and the Courtesan (*yellow*), i.e., the impulses of creative energy remaining in Ephesus. This means that Bohemia has been chosen for the accelerated activation of an alternative octagonal structure. In this way, there will be a possibility of using the Bohemian octagon to fix the problems in Italy, in Central Europe, and within the Cypriot link.

Viola has been sent from a newly activated higher state. This state has not been affected by the ancient demigods. This is why Viola is a manifestation of a perfect Black Lady, i.e., an impulse of unitive energy destined for the activation of a spiritual intellect:

> "she bore a mind that envy could not but call fair."
> (*Twelfth Night*, II.1)

This is the sort of impulse that was missing in Sicily after the transmission link was broken there.

The entire process has to be precisely directed. Both, the timing and the intensity of the initial exposure, have to be correctly administered. In accordance with the advanced methodology, Illyria is exposed to unitive energy prior to experiencing creativity. In other words, the assimilation of cruder energy may be accelerated by first exposing it to a purer energy. But exposure to the unitive energy has to be gradual. Initially, Illyria is exposed to a modulated impulse in the form of Viola disguised as a young boy named Cesario. At the beginning of the process, therefore, Cesario serves as a modulated impulse for both, Orsino and Olivia.

As always, a guide is needed to direct the process. The guide must diagnose the situation and administer the correct remedies. The role of the guide in "Twelfth Night" is assigned to Feste, a fool. After Olivia's father's death, Feste left Olivia's house. His return is triggered by the arrival of Viola and Sebastian. Feste is the first in the line of Fools who are directing the process within the Bohemian branch. Feste refers to his function in the following comment:

> "Well, God give them wisdom that have it; and those
> that are fools, let them use their talents."
> (*Twelfth Night*, I.5)

In order to achieve his goal, Feste has to work quite artfully on Orsino, Olivia, and their immediate environment. Like Pericles, Feste is a music master. The audience may see how Feste uses songs to monitor and carry out the process.

The final scene of "Twelfth Night" is executed in accordance with Othello's methodology. Viola's function is equivalent to that of Desdemona. Unlike Desdemona, however, Viola understands her situation very well. When Orsino threatens to kill her, Viola submits herself to Orsino's will without hesitation:

"And I, most jocund, apt and willingly,
To do you rest, a thousand deaths would die."
(*Twelfth Night*, *V.1*)

And then Viola explains to perplexed Olivia the nature of her untainted love:

"After him I love
More than I love these eyes, more than my life,
More, by all mores, than e'er I shall love wife.
If I do feign, you witnesses above
Punish my life for tainting of my love!"
(*Twelfth Night*, *V.1*)

As a result of Othello's teaching and Desdemona's previous experiences, Viola is free from earthly attachments. Viola's maturity allows her to neutralize Orsino's attack of jealousy nearly immediately.

At the end of the play the journey ends in a "lovers meeting": Olivia is married to Sebastian and Viola to Orsino. These two aspects of the heart and intellect faculties are united:

"... and golden time convents,
A solemn combination shall be made

148

Of our dear souls."
(*Twelfth Night, V.1*)

They form a spiritual quad, an intermediate form between a triad and an octagon. It is the first time that such a state of union ("a solemn combination ... of our dear souls") is activated directly within the ordinary state. The seed of a new spiritual being is formed and implanted into the fabric of Central European society.

However, spectators should be cautioned. Not everything has been "mended" in Illyria at the end of the play. For example, Malvolio, Olivia's puritanical steward, was not allowed to interfere with the final steps of the process. But he has not been removed from Illyria. Let's recall that Malvolio's last words were:

"I'll be revenged on the whole pack of you."
(*Twelfth Night, V.1*)

Feste's teaching did not have any effect on Malvolio. As the readers will find out, Malvolio's dogmatic and vengeful attitude will dominate the remaining plays of the Bohemian branch.

The evolutionary impact of the Illyrian quad will spread from the Balkans to Austria and then all the way to Denmark on the coast of the Baltic Sea. The next stage of the process is illustrated in "Measure for Measure".

Measure for Measure

The process moves from the Balkans further north towards Central Europe. "Measure for Measure" is set in Vienna. In accordance with the overall design of Shakespeare's plays, the city of Vienna presented in "Measure for Measure" is a reflection of the state of Illyria at the conclusion of "Twelfth Night". Although the action of the play takes place in Vienna, the main characters have Italian names. In this way the link to the Italian branch is further indicated.

The Duke of Vienna is the current projection of Duke Orsino. Juliet is the current manifestation of Olivia. Similarly to the situation in Illyria, one aspect of the heart is missing. It is referred to as Frederick, who was lost in a shipwreck. The readers may recognize that such a "lame heart" is a characteristic feature of the Bohemian branch. At the time of "The Winter's Tale" the missing aspect was represented by Mamillius; at the time of "Twelfth Night" it was Olivia's brother.

Lord Angelo, the Duke's cousin, is the current reflection of Malvolio. Let's remember that Malvolio's secret desire was to become a nobleman. As mentioned earlier, Malvolio's dogmatic and vengeful attitude would dominate the plays of the Bohemian branch.

To unfold the meaning of "Measure for Measure", it is necessary to reconstruct the events that took place during the previous nineteen years that shaped the current state of Vienna's affairs. Shakespeare introduces the character of Barnardine to symbolically represent the state of the Bohemian (Illyrian) quad. Like the Bohemian quad, Barnardine was "born" in Bohemia but was "raised" in Vienna:

"A Bohemian born, but here nursed up and bred; one
that is a prisoner nine years old.
(*Measure for Measure, IV.2*)

The Bohemian quad could not be sustained in Vienna for more than ten years after it was transferred from Illyria. After ten years the quad became dysfunctional. Symbolically this is presented as Barnardine being locked up in a jail for the last nine years. The behaviour of Barnardine is a reflection of the nature of spiritual experience. Such an experience serves as an imprint that may have a lasting effect, even for a long time after the termination of its original cause. If a spiritual state cannot be sustained, its effect will remain latent until the time is ripe for its reactivation. This is why Barnardine cannot "die" or "escape". While he is in the jail, Barnardine is a symbolic representation of such a latent state or "drunken sleep":

> "A man that apprehends death no more dreadfully but
> as a drunken sleep; careless, reckless, and fearless
> of what's past, present, or to come;"
> (*Measure for Measure, IV.2*)

The evolutionary impulses of unitive energy are now represented by Isabella (*black*) and her brother Claudio (*red*). They are the current replica of Viola and Sebastian from "Twelfth Night". Isabella is the current manifestation of an immaculate Black Lady.

During Barnardine's nine years of "drunken sleep", two impulses of creative energy were transferred from Ephesus to Vienna. This transfer was possible because the Bohemian branch was re-linked with the Realm at the time of "Twelfth Night". Let's recall that all previous evolutionary failures were caused by the inability to correctly assimilate creative energy. This is why these impulses are sent to Vienna only after the unitive energy has been partially absorbed, i.e., after the formation of the Bohemian quad. These impulses are needed for the formation of an octagonal inner structure. At the time of "The Comedy of Errors", these impulses were represented by Luciana (*white*) and the Courtesan (*yellow*). In Vienna, the Ephesian impulses are represented by Mariana and a woman called Kate Keepdown, respectively.

As indicated in the discussion of "The Winter's Tale", Luciana did not marry Antipholus of Syracuse; this impulse remained in Ephesus. Mariana's story is a repeat of Luciana's experiences. Five years before the beginning of the play, Mariana was engaged to Lord Angelo. But Angelo called the wedding off when Mariana lost her dowry in the shipwreck that killed Frederick, her brother. The loss of a "dowry" means that the circumstances were not ready yet for the constructive assimilation of this particular impulse. Afterwards, Mariana withdrew to "the moated grange at St. Luke's". Mariana has to wait until the overall conditions are correctly prepared for the fulfilment of her function.

The Courtesan of Ephesus appears in Vienna as Kate Keepdown. Kate is coloured for the heart (*yellow*). Kate was designated for Frederick, Marianna's brother. But after Frederick was lost at sea, Kate ended-up as a prostitute in Mistress Overdone's brothel.

The process implemented in Vienna follows the previously described advanced methodology. In accordance with this methodology, an impulse of unitive energy may be used as the means for the completion of the reformation. The impulse of unitive energy consists of Isabella and her brother Claudio. This means that Mariana and Kate may discharge their function only once Isabella and Claudio are united with their intended partners.

Juliet is coloured for Claudio. The play indicates that the assimilation of this purifying impulse has also been disturbed. This is symbolically illustrated by the untimely love affair between Claudio and Juliet. Claudio did not marry Juliet because of a problem also related to a "dowry". The fact that Juliet's dowry was "remaining in the coffer of her friends" indicates that marriage would be premature. Yet, Claudio "got possession of Julietta's bed". This is a sign of an error in the process.

Isabella with her "speechless dialect" and "reason and discourse" is coloured for the Duke of Vienna. Isabella's actions are entirely driven by her evolutionary purpose. Therefore, her actions cannot be judged or explained in terms of ordinary psychological, rational or moralistic criteria. "Freedom from choice" is a technical term that applies to Isabella's attitude. Isabella cannot give up her "virginity" for any other purpose except that which corresponds to her spiritual function.

At the beginning of the play the audience is informed that Isabella has decided to join Saint Claire convent. Let's recall that (i) Marianna is at St. Luke's; (ii) Juliet is pregnant but not married; (iii) Kate is a prostitute in a brothel. If Isabella withdraws to the convent, then none of the evolutionary impulses available in Vienna will be correctly assimilated. This means that Vienna would not be able to fulfil its evolutionary purpose.

The process in Vienna is directed by the Duke. His mission is to form an octagonal inner structure.

The Duke of Vienna commences his mission by announcing that he intends to leave the city on a diplomatic mission. He leaves the government in the hands of Lord Angelo. In fact, the Duke has not left the city, he remains in Vienna disguised as Friar Lodowick. He secretly monitors the city's affairs, especially the actions of Angelo. Angelo, like Malvolio, appears perfect only in his outward behaviour. Angelo's shutting down Vienna's liberties is the realization of Malvolio's threat: "I'll be revenged on the whole pack of you". Angelo is an example of a false "mystic" who immerses himself in the indiscriminate application of the outward form of laws. Such an approach does not lead to a meaningful change in his distractive characteristics. His hidden tendencies manifest themselves as soon as he is provided with the means to exercise his power. Angelo's flawed modus operandi is exposed during his encounters with Isabella. Isabella points out to him that misuse of authority is a form of self-importance and arrogance.

Claudio is arrested for impregnating Juliet. Lord Angelo sentences Claudio to death in order to serve as an example to the other Viennese citizens. Claudio's friend Lucio visits Isabella in the convent. He asks her to intercede with Angelo on Claudio's behalf. Isabella goes to Angelo to beg him for mercy. Angelo refuses, but suggests that there might be some ways to change his mind. When Angelo propositions her, saying that he will let Claudio live if she agrees to have sexual intercourse with him, she is shocked and immediately refuses. Afterwards, Isabella visits Claudio in prison and counsels him to prepare himself for death. At first Claudio agrees with Isabella's decision, but then changes his mind. He begs Isabella to save his life, but she refuses.

Disguised as Friar Lodowick, the Duke befriends Isabella and arranges a "bed trick" to thwart Angelo's intention. The Duke advises Isabella to send word to Angelo that she has decided to submit to him, but under the condition that their meeting occurs in darkness and silence. Mariana agrees to take Isabella's place. Angelo ends up having sex with his former fiancé.

We should note that the Duke is not a guide. He does not have the skills and foresights demonstrated by Othello, Don Pedro, or Feste. This is why his decisions are not always quite precise. On a couple of occasions he has to change his approach. Nevertheless, his mission is of great importance to the overall evolutionary process in this particular geographical area. The Duke symbolically represents one of the exceptional individuals who were developed "rapidly" and sent into the social, political, and religious streams of Europe. They demonstrated extraordinary knowledge and the most remarkable skills and inventiveness. At that time, their presence was required to give the European society a foretaste of the operation of supracognitive perception.

The Duke prepares the circumstances that are needed for the completion of his mission. The Duke faces quite a formidable challenge. He has to bring the four impulses together and then unite them with their designated partners. First, he has to delegate Isabella to play a more constructive role than her intention of becoming a nun. In his conversation with Friar Thomas, the Duke indicates that his purpose for pursuing Isabella is much deeper "than the aims and ends of burning youth":

> "No, holy father; throw away that thought;
> Believe not that the dribbling dart of love
> Can pierce a complete bosom. Why I desire thee
> To give me secret harbour, hath a purpose
> More grave and wrinkled than the aims and ends
> Of burning youth."
> (*Measure for Measure, I.3*)

The implementation of the process could not be realized without the help of Lucio. Lucio's role corresponds to that of Feste in "Twelfth Night". He is one of the Shakespearean fools. Lucio works in parallel with the Duke. He monitors the Duke's actions. When necessary, he intervenes and makes the necessary corrections. Lucio helps the Duke to implement his plan by bringing Isabella to Angelo's office. He guides her during her first encounter with Angelo, during which he seems to be invisible to the others.

As a guide, Lucio knows the Duke very well. As a matter of fact, he knows the Duke better that the Duke knows himself:

> "Friar, thou knowest not the duke so well as I do."

> "Sir, I was an inward of his."
> (*Measure for Measure, III.2*)

On a couple of occasions, the Duke and Lucio meet together and exchange information. However, Lucio's involvement must remain concealed from the others. This concealment will allow him to help the Duke execute the final scene: Lucio will unmask Friar Lodowick. This is why during their encounters, the Duke and Lucio communicate in their own language.

Lucio knows that the Duke was guilty of "getting a wench with child". Lucio tells the Duke that he knows it was the Duke who, during his earlier times of liberty, impregnated Kate, a prostitute in Mistress Overdone's brothel. But Lucio took the blame for it. Lucio suggests to the Duke how Kate and her child, whom we may call Lucianus, may be rescued from the brothel. Namely, Kate may be rescued by forcing Lucio to marry her. In this way, Lucio plays the role of a Joker. The Joker is the top trump card. This means that the Joker may be used as a temporary substitute for any "card", i.e., he may act as a substitute for a missing component of the octagon. And that is the role Lucio plays in the process. Indeed, a moment later, the audience is informed that it was Lucio who denounced Mistress Overdone's brothel to the authorities. As a result of Lucio's denouncement, the brothel was closed and Kate was released from Mistress Overdone's "custody". Therefore, it should not be a surprise that, at the end of the play, the Duke proclaims the following verdict on Lucio:

"Upon mine honour, thou shalt marry her.
Thy slanders I forgive."
(*Measure for Measure, V.1*)

Lucio acts as a substitute for Frederick. In this way, the impulse of creative energy could be temporarily assimilated within the being of Vienna.

At the end of the play the Duke manages to marry Angelo to Mariana; Claudio is released from prison and re-united with Juliet; Lucio is "forced" to marry Kate. The Duke marries Isabella. In this way, an octagonal union is formed.

The gains achieved are summarized in the final scene by the Duke's comment to Barnardine:

"Sirrah, thou art said to have a stubborn soul.
That apprehends no further than this world,

And squarest thy life according. Thou'rt condemn'd:
But, for those earthly faults, I quit them all;
And pray thee take this mercy to provide
For better times to come."
(*Measure for Measure, V.1*)

The above statement summarizes the outcome of the process described in "Measure for Measure". Namely, "for those earthly faults, I quit them all" and "take this mercy to provide for better times to come". In other words, the spiritual potential of the Bohemian branch has been advanced, at least temporarily, by the action instigated by the Duke. A patched-up octagonal union was formed. At that time, the important thing was to provide Bohemia, even for a brief period, with a taste of this particular experience. The impact produced by the Bohemian octagon was overlapped with a wave generated by the activation of a parallel octagon within the French branch. These two octagonal structures were needed to generate an energy field that affected the entire area of Western Europe. In this way, the overall process could be sustained.

"Take this mercy to provide for better times to come" offers some comfort and hope for future evolutionary gains in Central Europe. The Duke, representing the leading aspect of the intellect faculty, is definitively in control of Vienna. The Duke has managed to assemble four couples. The spectators may realize, however, that the Viennese octagon does not quite represent a balanced or harmonious arrangement. Unlike the octagon formed at the conclusion of "Pericles, Prince of Tyre", all components of the Viennese octagon are contained within the ordinary world. Therefore, this is a flat, i.e., two-dimensional structure. In addition, some of its components had to be patched up. The marriage of Angelo and Mariana is enforced; Claudio and Juliet have already consummated their relationship; Lucio's and Kate's marriage is simply a patch to provide the missing components of the octagonal structure. In summary, the outward shape of the union activated at the end of "Measure for Measure" is correct, but its inner content is not of the highest quality.

The details provided by Shakespeare in his other plays indicate that the marriage between the Duke and Isabella lasted happily for 30 years. Lucio adopted Lucianus, the child of the Duke and Kate. Claudio and Juliet became the parents of a boy named Claudius. However, the other two marriages did not last very long. After discharging their temporary function in Vienna, Mariana and Kate were transferred to Italy, i.e., their originally intended destination.

It was such a "lame" union that entered onto the sixth stage of the Bohemian branch. This stage of the process is presented in "Hamlet".

Hamlet

To unfold the inner structure of "Hamlet" it is necessary to reconstruct the events that followed "Measure for Measure". Let's recall that at the conclusion of "Measure for Measure" a Bohemian octagon was formed. A partially purified aspect of the intellect faculty (Duke Vincentio) ruled over Vienna. There was a strong presence of a corrupted aspect of the intellect (Lord Angelo). The heart faculty was severely weakened (Juliet).

At the end of "Measure for Measure", the illegitimate son of the Duke was one year and three months old. Lucio adopted the boy. Claudio's son was about to be born. The boys reappear in "Hamlet" as two brothers. Shakespeare refers to the adopted son of Lucio as Lucianus, and to the son of Claudio as Claudius.

Now the action moves from Vienna and goes further north to Elsinore in Denmark. The events that led to the current state of Elsinore are presented in "The Murder of Gonzago", the play-within-the play inserted into "Hamlet". Upon Hamlet's request, a travelling troupe of players stages an adaptation of "The Murder of Gonzago". Here is Hamlet's request to the First Player:

> "You could, for a need,
> study a speech of some dozen or sixteen lines, which
> I would set down and insert in't, could you not?"
> (*Hamlet, II.2*)

Hamlet's adaptation, which he called "The Mouse-trap", includes the story, which he heard from the Ghost. In this story the king's murderer married the king's wife:

> "you shall see anon how the murderer
> gets the love of Gonzago's wife."
> (*Hamlet, III.2*)

The players, however, presented their own adaptation of "The Murder of Gonzago". They augmented Hamlet's story by adding an episode that took place in Vienna after the conclusion of "Measure for Measure". In this way "The Murder of Gonzago" contains two sequential episodes. The players' performance starts with a dumb show, which illustrates Hamlet's adaptation according to the Ghost's report, i.e., the murder of Hamlet's father. The second episode follows the dumb show. It illustrates the story of the Duke of Vienna, i.e., the events that took place prior to the murder in Elsinore. At that time Gonzago was the Duke of Vienna:

> "This play is the image of a murder done in Vienna:
> Gonzago is the duke's name; his wife, Baptista."
> (*Hamlet, III.2*)

The Duke of Vienna is presented as a sick elderly man. He is liberal and considerate, and in this respect, very different, even opposite to the character of Hamlet's father. The Duke's wife, Baptista, is devotedly attached to her husband and there is no indication that she is deceiving him. The readers will recognize that Gonzago and Baptista represent Duke Vincentio and Isabella 30 years after the conclusion of "Measure for Measure". Lucianus, the Duke's nephew, is the murderer. In this way, we are informed of what happened between the conclusion of "Measure for Measure" and the beginning of "Hamlet".

Hecate, the goddess of witchcraft, also got involved in the process. Hecate used the same approach as in "Macbeth". Hecate identified Lucianus as her target and "whispered" to him the idea of murdering the Duke, Lucianus' natural father. Afterwards, she provided him with a poisonous mixture. Here is Lucianus' account of this event:

> "Thou mixture rank, of midnight weeds collected,
> With Hecate's ban thrice blasted, thrice infected,
> Thy natural magic and dire property,
> On wholesome life usurp immediately."
> (*Hamlet, III.2*)

Lucianus, following Hecate's whispering, poisoned the Duke:

> "He poisons him i' the garden for's estate. His
> name's Gonzago: the story is extant, and writ in
> choice Italian."
> (*Hamlet, III.2*)

After the murder of Gonzago, young Lucianus becomes the ruler. The fact that "The Murder of Gonzago" was "writ in choice Italian" further emphasizes its link to "Measure for Measure" and "Twelfth Night".

The players' changes to the play irritate Hamlet. Unhappy with their presentation, he himself takes on the role of the chorus. At one point he abruptly interrupts Lucianus' performance:

"Begin, murderer;
pox, leave thy damnable faces, and begin. Come:
'the croaking raven doth bellow for revenge'."
(*Hamlet, III.2*)

Hamlet's interruption prohibits the players from finishing their performance.

The play-within-the play allows us to identify the inner structure of Elsinore. Elsinore is the current reflection of Vienna from "The Murder of Gonzago". In the players' story the readers will recognize Hamlet's father as Lucianus. Lucianus was an illegitimate son of the Duke. Lucianus murdered his natural father, i.e., Hamlet's grandfather. Later, Lucianus was murdered by Claudius and Claudius became the king.

Elsinore is weak, fragmented, and severely degenerated. Its current modus operandi is driven by desire for power, revenge, greed, and ill-driven ambitions. Hamlet intuitively recognizes this state and compares it to "an unweeded garden":

"Fie on't! ah fie! 'tis an unweeded garden,
That grows to seed; things rank and gross in nature
Possess it merely."
(*Hamlet, I.2*)

Marcellus, one of the watchmen, summarizes the overall situation in the following comment:

"Something is rotten in the state of Denmark."
(*Hamlet, I.4*)

Such a degenerated or "rotten" state can be described as a leftover from the disintegrated octagonal structure. Such a state can be uplifted only by an incredible effort from its non-corrupted aspects.

The structure of the evolutionary impulse attached to the Bohemian branch consists of a sister and a brother. This structure was introduced as Viola and Sebastian in "Twelfth Night" and then continued with Isabella and Claudio in "Measure for Measure". The evolutionary impulse that is present in Elsinore is represented by Laertes and his sister Ophelia. Laertes is designated for an aspect of the spiritual heart (*red*). At this time there is no such aspect present in Elsinore. Such a "lame heart" is a characteristic feature of the Bohemian branch. This is why Laertes is prompted to go to France to look there for the fulfillment of his evolutionary purpose.

Ophelia represents an impulse of unitive energy (*black*) designated for the intellect faculty. After Viola and Isabella, Ophelia is the third manifestation of the untainted Black Lady. This impulse is designated for Hamlet but Ophelia is dominated by her father, Polonius. Polonius does not have any idea about Ophelia's function. In his ignorance, he interferes with the process by commanding her to distance herself from Hamlet. There is no need for Ophelia's presence in Elsinore if she cannot be united with Hamlet.

Hamlet represents a partially purified aspect of the intellect. He is the current "fruit" of the Bohemian developmental branch. His current state is a reflection of the previous "Dukes" of the Bohemian union, i.e., Orsino in "Twelfth Night" and the Duke of Vienna in "Measure for Measure". Hamlet is on the verge of experiencing a breakthrough to a higher state. His potential, however, is blurred by his immaturity, arrogance, and melancholy.

Ophelia is able to recognize Hamlet's spiritual potential, which she describes as "the expectancy and rose of the fair state" and the "mould of form". Hamlet's potential was formed as a result of his experiences as a courtier, soldier and scholar:

"The courtier's, soldier's, scholar's, eye, tongue, sword;
The expectancy and rose of the fair state,
The glass of fashion and the mould of form,
The observed of all observers."
(*Hamlet, III.1*)

These experiences parallel that of the Viennese Duke, i.e., Hamlet's grandfather, who was also "a scholar, a statesman and a soldier".

Hamlet intuitively recognizes that there is something wrong with Elsinore. He is able to pinpoint obvious inadequacies. It is clear, however, that he does not know how to approach the situation in which he finds himself. Hamlet's unfulfilled potential is reflected in his soliloquies, which contain an outward and an inward meaning. The outward meaning of his soliloquies is not satisfactory enough for him; the inward meaning is still beyond his comprehension. Here is Hamlet's famous soliloquy "To be, or not to be":

"To be, or not to be: that is the question:
Whether 'tis nobler in the mind to suffer
The slings and arrows of outrageous fortune,
Or to take arms against a sea of troubles
And by opposing end them? To die: to sleep;
No more; and by a sleep to say we end
The heart-ache and the thousand natural shocks
That flesh is heir to, 'tis a consummation
Devoutly to be wish'd. To die, to sleep;
To sleep: perchance to dream: ay, there's the rub;
For in that sleep of death what dreams may come
When we have shuffled off this mortal coil,
Must give us pause: there's the respect
That makes calamity of so long life;
For who would bear the whips and scorns of time,
The oppressor's wrong, the proud man's contumely,
The pangs of despised love, the law's delay,

The insolence of office and the spurns
That patient merit of the unworthy takes,
When he himself might his quietus make
With a bare bodkin? who would fardels bear,
To grunt and sweat under a weary life,
But that the dread of something after death,
The undiscover'd country from whose bourn
No traveller returns, puzzles the will
And makes us rather bear those ills we have
Than fly to others that we know not of?
Thus conscience does make cowards of us all;
And thus the native hue of resolution
Is sicklied o'er with the pale cast of thought,
And enterprises of great pith and moment
With this regard their currents turn awry,
And lose the name of action."
(*Hamlet, III.1*)

The soliloquy contains three parts. The first part introduces the two spiritual states "to be" and "not to be". The second part describes the struggles of a person who is in the state "not to be". The third part indicates a way leading to the state "to be".

The state "not to be" is developmentally sterile. It corresponds to ordinary life with all its suffering of "slings and arrows of outrageous fortune". This suffering is due to the dominant role of a corrupted self faculty. On the other hand, the state "to be" corresponds to a spiritually developed man. The state of "to be" is arrived at by following a path leading to the activation of subtle faculties. This approach requires an extraordinary personal effort. The soliloquy refers to such an effort as "to take arms against a sea of troubles, and by opposing end them". This means personal struggle against the corrupted self faculty and freeing oneself from worldly attachments. This part of the developmental process has previously been referred to as "to die before dying". Such experience of "dying" leads to the activation of the subtle faculties through assimilation of evolutionary energies.

It is important to realize that Hamlet's current state corresponds to "not to be". Therefore, Hamlet's behaviour is a reflection of his still underdeveloped state. When his father died, Hamlet hoped to become the king. Claudius, however, outmanoeuvred him and managed to be elected the new king. So, Hamlet hates Claudius and is disgusted with his mother. All of these made Hamlet depressed, bitter, and sarcastic. It is this unbalanced state that is reflected in the second part of the soliloquy. Hamlet perceives correctly that "dying" may end all the heartache and shocks that ordinary life brings. Therefore, such "dying" is a solution that one may wish for. But Hamlet does not understand the meaning of "dying". This is why he thinks that there is the catch: in this "death" who knows what kind of dreams might come? After all, who would put up with all life's sufferings, when one could simply take out a dagger ("a bare bodkin") and call it quits. It is the fear of the unknown combined with attachments to worldly pleasures that make people put up with their sometime outrageous fortunes and make them rather bear those ills than fly to others that they do not know. Hamlet concludes that it is our ordinary intellect ("the pale cast of thought") that induces such fearful thoughts that paralyse our actions and make us spiritual cowards. And this is as far as a person, who is in the state "not to be", can go, i.e., to explain and justify his or her own spiritual idleness by seemingly deep intellectual contemplation. Despite having an extraordinary intellectual ability, Hamlet is not able to figure out how to overcome the challenges associated with his struggle towards arriving at the state "to be". Hamlet does not know that he can fulfill his developmental potential and arrive at the state "to be" only by being united with Ophelia. This is emphasized by Ophelia's arrival which interrupts Hamlet's meditation:

"Soft you now,
The fair Ophelia! Nymph, in thy orisons
Be all my sins remembered."
(*Hamlet, III.1*)

Ophelia's arrival marks the third part of the soliloquy. Her appearance at this very moment symbolically indicates the approach that Hamlet should follow. Ophelia represents the impulse of unitive energy that would allow him to transmute his inner state. In other words, Hamlet could arrive at the state "to be" by getting married to Ophelia.

It seems that at the beginning of the play Hamlet is on the right track. He loves and nearly worships Ophelia ("Nymph, in thy orisons be all my sins remembered"). However, destructive forces interfere with the process by dispatching the Ghost. The Ghost's aim is to destroy Hamlet's potential by redirecting his priority from Ophelia to that of avenging his father's death.

It is important to note the following phrase in Hamlet's soliloquy:

"The undiscover'd country from whose bourn no traveller returns."
(*Hamlet, III.1*)

The term "the undiscover'd country" refers to the state "to be", i.e. a higher state. Hamlet is still ignorant of the possibilities offered by "the undiscover'd country" and does not realize that travel to "the undiscover'd country" is the only solution to his problems. But he would need a guide who would show him the way. A guide is a "traveler" who, like Pericles and Othello, has returned from "the undiscovered country", has "died before dying" and is capable of guiding others. With the help of a guide, Hamlet would be able to free himself from the destructive influence of the Ghost ("to take arms against a sea of troubles and by opposing end them"). Such a guide is present in Elsinore, but Hamlet is not able to recognize him.

Let's recall that Macbeth was destroyed by Hecate's prophesies. Elsinore is in a similar situation. Its weakness and fragmentation make it vulnerable to the destructive forces. The inner structure of Elsinore clearly indicates that Hamlet represents the only aspect that is capable of evolutionary growth. However, Hamlet's gross self, i.e., his impatience, melancholy, ambition, arrogance and hatred of Claudius make him an easy target. This is why a malignant and destructive Ghost is dispatched to corrupt Hamlet. The Ghost clearly describes its malignant state:

> "I am thy father's spirit,
> Doom'd for a certain term to walk the night,
> And for the day confined to fast in fires,
> Till the foul crimes done in my days of nature
> Are burnt and purged away."

> "O, horrible! O, horrible! most horrible!"
> (Hamlet, III.1)

The nature of the Ghost should not be a surprise for he is a projection of Lucianus, who committed "foul crimes". He murdered the Duke, his natural father.

Shakespeare points out that the Ghost's impact depends on the person's attachment to and respect for King Hamlet. Horatio and the watchmen have great respect for the former King. This is why they can see the Ghost. But the Ghost will not speak to Horatio because he approaches the apparition with a condition:

> "If there be any good thing to be done,
> That may to thee do ease and grace to me,
> Speak to me."
> (Hamlet, I.1)

Of course, "any good thing to be done" is not the Ghost's purpose. On the other hand, Hamlet's approach to the Ghost is unconditional:

> "Be thou a spirit of health or goblin damn'd,
> Bring with thee airs from heaven or blasts from hell,
> Be thy intents wicked or charitable,
> Thou comest in such a questionable shape
> That I will speak to thee."
> (*Hamlet, I.4*)

This is why the Ghost speaks to him. Hamlet considers the possibility that the Ghost "may be the devil" sent to abuse him. Therefore, he decides to apply a rational method to verify the Ghost's story:

> "I'll have grounds
> More relative than this: the play's the thing
> Wherein I'll catch the conscience of the king."
> (*Hamlet, II.2*)

Hamlet mixes up two different domains of knowledge, i.e., rational and perceptive. He assumes that the Ghost's command must be legitimate if his story is true. This is a similar situation to that of Macbeth. Macbeth believed in the witches' prophesy when he was made thane of Cawdor. Hamlet makes the same mistake. Hamlet becomes an "instrument of darkness" the moment he decides to fulfill the Ghost's command to avenge his father's death. The desire for revenge results in an internal rotting, which will eventually kill a man. Hamlet becomes a victim of the Ghost's whispering. He turns into a "wild prince" and becomes an instrument of the destructive forces. At this point Hamlet's developmental potential drastically diminishes.

An impulse of evolutionary energy cannot be wasted. Whenever there is a situation that does not allow for its constructive actualization, such an impulse is withdrawn. This is why Ophelia is "withdrawn" when Hamlet rejects her and leaves Elsinore. Ophelia's withdrawal from Elsinore is presented in three stages illustrated as her madness, death, and funeral. Ophelia drowned next to a willow tree, which symbolizes unfulfilled love. In this way, Shakespeare points out that Ophelia's madness was caused not so much by her father's death but by Hamlet's departure and his imminent death. The cause of Ophelia's madness is the same as Helena's sorrows in "All's Well That Ends Well":

> "I think not on my father;
> And these great tears grace his remembrance more
> Than those I shed for him. What was he like?
> I have forgot him: my imagination
> Carries no favour in't but Bertram's."
> (*All's Well That Ends Well*, I.1)

Helena's tears are not shed for the loss of her father; she laments the departure of her beloved Bertram.

While at the stage of "madness", Ophelia delivers prophesies. Her prophesies contain details and commentaries about past, present and future events that help us to understand the play. Ophelia's prophesies are delivered in the symbolic language of the flowers which she gives to Gertrude, Claudius, and Laertes. For example, Ophelia addresses Gertrude and she calls her "the beauteous majesty of Denmark". Then she discloses to the audience who Gertrude's "true love" is:

> "How should I your true love know
> From another one?
> By his cockle hat and staff,
> And his sandal shoon."
> (*Hamlet*, IV.5)

Gertrude's "true love" wears a pilgrim hat, staff and sandals. In other words, he is a man on a spiritual path. There is only one aspect of Elsinore that fits this description: Hamlet. In this way, Ophelia helps the audience to understand Gertrude's actions. It is very easy to misunderstand the character of Gertrude. Gertrude does not say much. She appears to be a very obedient wife. All we know about her is based on Hamlet's comments. But Hamlet is not a reliable source of objective judgment.

Gertrude represents a weakened and passive aspect of Elsinore. She has been dominated by her husbands. Although she was unaware of the murders committed by both of her husbands, she knew their manipulating skills very well.

Her first husband was proud, impulsive and violent (as "he smote the sledded Polacks on the ice"). The fact that Gertrude cannot see or hear the Ghost indicates that she was not too attached to her first husband. Gertrude realizes what Hamlet's true potential is and the role he should be capable of playing. She also understood the importance of Ophelia for Hamlet's future:

"I hoped thou shouldst have been my Hamlet's wife."
(*Hamlet, V.1*)

Definitively Gertrude is not driven by lust or sensual attraction to Claudius. It is the other way around. She takes advantage of Claudius' attraction to her in order to achieve her objective and she makes a deal with Claudius. It is this deal that leaves "black and grained spots" on her soul. Her secret objective is to protect Hamlet against the machinations of the Danish court and make him the future king of Denmark. After the death of the previous king, Gertrude knew that it would be too dangerous for Hamlet to be elected king, because he was still too young, naïve and immature.

The audience may presume that she agreed on her marriage to Claudius on the condition that Hamlet would be declared the "most immediate" heir to the throne. Claudius agreed to her request. Claudius' comment to Laertes further confirms Gertrude's feeling toward Hamlet and the nature of Gertrude's relationship with her second husband:

> "The queen his mother
> Lives almost by his looks; and for myself -
> My virtue or my plague, be it either which -
> She's so conjunctive to my life and soul,
> That, as the star moves not but in his sphere,
> I could not but by her."
> (*Hamlet, IV.7*)

Gertrude's only concern is Hamlet's future. Gertrude is unquestionably loyal to Hamlet. When Hamlet asks her not to disclose to Claudius that he only pretends to be mad, Gertrude promises to do so. And she keeps her promise.

***

Elsinore has reached such a low level that the only constructive available solution, regardless of how contradictory it may sound, is to remove all its corrupted aspects. Such a drastic form of reformation may provide the base for the renewal of this being. Only then will it be possible to bring in a new leading aspect. The play illustrates quite exactly, step by step, the preparation for such an event. Shakespeare marked the precise moment when such a preparation was initiated. This happened when King Hamlet killed his great rival Fortinbras of Norway. This means that at the time of King Hamlet's reign, the evolutionary potential of Elsinore was already seriously eroded. The corruption of Elsinore was caused by the "foul crimes" committed by Hamlet's father.

The Norwegian court is like a mirror reflection of Elsinore. The Old Norway is the brother of the killed king; young Fortinbras is the son of the previous king. Fortinbras' situation is very similar to that of Hamlet's. However, this aspect is not corrupted. His father was killed and Fortinbras seeks his revenge. But Fortinbras' approach is very different: he does not seek personal revenge. His eyes are on a higher aim: the well-being of the country. Fortinbras easily outmanoeuvres Claudius. Under the pretext of a war with the Polacks, Fortinbras secures Claudius' permission to bring his troops to Denmark. At this point Hamlet doesn't have any idea about Fortinbras' purpose. In his arrogance and ignorance, he assumes that Fortinbras, "a delicate and tender prince", is fighting for "an egg-shell".

Now we may realize that Elsinore is subjected to quite a sophisticated operation. On the one hand, there is a very precise preparation leading to the final scene in which the remaining elements of the Bohemian octagon will be removed. On the other hand, this preparation is coordinated with the movements of Fortinbras and his forces. It would be impossible to implement such a precise intervention without very advanced guidance. So, who does direct Elsinore's operation?

The developmental process requires the presence of a guide. However, a disciple has to recognize his guide. Otherwise, the guide will remain hidden and his function will be rather limited. This is Hamlet's challenge. The spectators watching the performance of "Hamlet" face the same challenge as Hamlet. Namely, in order to understand the play, it is necessary to recognize who the guide is and how he or she operates. The details are disclosed during Hamlet's encounter with the gravedigger. The gravedigger gives Hamlet a skull and tells him that it was Yorick's. Yorick was the previous king's jester. Hamlet exclaims:

"Alas, poor Yorick! I knew him, Horatio: a fellow
of infinite jest, of most excellent fancy."
(*Hamlet, V.1*)

Yorick, the Fool, was a spiritual guide. We have seen the Fool
performing such a function in the previous two plays of the
Bohemian branch, i.e., Feste in "The Twelfth Night" and Lucio in
"Measure for Measure". Yorick was the guide during the time of
King Hamlet's reign. Then, something went wrong. At the time of
King Hamlet's combat with Fortinbras, the octagonal inner
structure formed at the time of "Measure for Measure" was
disintegrated. The process was interrupted. Yorick spent the last
few years of his life training and preparing the young Hamlet for
his future role. At that time, Yorick transferred his mandate to his
deputy. The gravedigger told Hamlet about it in the following
quote:

"A pestilence on him for a mad rogue! a' poured a
flagon of Rhenish on my head once."
(*Hamlet, V.1*)

In the symbolic language of the teaching, "wine" represents the
unitive energy of love. In other words, by baptizing him with
"wine", Yorick passed his mandate to the gravedigger. It was then
that the Bohemian octagon was turned into a graveyard. Now the
gravedigger is in charge of completing the current phase of the
process.

The gravedigger is the wittiest character in the play. He is not only
asking sharp questions, he is giving answers without hesitation or
confusion. He seems to be on top of all issues. Even Hamlet
notices this:

"How absolute the knave is! we must speak by the
card, or equivocation will undo us. By the Lord,
Horatio, these three years I have taken a note of

it; the age is grown so picked that the toe of the
peasant comes so near the heel of the courtier, he
gaffs his kibe."
(*Hamlet, V.1*)

Hamlet comments sarcastically that the peasants have become so
clever and witty that they are overdoing the courtiers.

Hamlet's encounter with the gravedigger is another demonstration
of his non-readiness. The encounter takes the form of an interview,
a period of questions and answers. Hamlet is given several clues
that should help him recognize who the gravedigger really is. In
other words, by recognizing the guide he would demonstrate that
he is worthy of being guided. In the encounter with the
gravedigger, however, Hamlet appears to be clueless, even gullible.
The gravedigger clearly indicates that he knows Hamlet but Hamlet
does not notice it. Then, the gravedigger gives him another clue:

"I have been sexton here, man
and boy, thirty years."
(*Hamlet, V.1*)

Earlier on, the gravedigger said that he became a grave-maker on
the day when the young Hamlet was born. The above quote would
imply that Hamlet is now 30 years old. But Hamlet is a young
student (according to the Shepherd in "The Winter's Tale", Hamlet
is "between sixteen and three-and-twenty"). Therefore, the "30
years" is used to serve another purpose. Namely, it is a reference to
the performance of "The Murder of Gonzago". According to the
players' performance, Hamlet's father was killed when he
celebrated the 30 year anniversary of his marriage. In this way, the
gravedigger tries to draw Hamlet's attention to the players'
performance. The gravedigger is indicating to Hamlet that he
would be able to explain the inconsistency of "The Murder of
Gonzago". Furthermore, the gravedigger would be able to guide
Hamlet through his current situation but Hamlet would have to

pay attention to what the gravedigger is saying. Hamlet, however, completely ignores the gravedigger's hints and misses the opportunity to recognize the guide who would be able to help him to change the course of events. The gravedigger concludes the encounter with Hamlet by saying that Yorick's skull:

> "... has lain in the earth
> three and twenty years."
> (*Hamlet*, *V.1*)

For Hamlet to be 30 years old, Yorick would have had to be buried at least 23 years ago. The gravedigger has just told Hamlet that it takes some eight years for a dead body to rot but Hamlet notices that this particular skull is still smelly:

> "And smelt so? pah!"
> (*Hamlet*, *V.1*)

This means that the skull was buried no longer than 7-8 years ago, yet Hamlet still does not register this contradiction.

The gravedigger's comment is a summary of the current state of Elsinore. The "three and twenty" has the same meaning as in the Shepherd's remark; it symbolically marks the duration of an evolutionary branch or a cycle. The gravedigger indicates that, at this very moment, the "three and twenty years" of the Bohemian branch has been buried, and as Marcellus expressed it, only "rotten" stuff remains in Denmark.

All that can be done is to preserve a bare minimum of the previously achieved gains. Therefore, Hamlet will have to follow the "hard" way. Right after meeting with the gravedigger, Hamlet encounters Ophelia's funeral procession and he is shocked when he sees Ophelia's dead body. Ophelia's death and Laertes' lamentation over the loss of his beloved sister triggers in Hamlet a moment of true sincerity for the first time. He realizes that Ophelia was his real priority. At this moment he forgets about the Ghost, his father, and his revenge. He openly declares that he loved Ophelia:

> "I loved Ophelia: forty thousand brothers
> Could not, with all their quantity of love,
> Make up my sum."
> (*Hamlet, V.1*)

The current situation of Elsinore is such that the only constructive solution is to destroy all its destructive aspects together with those that did not fulfil their evolutionary potential. This is a required condition, before a new leading aspect may be brought onto the scene. The appearance of a new leading aspect is marked by the arrival of Fortinbras and the English ambassadors. The ambassadors' presence reinforces the link between Elsinore and England. Fortinbras becomes the leading aspect of this reformed being. The entire chain of events illustrated in "Hamlet" was the preparation for this event.

Hamlet, because of his moment of true sincerity, is granted a foretaste of a higher state. For a very brief moment he is able to experience the state "to be". The moment of his "awakening" is clearly defined. It commences when he "dies before dying":

> "I am dead, Horatio."
> (*Hamlet, V.2*)

It lasts until Hamlet's physical death. This moment is the quintessence of the play. At this moment the distinction between past, presence, and future disappears. Hamlet is able to "perceive" the meaning of the story of his father and the players' performance, the role of the Ghost, the functions of Ophelia, Claudius, Gertrude, Laertes, the gravedigger, and Fortinbras. Because of his awakened state of "to be", he is able to convey his understanding with a single sentence:

"I do prophesy the election lights on Fortinbras."
(*Hamlet*, *V.2*)

Hamlet is not only able to perceive the truth: during this brief moment of "to be" he is able to discharge the remaining fraction of his potential by expressing his support for Fortinbras' election as the next ruler of Denmark:

"he has my dying voice;
So tell him, with the occurrents, more and less,
Which have solicited. The rest is silence."
(*Hamlet*, *V.2*)

Hamlet's last words say everything. Nothing else needs to be added. Everything has been explained. Therefore, "The rest is silence".

***

Critical stages of the evolutionary process have their parallels in historical events. Whenever an evolutionary intervention is implemented, something happens on the historical scale. Although what happens takes the outward form of an ordinary event, there will always be some peculiar inner content qualitatively different from anything that can arise naturally in the interactions of ordinary life.

We may recognize such a parallel between the events described in Shakespeare's Bohemian plays and the situation of 16th century Central Europe. At that time, there were quite obvious signs that the development of European civilization was on the wrong track. Evolutionary growth was severely inhibited by corrupted doctrines and malpractices within the Church that dominated Europe. These malpractices culminated when the Church started to sell indulgences, i.e., "pardons" of particular sins. Shakespeare alludes to this fact in the following quote in "King John":

"Though you and all the kings of Christendom
Are led so grossly by this meddling priest,
Dreading the curse that money may buy out;
And by the merit of vile gold, dross, dust,
Purchase corrupted pardon of a man,
Who in that sale sells pardon from himself,
Though you and all the rest so grossly led
This juggling witchcraft with revenue cherish,
Yet I alone, alone do me oppose
Against the pope and count his friends my foes."
(*King John, III.1*)

Another major indication of such degeneration was the tremendous corruption within the Church's hierarchy, all the way up to the Bishop of Rome, who appointed individuals to the various titles of Bishops, Cardinals, etc., based upon financial contributions. In other words, the leading institution of Europe was severely degenerate as the overall situation had started to diverge from its evolutionary potential. At a certain stage of divergence, the evolutionary process could be seriously disturbed. At some point, it would become subject to the law of diminishing returns and finally it would be extinguished.

As indicated earlier, this situation was foreseen. A hundred years earlier, an evolutionary intervention was initiated. An evolutionary impulse was "rapidly" prepared on a higher level of the transmission chain. The impulse was sent to the Balkan Peninsula at the time of "Twelfth Night". This impulse was needed to form the octagonal union in Vienna at the time of "Measure for Measure". As previously indicated, the exposure to an octagonal inner structure has a constructive effect that neutralizes, at least partially, some destructive trends disturbing the evolutionary process. It is like a drop of oil that gradually spreads over a larger area. It was such a drop of "glory" generated by the Viennese octagon that led to the instigation of the European Reformation.

Historically, the Reformation was initiated by Martin Luther, a German monk, a scholar, and theologian. In 1517 Luther publicly exposed the abuses of the Church by posting on the door of the Castle Church in Wittenberg a copy of his famous 95 theses, which challenged the Church's doctrine. These 95 theses were quickly printed and widely distributed, making the controversy one of the first in history to be fanned by the printing press. Within two weeks, these papers spread throughout Germany; within two months throughout Europe. Luther's action deeply influenced the course of European civilization.

In this context, it is interesting to note that Martin Luther used a rose, a cross, and a ring in his seal. The seal was designed for Luther at the request of Prince John Frederick, Elector of Saxony. A rose, a cross, and a ring are symbolic representations of technical instruments used in the implementation of the evolutionary process. The "rose" is a breathing and visualization exercise, whose purpose is to activate man's subtle faculties. The "cross" indicates concentration points within the human body that are used during the rose exercise. The "ring", or the "garter", indicates the requirements needed for the effective performance of the rose exercise, i.e., the presence of certain people, the correct time and the right place. The appearance of these symbols within Luther's seal is a sign that the Reformation was one of the derivative effects of the evolutionary intervention initiated at that time.

The Church responded to Luther's challenge with the Diet of Worms. The Diet (Edict) was a decree issued by the Holy Roman Emperor Charles V, in 1521. This decree is known as "The Diet of Worms" because it was issued in the small town of Worms on the Rhine River. The decree declared Martin Luther an outlaw and a heretic and banned his literature. "The Diet of Worms" was an event which severely obstructed the original objective of the Reformation.

In "Hamlet", Shakespeare left a direct reference to "The Diet of Worms". Hamlet refers to it as "certain convocation of politic worms" that served "emperor for diet":

Claudius:

"Now, Hamlet, where's Polonius?"

Hamlet:

"At dinner."

Claudius:

"At dinner where?"

Hamlet:

"Not where he eats, but where he is eaten.
Certain convocation of politic worms are eaten at him.
Your worm is your emperor for diet."
(*Hamlet, IV.3*)

In other words, "Hamlet" symbolically illustrates the overall impact of the Bohemian union on the situation of 16th century Central Europe.

The Reformation was followed by a mild form of "renewal". This period is known in history as the Counter-Reformation. The Counter-Reformation was initiated at the Council of Trent in 1545, i.e., more or less at the time of Luther's death. The Counter-Reformation was a movement within the Church itself. A commission of cardinals was tasked with institutional reforms to address contentious issues such as corrupt bishops and priests, indulgences, and other financial abuses. As a result, the Church itself was forced to eliminate some of its worst corruptive aspects. This corresponds to the situation illustrated in the final scene of "Hamlet" when the corruptive aspects of the being of Elsinore were eliminated and only a tiny fragment of the evolutionary potential was realized.

In summary, the opportunity for a substantial evolutionary gain in Central Europe was not fulfilled. The results achieved fell short of the potential that was available there at that time. Shakespeare indicates that although the "better times" referred to by the Duke at the conclusion of "Measure for Measure" did not materialize, an evolutionary "catastrophe" was avoided.

***

Let's recall that the arrival of Viola and Sebastian in Illyria at the time of "Twelfth Night" was to serve several purposes. The first purpose was to bring the impulses of creative energy from Ephesus. This task was realized when Mariana and Kate were brought to Vienna from Ephesus at the time of "Measure for Measure". Afterwards, these two impulses were transferred to Italy.

The second purpose was to use the Bohemian octagon to counterbalance the destructive tendencies in Central Europe. This was partially achieved through its accelerated activation. Afterwards, the octagonal structure disintegrated.

The remaining two impulses of the octagon (Isabella and Claudio) stayed within the Bohemian branch. They served the third purpose, which was to reinforce the development of the leading aspect of the intellect within the English branch. These two impulses appear in "Hamlet" as Laertes and Ophelia. They played a critical role in Hamlet's experiences. After partially discharging their functions, these two impulses were removed from the physical world. Hamlet's experiences, however, were passed to Fortinbras. Afterwards, Fortinbras was able to make a journey to England and in this way Hamlet's experiences were transferred to England at the time of "The Merry Wives of Windsor".

Before Fortinbras could arrive in England, something else had to be developed in France. Therefore, let's take a look at the situation within the French evolutionary branch.

Cypriot link

The island of Cyprus was one of two intermediate states activated as a result of Pericles' mission. The Cypriot link was activated to act as an outpost for the expansion of the process to Moorish Spain and then to France and England. It was through this link that the chivalric sequence was downloaded from Pentapolis to Spain and then to the South of France. It was then that the French evolutionary branch was formed.

After downloading the chivalric sequence, Pentapolis was transformed into Mauritania. The new template took the shape of an octagon. The change of template required an adjustment of the transmitting vehicle: the triad was changed into a quad. A quad contains two aspects of the subtle faculties; it is formed by assimilating two evolutionary impulses. The octagon is obtained by overlapping two quads.

The evolutionary process implemented through the Cypriot link is illustrated in the French trilogy, i.e., "All's Well That Ends Well", "As You Like It", and "Love's Labour's Lost". Shakespeare uses the Kingdom of Navarre to represent Moorish Spain. Navarre was the kingdom that occupied lands on either side of the Pyrenees alongside the Atlantic Ocean. Navarre is referred to only in the last play of the French trilogy. However, events that previously took place in Navarre have influenced the situations in France that are illustrated in "All's Well That Ends Well" and "As You Like It".

Three impulses of evolutionary energies were transmitted via Cyprus to the Park in Navarre. These three impulses were complimentary to the fourth one, which remained in a standby position in Cyprus. As indicated in the discussion of "Othello", this fourth impulse (*yellow*) was represented by Bianca. From its first appearance as Cordelia in "King Lear", this particular impulse was designated for France.

At that time, the European royal families were to act as a transmission channel. In other words, the impulses invested in the Park were intended for the court of the King of Navarre. First, a veiled impulse of unitive energy (*red*) was sent from the Park to the court of Navarre. This impulse was designated for the King of Navarre. This impulse provided a seed for the network of chivalric ducal courts and generated ideas found in the Troubadours' poetry. Afterwards, the two remaining impulses (*white* and *black*) were to follow. These impulses were to be transmitted via the royal channel to England. But as is the way of man, he tends to interfere with the evolutionary process. Or like Lysander observed in "A Midsummer Night's Dream":

"The course of true love never did run smooth."
(*A Midsummer Night's Dream*, I.1)

There was a very strong resistance among the ruling royal family of Navarre against any ideas associated with the evolutionary process. This led to a transmission break between the Park and the court of Navarre. As a result, the other two impulses (*white* and *black*) could not be transmitted; they got trapped in the Park. Historically, the break was associated with the Reconquest of Moorish Spain and the collapse of the ducal courts in the South of France. The Reconquest was a period of nearly 800 years in the Middle Ages during which several Christian kingdoms, including Navarre, succeeded in retaking the Iberian Peninsula from the Moors. Navarre played a dominant role during the Reconquest of Spain.

The break between the Park and the court of Navarre meant that France and England were disconnected from the transmission chain. The French plays illustrate how, despite of all these interferences, the process was preserved and continued.

All's Well That Ends Well

The play is set in the 13th century, i.e., at the same historical time as "The Winter's Tale". "The Winter's Tale" is the third consecutive play of the Bohemian plays. This is an important pointer that helps us to understand the overall layout of the French plays. Namely, "All's Well That Ends Well" illustrates a later stage of the French branch. This means that Shakespeare did not describe the initial stages that were implemented in France. However, in his other plays he provided enough information to reconstruct the details of the early stages of the French branch.

The action of "All's Well That Ends Well" is set against the backdrop of the 13th century destruction of the ducal courts in the South of France. The play starts and finishes at the castle of the Count of Rousillon. It was partly in this region, famous for its high culture and tolerance that a network of chivalric ducal courts appeared in the 11th century. With the collapse of the ducal courts, the environment in which the Troubadours worked was destroyed. The last of the Troubadours is said to have been Guiraut Riquier, a native of Narbonne, who died in 1294. In the play, there is a reference to the death of Guiraut Riquier:

"He was famous, sir, in his profession, and it was
his great right to be so: Gerard de Narbon."
(*All's Well That Ends Well, I.1*)

In this way Shakespeare points out that this particular time corresponds to the period of the death of the last Troubadour.

The Count of Rousillon has also recently died. The King of France is terminally ill. The emphasis on death and illness indicates that France has reached a critical moment in its developmental cycle. This situation is a result of the break in the transmission with the Park in Navarre.

Because of the break, the evolutionary impulses designated for England could not be transmitted. This meant that the overall process would be greatly delayed or even interrupted. Therefore, it was decided to remedy the situation by forming a temporary octagon within the French branch. In this way, the formation of the French octagon would coincide with the activation of the Viennese octagon. The overlap of the waves generated by these two octagons would provide the needed reinforcement of the process.

After the break, the veiled impulse of unitive energy (*red*) was transferred from the court of Navarre to Rousillon. This was similar to the situation of Sicily, where Hermione managed to send Perdita to the Bohemian forest.

The remaining two impulses (*black* and *white*) were stored in the Park of Navarre.

The fourth impulse (*yellow*) remained in Cyprus. At that time it was decided to use the Sicilian link to deliver this impulse to France via Italy. When Sicily was reactivated at the time of "Much Ado About Nothing", this impulse was transferred from Cyprus to Sicily and then into the Italian evolutionary branch. At the time of "Much Ado About Nothing", this impulse was represented by Beatrice of Messina.

Gerard de Narbon was a guide and a custodian of the evolutionary process. After Gerard's death, Helena inherited her father's mandate and his function. At the same time she represents the impulse of unitive energy (*red*) that has been placed in Rousillon. The next step of the process requires this impulse to be assimilated in France. Bertram, the son of the Count of Rousillon, is the intended receptor of this impulse. According to the original plan, Bertram was to marry Maudlin, Lord Lafeu's daughter. Maudlin represents an earlier impulse of conscious energy. This marriage was suggested by the King when Bertram and Maudlin were very young:

> "…in the minority of them both,
> his majesty, out of a self-gracious remembrance, did
> first propose."
> (*All's Well That Ends Well*, IV.5)

Because of the change, Bertram is required to fulfil a much more demanding function. Instead of assimilating consciousness, he is required to absorb unitive energy. This may be accomplished when Bertram marries Helena. Bertram, however, is not ready to fulfill this function. Even worse, Bertram does not understand his situation at all. Bertram's spiritual "blindness" is expressed by his attitude towards Helena:

> "I know her well:
> She had her breeding at my father's charge.
> A poor physician's daughter my wife! Disdain
> Rather corrupt me ever!"
> (*All's Well That Ends Well*, II.3)

Bertram is not ready yet to recognize his role and responsibility. Therefore, he has to go through quite a difficult learning process. The overall purpose of the play is to illustrate how a spiritual guide may induce progress, even though, due to time and other factors, man is entirely ignorant of his own potential.

Gerard de Narbon passed to Helena precise instructions on how to handle the situation. According to these instructions, Helena should present herself at the royal court in Paris upon hearing that the King has been "touch'd with that malignant cause". Helena goes to Paris and offers to cure the King:

> "On's bed of death
> Many receipts he gave me: chiefly one.

Which, as the dearest issue of his practise,
And of his old experience th' only darling,
He bade me store up, as a triple eye,
Safer than mine own two, more dear; I have so;
And hearing your high majesty is touch'd
With that malignant cause wherein the honour
Of my dear father's gift stands chief in power,
I come to tender it and my appliance
With all bound humbleness."
(*All's Well That Ends Well, II.1*)

As payment for her service, she asks the King to allow her to marry a lord of her choice. Of course, she has to exclude "the royal blood of France"; a son of the King cannot be on her list:

"Then shalt thou give me with thy kingly hand
What husband in thy power I will command:
Exempted be from me the arrogance
To choose from forth the royal blood of France,
My low and humble name to propagate
With any branch or image of thy state."
(*All's Well That Ends Well, II.1*)

According to the original plan, a French Prince was supposed to be the recipient of this impulse. Now, however, the royal channel has been excluded from active participation in the process. This restriction is further indicated by another limitation that has been imposed on the French King. Namely, the King's actions are also restricted by his "cousin Austria":

"We here received it
A certainty, vouch'd from our cousin Austria,
With caution that the Florentine will move us
For speedy aid; wherein our dearest friend
Prejudicates the business and would seem

To have us make denial."
(*All's Well That Ends Well*, I.2)

This means that the King's son is also prevented from going to wars in Tuscany. But the King may send his French lords to Florence. The King encourages his lords to go:

"Not to woo honour, but to wed it."
(*All's Well That Ends Well*, II.1)

"Not to woo" but "to wed" marks a significant moment in the process. "Not to woo" but "to wed" is a reference to the change of the sterile triad of the Troubadours into an active one. The Troubadours' activity was limited to "wooing" because their Lady was still unattainable. Now the evolutionary potential has been advanced. The "lady" is available. This moment is marked by the arrival of Helena at the King's court in Paris. Up to this point, the particular function that is symbolically represented by Helena had been latent; it had been under Diana's protection. Helena describes the change in the following comment:

"Now, Dian, from thy altar do I fly,
And to imperial Love, that god most high,
Do my sighs stream."
(*All's Well That Ends Well*, II.3)

The protection period has ended. The Chivalric Knights, except for the royal Prince, are free to find and wed their ladies. This is a projection of the situation from Pentapolis when Pericles married Thaisa. It took fourteen centuries to project this event from Pentapolis onto the ordinary world.

The King accepts Helena's offer. Helena's treatment proves successful. The King is overjoyed and honours her condition. Of course, for a husband Helena chooses unwilling Bertram. Bertram is forced to marry Helena. Immediately after the marriage ceremony, Bertram demands that Helena go back home to Rousillon. He sends a letter in which he informs her that he will never be her true husband unless she can get his family ring from his finger and become pregnant with his child. These conditions, Bertram declares, will never happen. Bertram flees from France to Tuscany. In Tuscany he joins the army of the Duke of Florence and fights against the Duke of Siena.

Upon receiving the letter, Helena departs from Rousillon. She announces that she has decided to make a religious pilgrimage.

Helena carries an impulse of unitive energy (*red*). This impulse, however, is too subtle for the current state of Bertram. Therefore, an impulse of creativity (*yellow*) is needed to assist the implementation of this more advanced approach. In the meantime, this very impulse was transferred from Cyprus to Italy. It is present in 16th century Italy at the time of "Romeo and Juliet". This impulse is represented by Rosaline Capulet (Rosaline is described as she who "hath Dian's wit"). This is why the action of "All's Well That Ends Well" overlaps with "Romeo of Juliet". In "All's Well That Ends Well" this impulse appears as Diana Capilet, the daughter of an old widow who lives in Florence. Let's recall that from the perspective of the Realm, there is no such thing as past, present and future. Therefore, at the level of the Realm, it is possible to access the future in order to fix the present. The overlap of 13th century France with 16th century Italy is another example of a past-present-future intervention. The readers will notice that Helena's movements between France and Italy coincide with Posthumus' travels described in "Cymbeline". Posthumus also travelled via 13th century France to 16th century Renaissance Italy.

While in Florence, Bertram gets strongly attracted to Diana. He attempts to seduce her. It is then that Helena arrives in the city. Helena may use Diana to expose Bertram to the needed experience. The Widow's house in Florence serves the same purpose as Diana's temple in Ephesus. It is a temporary powerhouse where the available evolutionary impulses have been gathered. In addition to Diana Capilet, these impulses are represented by Violenta and Mariana. Shakespeare emphasizes the importance of Florence's role in the implementation of the European Renaissance by placing three impulses of creative energy there. They are all gathered in the Widow's house. These three impulses constitute nearly the entire charge of creativity that was invested in Europe at that time.

Violenta is another of Shakespeare's ghost characters. Violenta, like the Lady of Ephesus who appeared in the final scene of "Pericles, Prince of Tyre", is silent throughout the entire scene. Violenta is Diana's spiritual "twin", i.e., she represents the same evolutionary function (*yellow*). The only difference between them is their origin. Namely, Diana was sent from Cyprus; her intended destination is France. Violenta, on the other hand, belongs to the Sicilian link; her ultimate destination is Italy. Previously Violenta appeared as the Courtesan of Ephesus in "Pericles, Prince of Tyre" and then in "The Comedy of Errors". Afterwards she reappears as Kate in Vienna at the time of "Measure for Measure". From Vienna she is transferred to Florence.

Mariana represents an impulse of creative energy designated for the intellect faculty (*white*). Previously she also appeared in "The Comedy of Errors". At that time she was presented as Luciana. Afterwards, she reappeared as Mariana in Vienna at the time of "Measure for Measure". At that time Mariana took part in a bed-trick arranged by the Duke. Mariana's bitter outburst about the misery of "the wreck of maidenhood" alludes to her previous experiences:

"Beware of them, Diana; their promises,
enticements, oaths, tokens, and all these engines of
lust, are not the things they go under: many a maid

hath been seduced by them; and the misery is,
example, that so terrible shows in the wreck of
maidenhood, cannot for all that dissuade succession,
but that they are limed with the twigs that threaten
them. I hope I need not to advise you further; but
I hope your own grace will keep you where you are,
though there were no further danger known but the
modesty which is so lost."
(*All's Well That Ends Well, III.5*)

Violenta's and Mariana's transfer from Vienna to Florence is a step towards bringing them to their original intended environments. They will stay in Italy; they both will reappear in Verona.

The appearance of Mariana and Violenta explains the nature of the involvement of "our cousin Austria" into the process taking place in France. "Our cousin Austria" is a reference to the Bohemian branch. Specifically, this is related to the formation of the octagon in Vienna (Austria) at the time of "Measure for Measure". The wave of the Bohemian octagon reached Italy. It was this wave that brought Mariana and Violenta to Florence. But none of them was destined for the royal blood of France. This is why the French Prince was prevented from going to Tuscany.

Helena solicits the help of the Widow and Diana. She asks Diana to get from Bertram his ring and, in exchange, give him Helena's ring. Afterwards, Helena and Diana execute a bed-trick. The bed-trick is executed by inviting Bertram to Diana's bedchamber. In the darkness, Helena takes Diana's place, and Bertram has sex with Helena, his wife. Here is how Helena explains the rationale of the bed-trick:

"Why then to-night
Let us assay our plot; which, if it speed,
Is wicked meaning in a lawful deed
And lawful meaning in a lawful act,

Where both not sin, and yet a sinful fact."
(*All's Well That Ends Well, III.7*)

The above quote about "wicked meaning in a lawful deed" underlines a significant feature of a genuine developmental process. Namely, what matters is the spiritually constructive act that cannot be judged by simplistic and moralistic rules of what is "infidelity" and what is "religion" or what is "right" and what is "wrong".

Meanwhile, rumours have spread about Helena's supposed death. The rumours coincide with the death of Juliet in Verona that is described in "Romeo and Juliet". It should be pointed out that Juliet of Verona represents the same impulse as Helena (*red*). Therefore, the rumours about Helena's death are not entirely baseless. Upon hearing about Helena's death, Bertram decides to return to Rousillon. Unknown to him, Helena follows him, accompanied by Diana.

In Rousillon, everyone is mourning Helena's death. The King, who is visiting Rousillon, consents to Bertram marrying Maudlin. The King notices, however, the ring on Bertram's finger. This ring belonged to Helena; it was a gift from the King after she saved his life. Bertram is having difficulty explaining where the ring came from. At this moment Helena arrives. Helena informs Bertram that both his conditions have been fulfilled: she wears his family ring and she is pregnant with his child. In the final scene Bertram's change is completed. He recognizes the true nature of Helena:

"If she, my liege, can make me know this clearly,
I'll love her dearly, ever, ever dearly."
(*All's Well That Ends Well, V.3*)

Bertram promises to be a faithful husband to Helena. The impulse of unitive energy is assimilated within the French branch.

At the end of the play there is a new feature that is of great importance for the future of the French branch. Namely, the King of France decides that Diana will remain in France:

> "If thou be'st yet a fresh uncropped flower,
> Choose thou thy husband, and I'll pay thy dower."
> (*All's Well That Ends Well*, *V.3*)

In this way the impulse of creative energy (*yellow*) is transferred to its originally intended environment. After a long journey from Cyprus via Sicily and Italy, this impulse is embedded within the French branch. This impulse will be needed to form a spiritual quad.

As You Like It

"As You Like It" is a sequel to "All's Well That Ends Well". In accordance with Shakespeare's narrative, the state of France at the end of "All's Well That Ends Well" constitutes the initial state of France at the beginning of "As You Like It". The evolutionary impulses that are attached to France are the same as those present at the conclusion of "All's Well That Ends Well". Namely, the evolutionary charge consists of Rosalind and Celia. Rosalind's function is the same as Helena's. Rosalind represents an impulse of the unitive energy of love (*red*). Celia represents an impulse of creative energy (*yellow*). Celia was transferred from Italy to France at the conclusion of "All's Well That Ends Well". Celia points to her alien origin by changing her name to Aliena:

> "Something that hath a reference to my state
> No longer Celia, but Aliena."
> (*As You Like It*, *I.3*)

Both impulses are designated for the heart faculty. Within the evolutionary spectrum, the unitive energy is brighter and subtler than the creative energy. Celia's father gives the following account of the difference between these two impulses:

> "She is too subtle for thee; and her smoothness,
> Her very silence and her patience
> Speak to the people, and they pity her.
> Thou art a fool: she robs thee of thy name;
> And thou wilt show more bright and seem more virtuous
> When she is gone."
> (*As You Like It*, I.3)

One of Rosalind's uncles is a spiritual inheritor of Gerard de Narbon's mandate. Like Helena's father with Helena, this uncle has prepared Rosalind and her environment for the upcoming experiences. He has taught her the art of courtly love:

> "But indeed an old
> religious uncle of mine taught me to speak, who was
> in his youth an inland man; one that knew courtship
> too well, for there he fell in love."
> (*As You Like It*, II.7)

Presently Rosalind's uncle lives on the outskirt of the Forest of Arden.

The play illustrates the developmental sequence that leads to the accelerated activation of two spiritual quads. The first part of the sequence is focussed on the activation of the spiritual heart. Orlando and Oliver represent two aspects of the French heart. Rosalind, Celia, Orlando and Oliver may form such a quad. Before they can form the quad, they have to be trained in the Forest of Arden.

The developmental sequence follows the previously described methodology that includes a simultaneous exposure to unitive and creative energies. This sequence is symbolically illustrated as the experiences that Oliver and Orlando are going through. Here is Rosalind's description of the encounter of Oliver with Celia, i.e., the assimilation of creative energy:

> "There was never any thing so sudden but the fight of two rams
> and Caesar's thrasonical brag of 'I came, saw, and
> overcame:' for your brother and my sister no sooner
> met but they looked, no sooner looked but they
> loved, no sooner loved but they sighed, no sooner
> sighed but they asked one another the reason, no
> sooner knew the reason but they sought the remedy;
> and in these degrees have they made a pair of stairs
> to marriage which they will climb incontinent, or
> else be incontinent before marriage: they are in
> the very wrath of love and they will together; clubs
> cannot part them."
> (*As You Like It*, *V.2*)

Rosalind lists "degrees" or the seven developmental stages that Celia and Oliver went through during a single moment, i.e., they (1) met, (2) looked, (3) loved, (4) sighed, (5) asked, (6) knew, and (7) sought. Rosalind's reference to Caesar is quite appropriate. Within the Roman cycle, Julius Caesar was the only one who correctly assimilated creative energy. At that time, the impulse of creativity was represented by Calphurnia, Caesar's wife. We may note that Jaques' seemingly witty monologue about the seven stages of human life is in stark contrast to Celia's and Oliver's experience:

> "All the world's a stage,
> And all the men and women merely players:
> They have their exits and their entrances;
> And one man in his time plays many parts,

His acts being seven ages. At first the infant,
Mewling and puking in the nurse's arms.
And then the whining school-boy, with his satchel
And shining morning face, creeping like snail
Unwillingly to school. And then the lover,
Sighing like furnace, with a woeful ballad
Made to his mistress' eyebrow. Then a soldier,
Full of strange oaths and bearded like the pard,
Jealous in honour, sudden and quick in quarrel,
Seeking the bubble reputation
Even in the cannon's mouth. And then the justice,
In fair round belly with good capon lined,
With eyes severe and beard of formal cut,
Full of wise saws and modern instances;
And so he plays his part. The sixth age shifts
Into the lean and slipper'd pantaloon,
With spectacles on nose and pouch on side,
His youthful hose, well saved, a world too wide
For his shrunk shank; and his big manly voice,
Turning again toward childish treble, pipes
And whistles in his sound. Last scene of all,
That ends this strange eventful history,
Is second childishness and mere oblivion,
Sans teeth, sans eyes, sans taste, sans everything."
(*As You Like It, II.7*)

Jaques' monologue applies to ordinary, i.e., undeveloped man. This description parallels Macbeth's comment about the insignificance of human life:

"A tale told by an idiot, full of sound and fury, signifying nothing."
(*Macbeth, V.5*)

The play introduces the audience to the remaining impulses of the Cypriot link. Shepherdesses Phoebe and Audrey represent these two impulses coloured for the intellect faculty. They are designated for the second quad. Their presence in France indicates that the Forest of Arden is the current replica of the Park of Navarre. This means that, after the break between the court of Navarre and the Park, these two impulses were transferred to France.

Shakespeare gives a couple of hints that allow the audience to recognize their specific function. Audrey is *white* like a pearl; Phoebe is *black*:

> "He said mine eyes were black and my hair black."
> (*As You Like It*, III.5)

Phoebe's function is further indicated by her name. In Greek mythology, Phoebe was one of the Titans, representing oracular intellect. She represents an impulse of unitive energy designated for the intellect (*black*). Phoebe has been affected by impurities inherited from the ancient times. In her present outward manifestation, this Black Lady of the Forest of Arden is not of the same purity as Viola, Isabella, or Ophelia, i.e., the Black Ladies of the Bohemian branch. This is how Rosaline described Phoebe to Silvius:

> "You foolish shepherd, wherefore do you follow her,
> Like foggy south puffing with wind and rain?
> You are a thousand times a properer man
> Than she a woman: 'tis such fools as you
> That makes the world full of ill-favour'd children."
> (*As You Like It*, III.5)

Silvius is hopelessly in love with Phoebe. Silvius, a native of the forest, is still influenced by the conditions of the previous phase of the process. During the previous phase, an evolutionary impulse was symbolically represented by the unattainable mistress of the

Troubadours. This is why, for Silvius, his love is still made of fantasy and wishes. He is not the right partner for Phoebe. Yet, he may act as one of the temporary substitutes needed for the formation of the French octagon. Rosalind has to work on them both to bring them together. At the end, Rosalind plays a trick with Phoebe to force her to marry Silvius.

Touchstone, the Fool, is a custodian of the process. As indicated by his name, one of his functions is that of a touchstone. While Rosalind's role is to arrange the formation of an octagonal union, the Fool provides the assessment of those who are in the Forest. He acts as a point of reference in assaying their inner values. When the Fool meets Audrey, a simple goatherd girl, he recognizes that she is one of the impulses of evolutionary energy (*white*) that is needed for the formation of the octagon. But another native of the forest, William, claims his right to Audrey. After examining William, the Fool finds him unsuitable for Audrey:

> "Abandon the society of this female, or,
> clown, thou perishest; or, to thy better
> understanding, diest; or, to wit I kill thee, make
> thee away, translate thy life into death, thy
> liberty into bondage: I will deal in poison with
> thee, or in bastinado, or in steel; I will bandy
> with thee in faction; I will o'errun thee with
> policy; I will kill thee a hundred and fifty ways:
> therefore tremble and depart."
> (*As You Like It, V.1*)

It would be hard to miss that "William" is the first name of Shakespeare. This episode is a reference to the poet's own experiences. As a matter of fact, the Fool's quote alludes to Shakespeare's encounter with his White Lady, which he described in Sonnets 41-42. Like William, the poet lost the "White Lady" to his guide. Here is the bitter outcry of the poet from Sonnet 42:

"That thou hast her it is not all my grief,
And yet it may be said I loved her dearly"
(*Sonnet 42, 1-2*)

In an episode with Corin, another native of the Forest of Arden, the Fool explains the reason for William's unpreparedness. Corin, like William, is satisfied with living in the "forest" without any desire to experience another form of life. He indulges himself enjoying his simple life without performing any constructive function in the overall process. The Fool summarizes such an approach as incomplete and one-sided:

"Yep, you're damned like a roasted egg: all on one side."
(*As You Like It, III.2*)

Then the Fool further elaborates on the need for being both in the "forest" and at the "court":

"Why, if thou never wast at court, thou never sawest
good manners; if thou never sawest good manners,
then thy manners must be wicked; and wickedness is
sin, and sin is damnation. Thou art in a parlous
state, shepherd."
(*As You Like It, III.2*)

The Fool points out that it is necessary to be at the court and in the forest or to be in the world but not of the world. William could be fixed if he learned how to be of the world by being "at court". By the same token, a courtier, or a Prince, would have to spend some time in a "forest" to learn how "to be not of the world", because a court is not sufficient enough to provide the required training. Here is Duke Senior's description of learning while being in the "forest":

"And this our life exempt from public haunt
Finds tongues in trees, books in the running brooks,
Sermons in stones and good in every thing."
(*As You Like It, II.1*)

Only through balancing these two types of experiences is it possible to move forward. Yet, William thinks that he is somewhat smart:

"Ay, sir, I have a pretty wit."

The Fool, therefore, sends William away with the following advice:

"The fool doth think he is wise, but the wise man
knows himself to be a fool."
(*As You Like It, V.1*)

William did not know that the White Lady was not for him. His future function required a different sequence of experiences. William was not ready yet to experience the formation of the octagon. In other words, this particular aspect that is symbolically represented by William had to wait for another "forceful occasion".

Afterwards, the Fool discharges his most important role. This role is that of the Joker. This is the same role that Lucio played at the time of the formation of the Viennese octagon in "Measure for Measure". Audrey represents an impulse of creative energy designated for a subtle aspect of the intellect (*white*). There is none among those gathered in the Forest of Arden that could fill-in this role. By marrying Audrey, the Fool acts as a temporary substitute for the missing aspect that is needed to form the octagon. The Fool clearly indicates that this marriage is only a temporary patch:

"not being well married, it
will be a good excuse for me hereafter to leave my wife."
(*As You Like It, III.3*)

At the end of the play, an octagonal union is formed. Touchstone is married to Audrey and Silvius to Phoebe. Together with Rosalind, Orlando, Celia and Oliver they form a new structure that consists of four couples, or the "eight":

"Here's eight that must take hands
To join in Hymen's bands,
If truth holds true contents."
(*As You Like It*, *V.4*)

Together with the Viennese union, these two octagons are like two oil drops on the map of Western Europe. They will gradually spread over and coalesce, providing the needed evolutionary impact. Such an impact was needed to overcome the delays and interferences occurring within the Italian and English branches. Instead of the originally intended octagons along a North (England) – South (Italy) axis, the Viennese and the French octagons were activated along an East-West axis. The wave field generated by these two octagons was manifested in the ordinary world as the advent of the Renaissance and the Reformation.

Like the Viennese octagon, the French octagon formed in the Forest of Arden was also used to serve several functions. One of these was to affect the situation within the English branch. It is not a coincidence that, geographically, the region of Arden stretches into Northern France. It was not far from the Forest of Arden that, after the formation of the French union, Henry V fought the famous Battle of Agincourt. The Battle of Agincourt was used by Shakespeare as an example of a forceful occasion, i.e., an event when extraordinary forces were at work. Shakespeare used Prologue in "Henry V" to point out the relationship between the Forest of Arden and the Battle of Agincourt:

"Can this cockpit hold
The vasty fields of France? or may we cram
Within this wooden O the very casques

That did affright the air at Agincourt?"
(*Henry V, I. Prologue*)

The Prologue indicates that the octagonal structure, such as that symbolically represented by the octagonal wooden building ("this wooden O") of the famous Shakespeare's Globe Theatre, is capable of manifesting extraordinary forces which can break through the limitations of time and space. This is why "this wooden O" could hold within its walls the vast fields of France and thousands of soldiers that fought at Agincourt. Similarly, the octagon formed in the Forest of Arden provided an impact that was manifested during the Battle of Agincourt.

Another purpose of the French union was to attempt the reactivation of the process in Navarre. The details of this second purpose are described in "Love's Labour's Lost".

Love's Labour's Lost

The love's labour's won at the time of "All's Well That Ends Well" and further enriched in "As You Like It", can now be used to revitalize the developmental process in another place and in another situation.

"Love's Labour's Lost" takes place in Navarre. It was there that the original seed of the French branch was planted. With the collapse of the ducal courts, the developmental environment of that area was destroyed. The play illustrates an attempt at revitalizing this previously developmentally fertile region. The bedridden King of France sends an advanced evolutionary charge to restore the spiritual health of the ailing Navarre. It is an attempt at returning the transmission channel back to the European royals.

At the conclusion of "As You Like It" an octagonal union was formed in the Forest of Arden. It included the four impulses represented by Rosalind, Celia, Phoebe, and Audrey. Like the Viennese octagon, the French structure was flat and unbalanced. It did not last very long: it disintegrated. Afterwards, the four impulses were sent to Navarre to discharge their evolutionary function there. These impulses are symbolically represented by the Princess of France and her three attendants Rosaline, Katharine, and Maria. Shakespeare uses the colour code to specify the function of each of these four impulses.

Katharine represents the impulse of creative energy designated for the heart faculty (*yellow*, amber):

"Her amber hair"
(*Love's Labour's Lost, IV.3*)

Katharine is the current projection of Celia from "As You Like It" and Rosaline Capulet from "Romeo and Juliet".

Longaville, who is attracted to Maria, describes her as:

"What is she in the white?"
(*Love's Labour's Lost, II.1*)

and in this way he specifies that she represents the impulse of creative energy typed for the intellect faculty (*white*).

Rosaline is the impulse of unitive energy designated for the intellect faculty (*black*):

"By heaven, thy love is black as ebony."
(*Love's Labour's Lost, IV.3*)

In Rosaline's scornful attitude towards Berowne we may recognize disdainful Phoebe from the Forest of Arden.

The Princess, therefore, represents the impulse of unitive energy that is typed for the heart faculty (*red*).

The Princess of France, Katharine, Rosaline and Maria arrive in Navarre. According to the original plan, these impulses were to be transmitted from the Park to the court of the King of Navarre some 500 years before. The King of Navarre was the intended recipient of the unitive energy (*red*).

The composition of evolutionary impulses that are sent from France matches up with the current inner structure of Navarre. Namely, there are four aspects of Navarre: King Ferdinand, Berowne, Dumain, and Longaville. King Ferdinand and Dumain represent two aspects of the heart. Berowne and Longaville represent two aspects of the intellect.

From the very beginning, it is obvious that Navarre is not ready for such an experience. Although Navarre has previously been exposed to a genuine evolutionary impact, in the meantime it has deteriorated. We may presume that the corrective action was initiated as a last possible resort. This action aimed at reinstating some of the evolutionary gains in this previously fertile region which, at that time, was subjected to ruthless destruction.

Shakespeare clearly alludes to the effects of the developmental deterioration in the opening scene. These effects are marked by the approach adopted by King Ferdinand and his lords. The overall goal of their undertaking is naïve and simplistic:

> "Navarre shall be the wonder of the world;
> Our court shall be a little Academe,
> Still and contemplative in living art."
> (*Love's Labour's Lost*, I.1)

And so are the methods that are supposed to lead to this goal:

"To live and study here three years."

"Not to see ladies, study, fast, not sleep!"
(*Love's Labour's Lost, I.1*)

Such an approach corresponds to that of uninformed mystics who immerse themselves in severe exercises and studies without understanding the overall process. It was based on using one single medicine for every ailment without making a proper diagnosis and without taking into account the question of proportion. It was this naïve approach that previously led to the break with the Park. Now, however, Berowne starts to realize that there is another, more effective way to learn. Namely, man may learn through "women's eyes":

"From women's eyes this doctrine I derive:
They sparkle still the right Promethean fire;
They are the books, the arts, the academes,
That show, contain and nourish all the world:
Else none at all in ought proves excellent."
(*Love's Labour's Lost, IV.3*)

Berowne compares women's eyes to the source of the light of truth, which "contain and nourish all the world". Neither books and fasting nor any indiscriminate application of outward laws can lead to evolutionary progress. It is an impulse of evolutionary energy which is needed. It is the unitive energy of love that overrides the ordinary senses of seeing, hearing, touching, and tasting. It is the Love that "makes heaven drowsy with the harmony":

"And when Love speaks, the voice of all the gods
Makes heaven drowsy with the harmony."
(*Love's Labour's Lost, IV.3*)

Navarre, however, is not ready for exposure to Love, which is symbolically represented by the French ladies.

The artificially imposed barrier prevents the Princess and her ladies to access Ferdinand's court. Instead, their encounters take place in a park on the King's estate. According to Shakespeare's presentation, this particular Park in Navarre was the place where the evolutionary charge was first transferred from Cyprus. At that time, Navarre was provided with an evolutionary potential but it was incapable of actualizing it. During the Reconquest, the Park was deactivated and transferred to northern France. The Forest of Arden was a replica of this Park.

As always, a spiritual guide is needed if the process is to be successfully implemented. If the Forest of Arden was a replica of the Park of Navarre, a guide would operate in the Park as well. So, who is the guide and how does he operate?

Similar to the "old religious man" who lived in the Forest of Arden and who guided the process described in "As You Like It", there is such a man who inhabits the park. The Princess is able to spot him as soon as she arrives there to hunt. She spots a mysterious rider who "show'd a mounting mind". Here is the exchange between the Princess and Boyet:

Princess:

"Was that the king, that spurred his horse so hard
Against the steep uprising of the hill?"

Boyet:

"I know not; but I think it was not he."

Princess:

"Whoe'er a' was, a' show'd a mounting mind."
(*Love's Labour's Lost, IV.1*)

It was this rider with "a mounting mind" that preserved a link between the Park and Cyprus. It was this link that enabled to transfer the evolutionary charge from the Park of Navarre to the Forest of Arden. Neither Ferdinand nor his lords are aware of the presence of the rider. Therefore, the implementation of this particular phase of the process has been entrusted to Costard.

According to Longaville, Costard is the court jester:

> "Costard the swain and he shall be our sport;
> And so to study, three years is but short."
> (*Love's Labour's Lost, IV.1*)

Costard plays the same role as Touchstone in "As You Like It". He is the wittiest character of the play. Shakespeare underlines this by making him deliver the longest word spoken in all of his plays, i.e., honorificabilitudinitatibus:

> "O, they have lived long on the alms-basket of words.
> I marvel thy master hath not eaten thee for a word;
> for thou art not so long by the head as
> honorificabilitudinitatibus: thou art easier
> swallowed than a flap-dragon."
> (*Love's Labour's Lost, V.1*)

When Don Adriano asks Costard to deliver his love letter to Jaquenetta and, at the same time, Berowne gives him his letter written to Rosaline, Costard makes sure that the letters are mixed up and are delivered to the wrong hands. Don Adriano's letter is delivered to the Princess. Berowne's letter ends up with Jaquenetta. This sets up the entire plot of the play. The Princess is aware of Costard's role. When Costard finishes his role of Pompey the Great in the masque, he asks the Princess to acknowledge his contribution:

> "If your ladyship would say, 'Thanks, Pompey,' I had done."

The Princess gives him her thanks:

"Great thanks, great Pompey."
(*Love's Labour's Lost, IV.1*)

At the end of the play, the Princess and her attendants refuse to accept Ferdinand's and his lords' oaths of love. After testing them, the Princess concludes that Navarre is not ready for her and her ladies.

The Princess and her ladies, however, offer a recipe that may allow the lords of Navarre to fulfil their developmental potential. In accordance with the requirements of the process, the recipe must be customized. Depending on their initial states, the lords will have to follow different preparatory trainings. Namely, the Princess tells Ferdinand that he will have to abandon the comfortable environment of his court and spend his time in "some forlorn and naked hermitage". Only in this way he may be properly "roasted":

"Your oath I will not trust; but go with speed
To some forlorn and naked hermitage,
Remote from all the pleasures of the world;
There stay until the twelve celestial signs
Have brought about the annual reckoning."
(*Love's Labour's Lost, V.2*)

Berowne is told by Rosaline that he will have to learn how to use his biting wit in a constructive manner. He will have to visit hospitals and to make terminally ill patients laugh.

The recipe is a part of the advanced methodology that was referred to previously. It is focused on the purification of the selected faculties as a means of accelerating their reformation. Dumain and Longaville represent the non-reformed aspects. Therefore, their advancement is dependent on the progress made by Ferdinand and

Berowne, respectively. This is why Dumain will be able to win Katharine's love only after Ferdinand passes his trial successfully:

"Come when the king doth to my lady come;
Then, if I have much love, I'll give you some."
(*Love's Labour's Lost, V.2*)

The outcome of the play is summarized by Berowne's bitter comment:

"Our wooing doth not end like an old play;
Jack hath not Jill: these ladies' courtesy
Might well have made our sport a comedy."

When Ferdinand protests saying that:

"Come, sir, it wants a twelvemonth and a day,
And then 'twill end."

Berowne concludes:

"That's too long for a play."
(*Love's Labour's Lost, V.2*)

The question may be asked: what is going to happen next? What does the time period of "twelve celestial signs" mean?

The Navarre operation involved quite an advanced evolutionary charge. Such an occasion does not happen very often. It may occur only once during an evolutionary cycle. This may be compared to the changing of the seasons, like the winter that follows the spring in the songs that are presented at the end of the Worthies' masque. No progress can be made during a spiritual winter. Therefore, another forceful occasion of the same kind can occur only at the next turn of the evolutionary season. Historically, it took several centuries before this particular region could be exposed again to a similar impulse. It seems that Berowne knew quite well that this definitely was "too long for a play".

The royal channel could not be reactivated. The French impulse is withdrawn from Navarre. Instead, it will be transferred to England at the time of "The Merry Wives of Windsor". It is then that the ultimate purpose of the French octagon will be accomplished.

Italian evolutionary branch

According to the original plan, the Italian branch was to be developed in parallel with the English branch. As it has been mentioned previously, there were problems within both of these branches. Let's take a look at how these various interferences affected the implementation of the process in Italy.

After the restoration of Sicily at the time of "Much Ado About Nothing", the process may be brought back to Italy. The next episode of the Italian branch is illustrated in "The Merchant of Venice". This episode takes place in Venice. In this way, the ascending-descending loop initiated at the time of "Othello" is completed. The Sicilian link has been re-established: Italy has been connected to the evolutionary transmission chain.

The Merchant of Venice

The city of Venice represents an ordinary state within the Italian branch. Through Messina, the Italian branch has been connected to the transmission chain. Now, therefore, an advanced evolutionary charge may be transmitted to Venice. The play illustrates the challenges associated with the expose of Venice to this advanced charge.

At the beginning of the play Venice seems to be balanced and stable. However, under closer examination, it is possible to detect some subtle movements within this being. Some insignificant and seemingly unrelated events are starting to take place, which may indicate that something is being instigated:

- Antonio, Bassanio's kinsman and friend, becomes sad and melancholic; he is not able to identify the source of his depression.

- Bassanio asks Antonio for a loan so he may travel in style to Belmont to win Portia; in this way he expects to fix his financial troubles and to pay back his debts.

- Shylock's servant, Launcelot, decides to run away from his master and work for Bassanio.

- Shylock's daughter, Jessica, plans to escape from her father and marry Lorenzo, Bassanio's friend.

- Gratiano, who is helping Lorenzo arrange Jessica's escape, asks Bassanio to be allowed to accompany him on his trip to Belmont.

It looks like Bassanio is at the centre of all these happenings. Bassanio seems to be connected to the source of these subtle movements. This could be compared to a situation where suddenly an invisible magnetic-like force is switched on and some constituents, that were previously "synthesized" but latent, are activated. Let's note that, at the time of "The Merchant of Venice", two octagonal inner structures have already been activated, one in Vienna and the other in the Forest of Arden. It may be assumed that these two "oil spots" spread over to Venice. They are a source of this magnetic-like force. Perceptive Lorenzo compares this force to a "harmony" generated by the heavenly spheres:

"There's not the smallest orb which thou behold'st
But in his motion like an angel sings,
Still quiring to the young-eyed cherubins;
Such harmony is in immortal souls;
But whilst this muddy vesture of decay
Doth grossly close it in, we cannot hear it."
(*The Merchant of Venice, V.1*)

Lorenzo points out that not everybody is able to perceive "such delightful pleasing harmony". Some may be only partially affected by it. For example, Jessica says that sweet music does not make her happy:

> "I am never merry when I hear sweet music."
> (*The Merchant of Venice, V.1*)

Jessica's comment also explains the reason for Antonio's recent melancholy. Antonio is still veiled by "this muddy vesture of decay". Like Jessica, he is affected by this heavenly "harmony" but his reaction is blurred. His melancholy is one of the signs that an invisible magnetic-like force has been switched on.

***

It helps to understand the play to compare the state of Venice at two different stages of its evolutionary path, i.e., at the time of "Othello" and at the time of "The Merchant of Venice". This will allow us to identify the evolutionary structure of Venice that resulted from the activities implemented previously by Othello and Don Pedro.

At the time of "Othello", Cassio and Roderigo represented two aspects of the heart faculty. For Cassio and Roderigo, Desdemona was an unattainable Princess who symbolized a spiritual quality to which they were strongly attracted, but which was essentially beyond their reach in their current state. In this context Othello, Desdemona, Cassio and Roderigo constitute a "ménage a trois" of the Troubadours. However, there was a substantial difference between Cassio's and Roderigo's attractions to Desdemona. For Cassio, Desdemona represented an unattainable divinity. Like the Knights of the Chivalry, Cassio nearly worshiped her. Roderigo, on the other hand, represented an unreformed aspect of the heart. He was entirely driven by his cruder attractions.

Now, Cassio and Roderigo appear in Venice as Bassanio and Lorenzo. They both have been constructively affected by their previous experiences. They have been prepared for their encounters with more advanced evolutionary impacts.

Although Bassanio is presented as an ineffectual businessman, his former experiences are referred to as a scholar (Cassio in "Othello") and a soldier (Benedick in "Much Ado About Nothing"). Here is Nerissa's comment about Bassanio's previous experiences:

> "Do you not remember, lady, in your father's time, a
> Venetian, a scholar and a soldier, that came hither
> in company of the Marquis of Montferrat?"
> (*The Merchant of Venice, I.2*)

In other words, Bassanio encompasses the experiences that Cassio and Benedick previously went through. Bassanio is young, immature, and rather irresponsible. He easily spends the money that he borrows from Antonio. Nevertheless, Bassanio is loyal, straightforward and shows some signs of intuitive perception. In addition, he manifests an inner quality that attracts other people.

Lorenzo appears as a perceptive and gentle young man. His present state is the result of his rather painful experiences as Roderigo in "Othello" and Claudio in "Much Ado About Nothing".

The inner structure of Venice's heart is reflected in the spectrum of evolutionary impulses that are now available in Italy. Namely, there are two impulses designated for the Venetian heart. They are represented by Portia and Jessica. At the time of "Othello", these two impulses were represented by Desdemona and Bianca, respectively.

Portia of Belmont represents an impulse of unitive energy (*red*). She is the current manifestation of Desdemona. After the completion of Othello's mission, this impulse was transferred from Mauritania via Messina to Belmont, near Venice. Similar to the situation within the French branch, the transfer was arranged by the previous guide, i.e., Portia's father. Portia plays the same role as Helena in "All's Well That Ends Well". Like Helena's father, Portia's father prepared a recipe for the current state of Venice. The recipe is in the form of a test for Portia's suitors. The lady may get married. But only the man who correctly chooses one of three caskets may marry her.

Jessica represents the ancient impulse of creativity (*yellow*) that was transferred from Cyprus via Messina to Venice. Jessica is the current representation of Bianca of Cyprus and Beatrice of Messina. Shakespeare uses "gold" to indicate the presence of creative energy. Shylock, Jessica's father, likens his daughter to his ducats ("gold") when he cries:

> "My daughter! O my ducats! O my daughter!"
> (*The Merchant of Venice, II.8*)

Shylock has inherited the responsibility to preserve the "gold" until the next evolutionary phase occurs. His function is similar to that of the Shepherd in "The Winter's Tale" when he found Perdita and inherited Timon's gold. Unlike the Shepherd, Shylock is incapable of discharging his function correctly. Shylock is presented as an "usurer", because he has corrupted his responsibility.

The readers will notice that there are no impulses coloured for the inner layers of the intellect faculty. There is neither a *white* nor a *black* impulse in Venice. This is a consequence of the breaking of the Sicilian link at the time of "The Winter's Tale". At that time, the *black* impulse could not be activated; the *white* impulse remained in Ephesus. The absence of these two impulses prevents the formation of an octagonal inner structure within the Italian branch. Instead, efforts have been focussed on the activation of a spiritual quad of the heart.

Belmont, Portia's estate, symbolically represents a spiritual power house, i.e., a place where interactions with the evolutionary impulses may take place. Belmont and Portia attract a lot of attention. There are many candidates who wish to be accepted to her "school". To be accepted to her "school", a candidate has to pass a test. The test consists of choosing one of three caskets made respectively of gold, silver and lead. There are three types of candidates who intend to take the test, i.e., (i) a group of Western aristocrats, (ii) the Prince of Morocco and the Prince of Aragon, and (iii) Bassanio. These three groups of candidates represent three different initial states of potential disciples. The European aristocrats are represented by the Neapolitan Prince, the County Palatine, the French Lord, the young Baron of England, the Scottish Lord, and the Duke of Saxony's nephew. They all gathered in Belmont to woo Portia. This is another sign that the overall evolutionary situation has changed. Portia, who represents an impulse of the unitive energy of love, is no more the unattainable lady of the Troubadours. As stated by the King of France in "All's Well That Ends Well", now is time not to woo but to wed. However, for these Western European aristocrats gathered in Belmont, this stage of the process is still too advanced. They are not capable of benefiting from it. All of them shy away from taking the test. They skip the trial and go back to their homes. Their departure is a symbolic indication of the overall evolutionary impotence of Western Europe at that time.

The Prince of Morocco and the Prince of Aragon represent remnants of genuine developmental schools from the past, which in the meantime, have deteriorated. We may recognize in Morocco's attitude a frozen form of Othello's teaching and in Aragon's approach a sterilized form of Don Pedro's school. When an activity related to a certain developmental stage is institutionalized and acquires a label, e.g., *Moorism* or *Aragonism*, it loses its dynamic component and becomes developmentally sterile. We have seen an example of such deteriorated systems in Navarre at the time of "Love's Labour's Lost". We may notice that Morocco and Aragon came from the same region that was influenced by Moorish Spain. At the time of "The Merchant of Venice", the Park of Navarre was deactivated. This is why Aragon and Morocco travel to Belmont to try their luck there. Ironically, unlike the Western aristocrats, Morocco and Aragon are determined enough to take the test. However, they are not fitted yet for Portia's school. They fail the test and are sent away.

Portia is another example of a beautiful young woman in love with a man who, at the beginning of the play, is not yet ready for her. Bassanio, however, has an inner quality that makes him fit for discipleship. But this is going to be a long and challenging way for this young and a bit spoiled man.

Before Bassanio is allowed to take the casket test, he is tested for his patience. Portia suggests that he should take time before making his commitment:

"I pray you, tarry: pause a day or two
Before you hazard;"

"I would detain you here some month or two
Before you venture for me."
(*The Merchant of Venice, III.2*)

It seems that Portia knows that Bassanio is in a hurry to go back to Venice to pay back his loan to Antonio. At this time, financial issues are Bassanio's top priority. Therefore, Portia puts him through a test to demonstrate to him that his affection for her is still superficial. Bassanio, however, fails to notice it. He insists on taking the test right away. Portia indicates to him that he is not quite honest with her:

"Upon the rack, Bassanio! then confess
What treason there is mingled with your love."

And when Bassanio comes out with a silly explanation:

"None but that ugly treason of mistrust,
Which makes me fear the enjoying of my love,"

she clearly indicates to him that she knows he is lying:

"Ay, but I fear you speak upon the rack,
Where men enforced do speak anything."
(*The Merchant of Venice, III.2*)

Nevertheless, Portia allows Bassanio to take the casket test. The test is not to judge the candidate's ability. Portia knows very well what Bassanio's ability is. The test is an exercise for the candidate, so he may learn something from such an experience. In the case of Bassanio, Portia is even helping him to make the right choice but Bassanio cannot know about it. He has to be convinced that he is on his own. This is an integral part of this particular exercise. This exercise is designed in such a way that it may help Bassanio to get in touch with his inner feelings. Portia is using music to guide Bassanio to the right casket:

"If you do love me, you will find me out.
Nerissa and the rest, stand all aloof.
Let music sound while he doth make his choice."
(*The Merchant of Venice, III.2*)

Let's remember that Portia, as a custodian of the evolutionary process, has access to the "music of the spheres", i.e., music that allows one to break through the ordinary limitations of time and space. It should be pointed out that music was not played when Morocco and Aragon were taking the test; it was not necessary for them to experience this test in such a way.

While Bassanio is examining the caskets, a singer is singing the following verses:

218

> "Tell me where is fancy bred,
> Or in the heart, or in the head?
> How begot, how nourished?"
> (*The Merchant of Venice, III.2*)

We may notice that the lines of the song rhyme with "lead", i.e., bread, head, nourished. The entire environment around the casket trial, which has been prepared by Portia, induces an inner feeling in Bassanio that allows him to make the right choice.

As soon as Bassanio passes the test, Portia sets him up for the next trial. She gives him her ring:

> "I give them with this ring;
> Which when you part from, lose, or give away,
> Let it presage the ruin of your love
> And be my vantage to exclaim on you."
> (*The Merchant of Venice, III.2*)

It seems that she knows that he will not be able to keep his word. Therefore, the expected penalty is not too severe: "be my vantage to exclaim on you". All of this is lost on Bassanio. His answer to this challenge sounds phoney and even embarrassing:

> "But when this ring
> Parts from this finger, then parts life from hence:
> O, then be bold to say Bassanio's dead!"
> (*The Merchant of Venice, III.2*)

Right after the casket test, Bassanio receives a letter from Antonio in which Antonio describes his dramatic situation. Bassanio decides to leave right away. When he tells Portia that he has to go back to Venice, she encourages him to go and she gives him money to pay for the bond. Now we may realize that Bassanio's return to Venice is part of the training curriculum that has been prepared and is directed by Portia.

Portia has to arrange a set of circumstances which will allow Bassanio, and Venice, to go through a series of constructive experiences. Portia is in control of the entire plot. But it is only at the end of the play that the audience finds out how Portia was able to set it up. In the final scene of the play, Portia gives a letter to Antonio. The letter informs Antonio about the sudden recovery of his ships:

> "Antonio, you are welcome;
> And I have better news in store for you
> Than you expect: unseal this letter soon;
> There you shall find three of your argosies
> Are richly come to harbour suddenly:
> You shall not know by what strange accident
> I chanced on this letter."
> (*The Merchant of Venice, V.1*)

Assisted by the "music of the spheres", Portia was able to break through the limitations of time and space to destroy and then miraculously recover Antonio's ships. The disappearance of Antonio's ships led to the experiences that were needed to advance the process in Italy.

***

Let's go back to the time when the impulse of unitive energy was removed from Rome and transferred into the Celtic branch. At that time this impulse was represented by Imogen. This event is illustrated in "Cymbeline". Let's recall that the action of "Cymbeline" is taking place in 1st century Britain at the time of Caesar Augustus. In one of the scenes in "Cymbeline", Posthumus arrives in 16th century Renaissance Rome.

At the time of "The Merchant of Venice", Portia represent an impulse of unitive energy. She arrives in Venice disguised as Balthasar, a young doctor of Rome, i.e., she comes from Rome. In this way Shakespeare points out that Posthumus' arrival in Renaissance Rome corresponded to the time of "The Merchant of Venice".

In the scene from "Cymbeline", a Frenchman, a Dutchman, a Spaniard, an Italian, and a Briton gathered together at Philario's house in Rome. They were representing the European aristocrats who came to Italy to woo Portia. The discussion in Philario's house, therefore, provides an insight into the conversations that took place in Portia's courtyard. Namely, the men were arguing about the virtues of their country mistresses:

> "It was much like an argument that fell out last
> night, where each of us fell in praise of our
> country mistresses."
> (*Cymbeline, I.4*)

This explains why those who gathered in Belmont were incapable of taking the casket test: they all were still at the earlier stage of "wooing" their respective chivalric mistresses. Posthumus was among those wooers who were visiting Italy. It was then that Iachimo provoked him by making the following comment about "ours of Italy":

> "You must not so far prefer her 'fore ours of Italy."

Posthumus, like the European "wooers", was boasting about the virtues of his mistress. In other words, there was no difference between Posthumus and the other "wooers". They all were incapable of recognizing inner beauty. Their perceptions were still veiled.

Prior to his arrival in Italy, Posthumus travelled in France. While in France, he had a quarrel with the Frenchman. Here is the Frenchman's comment about it:

"this gentleman at that time
vouching -and upon warrant of bloody
affirmation- his to be more fair, virtuous, wise,
chaste, constant-qualified and less attemptable
than any the rarest of our ladies in France."
(*Cymbeline, I.4*)

The entire context of this scene indicates that Posthumus was in France when the King of France in "All's Well That Ends Well" was presenting Helena to his lords at the court in Paris. Here is Lord Lafeu's comment about the French lords' inability to recognize Helena's true beauty:

"These boys are boys of ice, they'll none have her:
sure, they are bastards to the English; the French
ne'er got 'em."
(*All's Well That Ends Well, II.3*)

Posthumus' quarrel indicates that he, like Bertram and the other French lords, was not able to recognize Helena's inner beauty. Like in Italy so in France, he was not ready to perceive true beauty.

Imogen, Helena, and Portia represent impulses of the unitive energy of love (*red*). These impulses were made available in various geographical regions at different times. Namely, they appeared as Imogen in Celtic Britain in the 1st century; as Helena in 13th century France; and as Portia in 16th century Italy. Their external appearances may be different. But they are all the manifestations of the same quality of inner beauty. The interesting thing to notice is that, during his journey, Posthumus was exposed to all three manifestations of this energy. Yet, he was incapable of recognizing it.

Now we may answer the question concerning the purpose of the Celtic intervention and Posthumus' travels. Namely, Posthumus' travels served as a test to determine how man would respond to exposure to unitive energy at the times when this energy was going to be available within the Cypriot and the Sicilian links. Posthumus' reactions indicated that direct exposure to unitive energy was too subtle to have a constructive effect on ordinary man. As illustrated in the final scene of "Cymbeline", Posthumus' attraction to Imogen was mostly driven by her outward appearance; he remained blind to her inner beauty. A more sophisticated procedure would be needed to prepare man correctly for such an experience.

Afterwards, a methodology based on the "modulation of beauty" was implemented within the modern evolutionary branches. In this approach woman's beauty is modulated, so the intended recipient is exposed to a diluted dose of the evolutionary charge. The "modulation" may be realized by disguising the woman as a boy. We may notice that after Posthumus' encounters in France and Italy, the women representing the unitive energy within the French, the Italian and the Bohemian branches appear disguised as boys. For example, Portia arrived in Venice disguised as Balthasar, a young doctor of Rome; Rosalind went to the Forest of Arden disguised as a young boy named Ganymede; Viola appeared at Orsino's court disguised as Cesario. In this way the efficiency of the implemented approach was greatly improved.

The Taming of the Shrew

The play "The Merchant of Venice" concluded the descending part of the loop that was initiated by Othello. The transmission chain was restored and the evolutionary spectrum was made available on the level of ordinary man. After several millennia and the extraordinary work done by the custodians, man's evolutionary situation was finally restored. Now it is up to man himself to make an effort to earn his return to the Realm.

The remaining Italian plays illustrate man's challenges and his struggles along the path leading towards his ultimate purpose. The next stages lead through a series of cities located in the northern part of Italy. These cities are located along Shakespeare's "route of the heart" that goes westwards from Venice through Padua and Verona to Milan. After Venice, therefore, the next city on Shakespeare's route of the heart is Padua. It is there that the action of "The Taming of the Shrew" takes place.

The current developmental state of Padua is summarized by Petruchio during Lucentio's wedding banquet:

> "Nothing but sit and sit, and eat and eat!"
> (*The Taming of the Shrew, V.2*)

The dominating characteristics of Padua may be described as "Nothing but sit and sit, and eat and eat!" Padua is presented, therefore, as a spiritually idle state. This corresponds to the spiritual state of ordinary man. The restoration of the transmission chain has not changed man's spiritual state.

The inferior environment of Padua, therefore, has distorted the spiritual impact that was projected from Belmont. Such a distortion is symbolically illustrated by the partial blurring of the evolutionary impulses that have been placed in Padua. The daughters of Baptista, Katharina and Bianca, represent the currently available impulses. Both impulses are coloured for the heart faculty. Bianca is a blurred projection of unitive energy (*red*). At the time of "The Merchant of Venice", this particular energy was represented by Portia of Belmont. Katharina, the elder daughter of Baptista, represents a blurred impulse of creative energy (*yellow*). Katharina is the current projection of Jessica of Venice. Katharina's shrewdness is reminiscent of the unhappy experiences that this particular impulse was exposed to previously.

This means that Shakespeare's route of the heart is marked by the colours *red* and *yellow*. These two impulses are driving the events that are illustrated in the remaining Italian plays.

Baptista insists that no one may woo Bianca before he finds a husband for Katharina, his ill-tempered elder daughter. This puts Padua in a rather stagnant situation, as it seems that there is no possibility of resolving the current impasse. The situation changes with the arrival of Petruchio and Lucentio. Lucentio is the current projection of Cassio of Florence from "Othello", Benedick of Padua from "Much Ado About Nothing", and Bassanio of Venice from "The Merchant of Venice".

The leading character of the play is Petruchio. Petruchio seems to be a boastful, selfish and greedy man. He appears to be nothing more than an uncaring chauvinist who treats marriage as an act of domination and enrichment. Such assessment of Petruchio may be arrived at if one looks at the play from a social, emotional, or intellectual point of view. However, there is another way to look at and interpret Petruchio's actions. Petruchio arrives in Padua with a certain goal. When his friend Hortensio asks him:

"And tell me now, sweet friend, what happy gale
Blows you to Padua here from old Verona?"

Petruchio gives the following answer:

"Such wind as scatters young men through the world,
To seek their fortunes farther than at home
Where small experience grows."
(*The Taming of the Shrew*, I.2)

Petruchio knows perfectly well what he is looking for. Petruchio is looking for *fortune*. This fortune has to do with a certain *experience* that is not usually found at *home*. Petruchio is a wealthy man. However, when he hears from Hortensio about Katharina, he right away describes his own quest in such a way that Hortensio immediately becomes his ally. Petruchio offers to woo and marry Katharina.

Why then does Petruchio seize on Katharina and pursue her so decisively? He is, after all, a young man of wealth and social position, and Italy offers many beautiful, docile, well-dowered young ladies for him to marry. And yet, when he hears, for instance, that Katharina has broken a lute over Hortensio's head, Petruchio exclaims:

"Now, by the world, it is a lusty wench;
I love her ten times more than e'er I did:
O, how I long to have some chat with her!"
(*The Taming of the Shrew, II.1*)

It seems that Petruchio has perceived in Katharina's behaviour a certain inner beauty. And it is this inner beauty that Petruchio is interested in.

Katharina represents an impulse of creative energy. This impulse remained dormant in Cyprus until the arrival of Othello. It was reactivated in Messina as Beatrice at the time of "Much Ado About Nothing". Then it appeared as Jessica in "The Merchant of Venice". Originally, this particular impulse was intended for the French branch. This is why Katharina feels out of place in her current environment.

In Petruchio's vocabulary, an ordinary mind is called *home*; knowledge is referred to as *fortune*; the means of learning knowledge is equated with *experience*. A blurred evolutionary impulse is represented by a *shrew*, and *marriage* symbolically indicates unconditional commitment to the guide's protection. In other words, Petruchio is a spiritual guide and a teaching master:

"Ay, mistress, and Petruchio is the master;
That teacheth tricks eleven and twenty long,
To tame a shrew and charm her chattering tongue."
(*The Taming of the Shrew, II.1*)

Petruchio has been mandated to direct this particular stage of the evolutionary process. It is up to Petruchio to unveil Katharina's inner beauty. Like in "Othello", the process of unveiling is illustrated as Petruchio's wooing of Katharina. At the moment when we recognize that Petruchio is a spiritual guide, the entire play becomes easy to follow and understand. At the same time, any trace of supposed controversy related to any form of political incorrectness disappears entirely.

Because of the inferior environment of Padua, Katharina and Bianca represent blurred evolutionary impulses. As a matter of fact, it would be impossible for an ordinary man to recognize their evolutionary essence. Only a guide is able to perceive their inner beauty. Despite the fact that Katharina is widely reputed throughout Padua to be a shrew, foul-tempered and sharp-tongued, Petruchio is able to recognize her inner beauty, which is hidden from the others. When Petruchio tells Baptista that Katharina has consented to marry him, Katharina does not seem to protest. Like her previous manifestations within the Roman evolutionary branch, she becomes "eloquently" silent. This is the first sign that Katharina starts to realize that Petruchio is not an ordinary man.

As illustrated in "Othello", sometimes a guide has to adopt "blameworthy" behaviour. This is illustrated in the wedding scene. Petruchio seemingly humiliates Katharina by arriving late. He arrives riding on a broken-down horse. He looks and behaves like a clown. By no means, however, is he ignoring her or the wedding ceremony. Quite the contrary, he is very well prepared for it. He arrives dressed in an elaborate although ridiculous outfit. Petruchio tells Katharina that she is "marrying" him and not his clothes. He indicates that the man beneath the attire is not the same as the attire itself. When later in the play her dress is the issue, he tells her:

"Our purses shall be proud, our garments poor;
For 'tis the mind that makes the body rich;
And as the sun breaks through the darkest clouds,
So honour peereth in the meanest habit."
(*The Taming of the Shrew, IV.3*)

By behaving in such a way, Petruchio is able to produce a certain constructive effect on those around him. It is an example of a shock technique, by which a disciple is exposed to a certain impact that affects his or her inner being. Petruchio does not care about himself and what others will think about him. He is helping others to realize that there is another way of looking at the situation, another way of thinking, another way of evaluating themselves and those around them. The audience watching the play is subjected to the same impact.

Following the wedding, Petruchio goes to seemingly strange ways of imposing his teaching on Katharina. He uses a number of different techniques to "tame" her. When they arrive at his house, he declares he will "kill her with kindness" by pretending that he cannot allow her to eat his inferior food or sleep in his inferior bed. Because Petruchio couches his attempt to tame her in the rhetoric of love and affection, it is impossible for her to confront him with outright anger. Only when she realizes that it is beneficial for her to be fully obedient, is Petruchio able to remove her veil of shrewishness. As a result, she is gradually awakened from her "sleep". Thus, Katharina's eventual compliance with Petruchio's taming brings her to a position where she slowly starts to realize that she is discovering something that is beyond the ordinary.

At the end of the play Katharina gives her famous speech. The once shrewish Katharina now declares that:

"Thy husband is thy lord, thy life, thy keeper,
Thy head, thy sovereign; one that cares for thee,
And for thy maintenance commits his body
To painful labour both by sea and land,
To watch the night in storms, the day in cold,
Whilst thou liest warm at home, secure and safe;
And craves no other tribute at thy hands
But love, fair looks and true obedience;
Too little payment for so great a debt.
Such duty as the subject owes the prince
Even such a woman oweth to her husband;
And when she is froward, peevish, sullen, sour,
And not obedient to his honest will,
What is she but a foul contending rebel
And graceless traitor to her loving lord?"
(*The Taming of the Shrew, IV.3*)

It is obvious that Katharina's speech does not apply to ordinary marriage. If we remember that in Petruchio's vocabulary "husband" means a spiritual guide and an exemplar of a fully developed man, then Katharina's speech becomes suddenly pregnant with an entirely different meaning. She describes the spiritual guide as a disciple's lord, king, and governor. The guide is to his disciple as a king is to his subject, and if a disciple proves shrewish, then he, or she, is like a traitor to a loving king. In return, the guide asks only for the disciple's kindness and true obedience, which represents but tiny payment for "so great a debt". She says that the guide supports and protects mankind, while living a life of hard work and responsibility.

Katharina's final speech demonstrates the effect of the unveiling of her inner beauty that was realized over the course of the play. It also shows that Katharina developed an understanding that does not correspond to a tamed shrew, but rather to a person who arrived at a higher level of being. One cannot arrive at such an understanding by following social etiquette. Katharina has arrived at her current understanding by a spiritual method. This kind of understanding is a by-product of Petruchio's "taming".

Similarly to Lucio in "Measure for Measure" and Touchstone in "As You Like It", Petruchio acts as a Joker. He fills-in for the missing aspect of the heart faculty. Petruchio has to marry Katharina, so Italy may be correctly prepared for exposure to unitive energy. Let's recall that all the previously described evolutionary fiascos resulted from man's failure to correctly assimilate the particular impulse of the evolutionary spectrum that is represented by Katharina. In other words, Katharina's shrewishness is a result of man's previous mistreatment of this particular impulse. The taming of Katharina is in reality the process of removing the spiritual "blindness" of those who are around her. This means that the taming of Katharina is only an intermediate step in the process.

It is important to draw the reader's attention to the fact that Petruchio has tamed Katharina, so she could play a critical role in the current as well as in the future stages of the process. Her role is twofold: as Kate (an active impulse) and as Dian (a passive impulse). Petruchio alludes to this in the following comment:

"O, be thou Dian, and let her be Kate;
And then let Kate be chaste and Dian sportful!"
(*The Taming of the Shrew, II.1*)

In the case of Lucentio, Katharina plays a passive role. Although Lucentio and Bianca are married, the impulse of unitive energy (*red*) remains blurred. This is indicated by Lucentio's bitter comment about Bianca's disobedience:

"But a harsh hearing when women are froward."
(*The Taming of the Shrew, V.2*)

The future development of the being of Italy depends upon the impact of tamed Katharina on Lucentio. This is why, immediately after Katharina's speech, Petruchio leaves the scene. This is in accordance with the teaching methodology that, at this point, the guide has to withdraw. Now it is up to Lucentio to digest the impact. The last line of the play contains Lucentio's ambivalent comment about the impact:

" 'Tis a wonder, by your leave, she will be tamed so."
(*The Taming of the Shrew, V.2*)

Lucentio's comment is a mixed reaction of wonderment, of doubt, and a hint of the possibility of taming ... Bianca, i.e., his wife, and unveiling her still blurred inner beauty.

Now, the being of Italy must move along Shakespeare's route of the heart from Padua to the next developmental stage. The next stage is symbolically represented by the city of Verona. It is illustrated in "Romeo and Juliet". It is there that the audience will find out the meaning of Lucentio's final comment.

Romeo and Juliet

This play is the developmental sequel to "The Taming of the Shrew". It describes the sixth consecutive stage of the Italian branch. (The Italian branch sprouted out of the Bohemian branch at the time of "The Winter's Tale"). Therefore, "Romeo and Juliet" should be analyzed in the context of the other Italian plays if its original intent is to be understood. This is the most challenging stage, corresponding to an interval or a gap within a branch or a cycle. In this respect, the play parallels "Titus Andronicus" within the Roman branch, "Macbeth" within the Celtic branch, and "Hamlet" within the Bohemian branch. In other words, the play describes an unavoidable difficult experience of the evolutionary process. Such experience is a preparation for the next ones, which lead to constructive outcomes.

Like Venice and Padua, the city of Verona represents the ordinary state of Italy. This state is the result of the previous experiences described in "The Taming of the Shrew". Specifically, the play indicates that its action takes place "some five and twenty years" after Lucentio's wedding:

> "What, man! 'tis not so much, 'tis not so much:
> 'Tis since the nuptials of Lucentio,
> Come pentecost as quickly as it will,
> Some five and twenty years; and then we mask'd."
> (*Romeo and Juliet, I.5*)

The determining feature of Verona, or its current malady, is indicated by Chorus in the Prologue. The malady is referred to as an ancient grudge, i.e., the same malady that led to the collapse of the ancient Greek civilization described by Shakespeare in "Troilus and Cressida". Shakespeare further underlines this link to "Troilus and Cressida" by including Paris and "the lively Helena" among the guests that are invited to the "ancient feast of the Capulet's". Like the Trojans and the Greeks, the feuding families of Capulet and Montague in "Romeo and Juliet" represent various corrupted and distracting aspects. However, there is a significant difference between the Greece of "Troilus and Cressida" and the Italy of "Romeo and Juliet". At the time of "Troilus and Cressida", Greece was disconnected from the chain of transmission. The Italian branch, on the other hand, has been carefully designed and prepared. At the time of "Romeo and Juliet" the evolutionary infrastructure has been rebuilt and Verona has been linked to the transmission chain. The present state of Verona is the result of the preparatory work done previously by Othello, Don Pedro, Portia, and Petruchio. In other words, the story of "Troilus and Cressida" is replayed in "Romeo and Juliet" but within a context that belongs to a higher turn of the evolutionary spiral.

The evolutionary charge that is present within Verona is represented by Juliet and her cousin Rosaline. In "The Taming of the Shrew", these two impulses were represented by two sisters, Bianca and Katharina, respectively. Juliet and Rosaline are members of the house of Capulet. Rosaline signifies a fully unveiled but passive impulse of creative energy (*yellow*). She does not appear in the play; she is only referred to. In this respect she is, as her predecessors, eloquently silent. At the beginning of the play, Romeo is in love with her. But Rosaline ignores him. Romeo complains that Rosaline is beyond his reach; Rosaline "hath Dian's wit".

Let's recall that this particular stage of the Italian branch is overlapped with "All's Well That Ends Well" of the French branch. At the time of "All's Well That Ends Well", Rosaline Capulet reappeared as Diana Capilet in Florence. Afterwards she was transferred to France. Rosaline's transfer was in reality her return to her originally intended environment. This is why she could not be assimilated permanently within the Italian branch.

Juliet symbolizes an impulse of unitive energy (*red*). Bianca in "The Taming of the Shrew" represented a blurred manifestation of this impulse. Now, however, Bianca as Juliet went through quite a significant change. This is manifested by her comment about her boundless love:

"My bounty is as boundless as the sea,
My love as deep; the more I give to thee,
The more I have, for both are infinite."
(*Romeo and Juliet, II.2*)

This would indicate that, in the meantime, this particular impulse went through an unveiling process. This confirms that Bianca has been "tamed". This fact clarifies Lucentio's ambivalent comment at the conclusion of "The Taming of the Shrew". The appearance of a "tamed" Juliet provides another indication that "Romeo and Juliet" is the continuation of the process described in "The Taming of the Shrew".

According to Shakespeare's code concerning the evolutionary impulses, Juliet has to be a half-orphan. This would indicate that Lady Capulet cannot be her mother. Indeed, Capulet alludes to the death of Juliet's mother:

"The earth hath swallow'd all my hopes but she,
She is the hopeful lady of my earth."
(*Romeo and Juliet*, I.2)

The Nurse, in her conversation with Lady Capulet, indicates that Capulet remarried when Juliet was three years old.

Romeo is the current projection of the aspect which was previously represented by Lucentio of Padua. Lucentio was linked to Cassio of Florence in "Othello", Benedick of Padua in "Much Ado About Nothing", and Bassanio in "The Merchant of Venice". Romeo's family name, Montague, reconfirms the link to Cassio of Florence (Montano was the Duke's representative in Cyprus; Cassio was promoted to this position at the conclusion of "Othello") and to Benedick of Padua (Signior Mountanto in "Much Ado About Nothing"). Similarly to Lucentio, Romeo represents a partially purified but still unreformed aspect of the heart faculty. Romeo's unbalanced state is compared by his father to "the bud bit with an envious worm". In accordance with the advanced developmental methodology, the reformation of Verona's heart can be accomplished by a simultaneous exposure to reforming and purifying impulses. This is presented as Romeo's attraction to Rosaline and Juliet.

At the beginning of the play, Romeo is attracted to Rosaline. But he is not able to recognize her inner beauty. Romeo is driven by sensuality and ordinary obsession. Rosaline knew that Romeo's love was false. Rosaline's coldness leads Romeo to confusion, sadness and melancholy. When Romeo meets Juliet, his attraction to Rosaline melts right away:

> "It is the east, and Juliet is the sun.
> Arise, fair sun, and kill the envious moon,
> Who is already sick and pale with grief,
> That thou her maid art far more fair than she."
> (*Romeo and Juliet*, II.2)

Juliet's effect is much stronger. This is why Romeo compares Juliet to the sun, while Rosaline for him becomes like "the envious moon".

Perceptive Mercutio is able to identify the cause of Romeo's and Juliet's troubles. He names Queen Mab as the prime culprit. Mercutio's description of Queen Mab's influence equates with that of Cupid. Like Cupid, Queen Mab operates through dreams and fantasy:

> "she gallops night by night
> Through lovers' brains, and then they dream of love.
>
> ...
>
> O'er ladies' lips, who straight on kisses dream,
> Which oft the angry Mab with blisters plagues,
> Because their breaths with sweetmeats tainted are."
> (*Romeo and Juliet*, I.4)

Imagination, desires, and fantasy induced by Queen Mab trigger a passionate love between Romeo and Juliet. The main difficulty that Romeo and Juliet are faced with is that neither of them is ready yet for such an encounter. At the beginning of the play Juliet is not mature enough to discharge her function correctly. Juliet's insistence on immediate marriage with Romeo triggers tragic events. In "Love's Labour's Lost" Shakespeare inserted a brief episode that further alludes to the cause of Juliet's death. Katharine, who appears in "Love's Labour's Lost", is a projection of Rosaline, Juliet's cousin. In this episode, Katharine indicates that the death of her "sister", was caused by Cupid, i.e. "five thousand years a boy":

> "He made her melancholy, sad, and heavy;
> And so she died."
> (*Love's Labour's Lost*, V.2)

In this context is it interesting to take a closer look at Friar Laurence. Friar Laurence is a well-intentioned but unqualified spiritual counsellor. He is familiar with the overall spiritual process. He studied it. He has acquired certain knowledge about it. Friar Laurence considers Romeo to be his pupil. He introduced Romeo to the concept of love. He indicated to Romeo the difference between sensual obsession and true love. He is also familiar with the experience of "to die before dying" and with the overall sequence of the evolutionary process:

> "She's not well married that lives married long;
> But she's best married that dies married young."
> (*Romeo and Juliet*, IV.5)

In this quote "marriage" means discipleship; "death" refers to the spiritual experience "to die before dying" or "to die to live". In other words, Friar Laurence says that a successful "marriage" is completed with "death", i.e., the ultimate goal of a disciple is to overcome his selfish desires. However, Friar Laurence's theoretical knowledge is not coupled with a true understanding of the process. He does not have the capacity and the skills to be a guide; he is not capable of perceiving the currently operating design. He does not understand this particular developmental stage. This is why he becomes confused by Romeo's actions. Friar Laurence hopes to reconcile the two families through their children's marriage. As Friar Francis in "Much Ado About Nothing", Friar Laurence tries to achieve his objective by applying a stratagem. He proposes to Juliet a copy of Friar Francis' remedy. In its outward form the remedy of "die to live" is identical to the one devised by Friar Francis in "Much Ado About Nothing". Friar Laurence, with the best intention, offers this approach without realizing what is needed to administer an effective remedy. Friar Laurence acts similarly to those supposed mystics, who simply repeat mechanically certain procedures from the past without understanding the entire process and unaware of the current projection of the developmental design. Each step instigated by Friar Laurence leads to new complications and seemingly unexpected consequences. He follows a path of trial and error.

Romeo and Juliet gradually start to understand that they are following a rigid path with an inescapable fate. They both realize that they cannot escape from it. Their choices are limited; they have to accept and follow their destiny. They both have to die. They have to die to generate a shocking and awakening rebuke to Verona. Only in this way may the overall environment of Verona be prepared for the next stage of the process.

At the end of the play the Prince summarizes the effect of the rebuke:

> "Where be these enemies? Capulet! Montague!
> See, what a scourge is laid upon your hate,
> That heaven finds means to kill your joys with love."
> (*Romeo and Juliet, V.3*)

The story of Romeo and Juliet would be meaningless if considered outside of the context of the other Italian plays. Indeed, if analyzed as a play on its own, it can be easily classified as an emotionally charged and tragic love story with no inner meaning. In fact, "Romeo and Juliet" is only one episode of the story. Juliet and

Romeo reappear within a more advanced environment. Then they are able to complete their spiritual journey. The audience meets them again in "Two Gentlemen of Verona".

Two Gentlemen of Verona

The Italian route of the heart leads from Venice to Padua, from Padua to Verona, and from Verona to Milan. Milan symbolically represents the final stage of the Italian plays. At one time, Milan was known as the New Athens. Let's recall that the Italian branch sprouted from the Bohemian branch that was initiated in Athens.

There are two evolutionary impulses in "Two Gentlemen of Verona". These two impulses are represented by Silvia and Julia. Here is Julia's comment about Silvia:

> "Her hair is auburn, mine is perfect yellow."
> (*Two Gentlemen of Verona, IV.4*)

This indicates that Silvia represents an impulse of unitive energy (*red*, auburn). Julia, on the other hand, represents an impulse of creative energy (*yellow*).

Julia is the current equivalent of Rosaline from "Romeo and Juliet". As indicated in the discussion of "All's Well That Ends Well", this particular impulse was represented by Violenta who was present in the Widow's house in Florence. Let's recall that Violenta was a spiritual "twin" of Rosaline. Rosaline was designated for the French branch; Violenta was marked for the Italian branch. This is why it was necessary to exchange Rosaline and Violenta. The exchange took place in Florence at the time of "All's Well That Ends Well". Now Violenta appears in Verona as Julia.

Silvia is the current projection of Juliet Capulet from "Romeo and Juliet". Her previous experiences as Juliet have allowed her to mature. Silvia, unlike Juliet, realizes that it is not her personal affair that is at stake. Her marriage is a matter for the entire Italy. Silvia does not allow herself to be driven by sensual desires. Silvia's handling of her love affair bears a resemblance to Portia's dealing with Bassanio in "The Merchant of Venice". Silvia knows that her marriage is part of a bigger picture:

"And on the justice of my flying hence
To keep me from a most unholy match,
Which heaven and fortune still rewards with plagues."
(*Two Gentlemen of Verona*, IV.3)

Therefore, her "unholy match" would lead to disasters ("plagues"). On the other hand, a correctly executed "holy match" will bring peace and harmony. A "holy match" means a complete assimilation of the evolutionary impulse. Such assimilation may be realized only by the formation of a quad of the heart faculty. The quad consists of two aspects of the heart faculty. Only then can the unitive energy of love be correctly assimilated.

The reformation of Verona at the time of "Romeo and Juliet" led to the appearance of two aspects of the heart faculty. Now Romeo appears as Proteus and Valentine. Here is Valentine's comment about the common origin of these two aspects:

"I know him as myself; for from our infancy
We have conversed and spent our hours together."
(*Two Gentlemen of Verona*, II.4)

Valentine and Proteus encompass the experiences that Romeo went through. Valentine represents a more mature Romeo. This advanced aspect of the heart faculty has been formed as a result of the experiences described in "Romeo and Juliet". Valentine alludes to these previous experiences during his encounter with the outlaws in the forest near Mantua:

"I kill'd a man, whose death I much repent;
But yet I slew him manfully in fight,
Without false vantage or base treachery."
(*Two Gentlemen of Verona, IV.1*)

This quote refers to the duel in which Romeo killed Paris.

Proteus, on the other hand, encompasses the characteristics of immature Romeo.

At the beginning of the play, Valentine is getting ready to leave Verona to go to Milan. Valentine is eager to travel and seek "the wonders", which he cannot find in Verona:

"To see the wonders of the world abroad,
Than, living dully sluggardized at home,
Wear out thy youth with shapeless idleness."
(*Two Gentlemen of Verona, I.1*)

Proteus recognizes that Valentine is prompted to hunt for "honour", and in this way he may dignify himself as well as his friends:

"He after honour hunts, I after love:
He leaves his friends to dignify them more,
I leave myself, my friends and all, for love."
(*Two Gentlemen of Verona, I.1*)

This quote provides an important clue to the story. It indicates that Valentine's quest contains an element of generosity, whereas Proteus' actions are driven entirely by his selfish and sensual desires. Valentine begs Proteus to come with him. But Proteus refuses because he is in love with Julia. Valentine goes to Milan alone. While in Milan, Valentine meets Sylvia, the daughter of the Duke. He falls in love with her.

Proteus is still driven by his emotions and sensual desires. In this context, it is interesting to quote a conversation between Proteus's father, Antonio, and Antonio's servant Panthino. In this conversation Panthino delivers Antonio brother's message concerning Proteus' education:

> "He wonder'd that your lordship
> Would suffer him to spend his youth at home,
> While other men, of slender reputation,
> Put forth their sons to seek preferment out:
> Some to the wars, to try their fortune there;
> Some to discover islands far away;
> Some to the studious universities.
> For any or for all these exercises,
> He said that Proteus your son was meet,
> And did request me to importune you
> To let him spend his time no more at home,
> Which would be great impeachment to his age,
> In having known no travel in his youth."
> (*Two Gentlemen of Verona, I.1*)

Proteus' uncle seems to be quite familiar with the developmental process. In his message to Antonio he mentions several developmental stages, e.g., "the studious universities", "the wars", and "discovering islands". Enrolling into "the studious universities" indicates introductory studies; "the wars" mark the stage of reformation; discovering "islands far away" corresponds to the activation of higher states. Proteus' uncle discreetly monitors and directs the developmental process that is described in "Two Gentlemen of Verona". He intervenes in the process immediately after Julia and Proteus have exchanged vows of love. It is then that Proteus is sent to the Duke's court in Milan. Proteus and Julia are devastated by this decision. Before leaving Verona, Proteus promises never to stop loving Julia.

The following events should not surprise the audience. Proteus' initial characteristics clearly indicate that he is not capable of keeping his oath. It is not because of his intention or willingness; it is a matter of capacity. His present state of development, emphasized by the meaning of his name, is such that he is incapable of such a commitment. He, like Romeo, is still driven by his base desires. This is why he will have to go through a specifically designed set of experiences.

The inconstancy of Proteus' desires is manifested as soon as he arrives in Milan and meets Silvia. He instantly forgets about his love for Julia:

"At first I did adore a twinkling star,
But now I worship a celestial sun."
(*Two Gentlemen of Verona*, II.6)

Proteus compares Julia to a "twinkling star" which is dimmed by Silvia, whom he equates with "a celestial sun". This is very similar to Romeo's experiences when he meets Juliet and compares her to the sun and Rosaline to the moon. In other words, the process described in "Two Gentlemen of Verona" follows the same sequence as described in "Romeo and Juliet". At one point, however, these two plays start to diverge. They start to diverge because the action of "Two Gentlemen of Verona" takes place in a very different environment. As the result of the experiences described in "Romeo and Juliet", Verona has been cleansed from its negative and distracting tendencies. This is why Julia, unlike Rosaline, responds to Proteus' love. When Proteus falls in love with Silvia, Julia intuitively perceives that there is something wrong. She disguises herself as a boy named Sebastian and goes to Milan.

The Duke's court in Milan is referred to as "our royal court" and "the emperor's court". The Duke is the leading aspect of the intellect faculty. It is the first time within the Italian plays that the Duke gets personally involved in the implementation of the process. The Duke's advanced state is further indicated by his attraction to "a lady in Verona". He refers to her in his conversation with Valentine:

> "There is a lady in Verona here
> Whom I affect; but she is nice and coy
> And nought esteems my aged eloquence."
> (*Two Gentlemen of Verona, III.1*)

The lady is the current projection of Mariana who, like Violenta, appeared in Italy at the time of "All's Well That Ends Well". Mariana was present in the Widow's house in Florence. Afterwards she ended up in Verona. The lady of Verona represents an evolutionary impulse (*white*) that is coloured for the intellect.

The Duke is well aware of the affection between Silvia and Valentine. He keeps his eyes on the lovers and monitors their actions. This is why Silvia feels that she is being watched:

> "I fear I am attended by some spies."
> (*Two Gentlemen of Verona, V.1*)

The Duke purposely uses the boorish Thurio as an instrument in the process. The Duke's insistence on the marriage of Silvia with Thurio is a test for the young lovers. If their love is really true, they will be able to overcome the obstacle that the Duke has thrown in their way. When the Duke discovers that Valentine intends to escape with Sylvia, he banishes him from Milan.

While travelling from Milan to Mantua, Valentine is apprehended in a forest by a group of outlaws. The outlaws are also banished for "practising to steal away a lady":

> "Know, then, that some of us are gentlemen,
> Such as the fury of ungovern'd youth
> Thrust from the company of awful men:
> Myself was from Verona banished
> For practising to steal away a lady,
> An heir, and near allied unto the duke."
> (*Two Gentlemen of Verona, IV.1*)

The outlaws symbolically represent the experiences that the various aspects of the Italian heart went through previously. Let's recall that Lorenzo in "The Merchant of Venice", Lucentio in "The Taming of the Shrew" and Romeo in "Romeo and Juliet" were all guilty of stealing a lady from her father. They all followed Othello's example. These outlaws were waiting in the forest for the appearance of their king, i.e., a correctly developed aspect that would be capable of completing the process, so they would be able to earn their true nobility.

The entire plot of the play is designed in such a way as to bring the two aspects of the heart faculty into a state of union. If both of these aspects are correctly aligned, and if there is no interruption of the process caused by negative and distracting tendencies, then they may form a quad and experience a state of spiritual union. The quad may be formed by the assimilation of two impulses. In this particular case, the quad consists of Silvia, Valentine, Julia and Proteus. This is why Valentine cannot be united with Silvia while Proteus is still oblivious to Julia's inner beauty. Both Silvia and Valentine understand the situation; they cannot be married prior to the reformation of the other aspect of the heart faculty. This is very similar to the formation of the union described in the French branch at the conclusion of "As You Like It", where Orlando could not be united with Rosalind before Oliver's reformation.

After Valentine's banishment, Silvia escapes from Milan and goes in search of him. While traveling through the forest, she is overtaken by the outlaws. She tries to defend herself. By this time, the Duke, Julia (who is still disguised as Sebastian) and Proteus also arrive in the forest to search for her. While Valentine watches the action unseen, Proteus wrests Silvia away from the outlaws. Then Proteus demands that Silvia gives him some sign of favour for freeing her. Sylvia decisively refuses. When Proteus tries to rape her, Valentine jumps out and stops him. Proteus' attempt to rape Silvia is a symbolical indication of his destructive tendency. It is this tendency that prevents the being from completing the process. In the following comment Silvia indicates the challenge they are all faced with:

> "Had I been seized by a hungry lion,
> I would have been a breakfast to the beast,
> Rather than have false Proteus rescue me."
> (*Two Gentlemen of Verona*, V.4)

Silvia alludes to the fact that an unfulfilled spiritual potential ("false Proteus") reduces man to a level below his ordinary beastly state of "a hungry lion". Proteus' sensual attraction to Silvia does not allow him to see the evolutionary essence that is contained in Julia. In other words, at this moment, the being is still prevented from experiencing the state of union. Proteus' reformation can only be completed through an artfully delivered rebuke. It is up to Valentine to instigate it. When Valentine sees Proteus's attempt to rape Silvia, he delivers this rebuke:

> "Who should be trusted, when one's own right hand
> Is perjured to the bosom? Proteus,
> I am sorry I must never trust thee more,
> But count the world a stranger for thy sake."
> (*Two Gentlemen of Verona*, V.4)

This is similar to Orlando saving Oliver from a hungry lioness prior to the formation of the French union. Because of the preparatory experiences, Proteus' response to the rebuke is immediate:

"My shame and guilt confounds me.
Forgive me, Valentine: if hearty sorrow
Be a sufficient ransom for offence,
I tender 't here; I do as truly suffer
As e'er I did commit."
(*Two Gentlemen of Verona, V.4*)

At this moment the aspect represented by Proteus is instantly reformed. Then Valentine prepares the ground for the second rebuke. Its aim is spiritual union:

"Then I am paid;
And once again I do receive thee honest.
Who by repentance is not satisfied
Is nor of heaven nor earth, for these are pleased.
By penitence the Eternal's wrath's appeased:
And, that my love may appear plain and free,
All that was mine in Silvia I give thee."
(*Two Gentlemen of Verona, V.4*)

The last two lines of this quote are the most significant in the entire canon of the Italian plays. However, their meaning is difficult to comprehend if one tries to analyse them from an ordinary or conventional point of view. It is only when analysed in the context of the process described above that the scene can be correctly interpreted. Namely, this scene illustrates the moment when the aspect of the heart faculty represented by Valentine has been completely purified ("that my love may appear plain and free"). In this state Valentine is capable of assimilating the impulse of unitive energy. Silvia represents this impulse of the unitive energy of love that is designated for him. Let's recall Juliet's description of this impulse's potential:

"My bounty is as boundless as the sea,
My love as deep: The more I give to thee

The more I have, for both are infinite."
(*Romeo and Juliet, II.2*)

The previous attempt by Juliet to pass the "bounty" onto Romeo could not be realized. Neither Verona nor Romeo was ready for it. Now, however, Valentine is able to assimilate it. Moreover, because of his spiritual purity, Valentine is capable of passing it on to Proteus. This is the meaning of his words: "All that was mine in Silvia I give thee". Of course Silvia does not protest against Valentine's gesture, because "the more I give to thee, the more I have". It is then that Julia swoons. When Julia recovers, she removes her disguise and delivers the final rebuke:

"O Proteus, let this habit make thee blush!
Be thou ashamed that I have took upon me
Such an immodest raiment, if shame live
In a disguise of love:
It is the lesser blot, modesty finds,
Women to change their shapes than men their minds."
(*Two Gentlemen of Verona, V.4*)

At this moment Proteus' veil, which had blinded him, is removed. Now he is able to see the true beauty in Julia:

"O heaven! were man
But constant, he were perfect. That one error
Fills him with faults; makes him run through all the sins:
Inconstancy falls off ere it begins.
What is in Silvia's face, but I may spy
More fresh in Julia's with a constant eye?"
(*Two Gentlemen of Verona, V.4*)

This beauty is of the same nature as Silvia's, but is targeted, or coloured, for Proteus. And only now is Proteus able to see it. This is why Proteus perceives it as "more fresh". Proteus' constructive response to the rebuke allows the union of the heart. This is indicated by Valentine's final comment:

"One feast, one house, one mutual happiness."
(*Two Gentlemen of Verona*, *V.4*)

The Italian union consists of two simultaneously married couples. Because of the break in the transmission chain at the time of "The Winter's Tale", a part of the evolutionary potential was lost. There is no Black Lady within the Italian plays. The absence of the *black* impulse did not allow for the formation of a second quad. Only the quad of the heart could be activated at the conclusion of the Italian plays. It was this united spiritual heart that was used to activate a new evolutionary cell in the New World. The details of the next episode are illustrated in "The Tempest".

The Tempest

The overall purpose of spiritual development is to form an advanced being that is capable of assuming a new evolutionary function. This is why a newly formed advanced being has to either return to the ordinary world to discharge its acquired evolutionary function, or be sent to another place to initiate or revitalize the evolutionary process there.

Prospero is the current projection of the Duke of Milan from "Two Gentlemen of Verona". It may be presumed that the Duke of Milan's elevated state was activated through his marriage with "a lady in Verona", who represented an impulse of creative energy (*white*). Afterwards, Prospero, guided by "a most auspicious star", is taken away from Milan and tossed together with his infant daughter upon an Island. An Island symbolically represents a higher state. Miranda, Prospero's daughter, represents an impulse of unitive energy (*red*). At the time of "Two Gentlemen of

Verona", this impulse was split into Silvia (*red*) and Julia (*yellow*). At the conclusion of "Two Gentlemen of Verona", the impulse was united.

While on the Island, Prospero perfects his "art" and then discharges his evolutionary function. His role is to accomplish several tasks.

First, Prospero has to experience a new higher state. The Island, an imaginary place, represents this higher state. This higher state is needed to initiate a new evolutionary cell. Like Pentapolis, this particular state will be projected into the future. It will provide a new cell within the New World. The Island's spiritual quality is a reflection of the spiritual development within the Italian branch. Let's recall that because of the break with Sicily at the time of "The Winter's Tale", the Italian branch was without the impulse of unitive energy (*black*) needed for the purification of the intellect faculty. While on the Island, Prospero can be exposed to such an impulse. This impulse is symbolically represented by mythical goddesses. In this way he may be able to bridge the gap that was caused by the Sicilian break. But such an encounter is more challenging, because it involves an ancient, therefore a maculated impulse.

Secondly, Prospero may revitalize part of the former Kingdom of Sicily. The Kingdom of Naples represents that part of the Kingdom that was separated from Sicily at the time of "The Winter's Tale". Since the break, the Kingdom of Naples has remained spiritually sterile. The inner structure of Naples presented in "The Tempest" is a reflection of Sicily described in "The Winter's Tale". At that time, Sicily was represented by King Leontes, his "brother" Polixenes, Leontes' children Mamillius and Perdita, and Lord Camillo. Now Leontes reappears as Alonso, the King of Naples. Sebastian is his brother. Leontes' children are represented by Ferdinand and Claribel. Like Perdita in "The

Winter's Tale", Claribel symbolically represents an impulse of creative energy (*white*). Prince Ferdinand represents an aspect of the heart faculty. Previously, this particular aspect was dormant; it was represented by Mamillius. Lord Camillo reappears as Lord Gonzalo. Like Camillo, who acted as a mediator between Bohemia and Sicily, Gonzalo plays a similar role between Naples and Milan. The Kingdom of Naples may be revitalized by the activation of its spiritual heart, the purification of its intellect, and the reformation of its self faculty.

Thirdly, and most importantly, Prospero experiences on the Island are needed for all of Western Europe. From the Island, Prospero will return to Milan. Milan, or New Athens, was the final stage of the Italian branch. Prospero's experiences will be needed for a delayed activation of the Italian octagon.

The process described in "The Tempest" is linked to events that previously took place in the Italian Peninsula. These events were related to the initiation and the termination of the Roman evolutionary branch. Shakespeare used Dido, the legendary founder and the first Queen of Carthage, to explain events leading to the foundation of Rome. In "The Tempest" Shakespeare draws the audience's attention to Dido by inserting the following exchange between Gonzalo and Adrian, one of the Neapolitan courtiers:

Gonzalo:

"Methinks our garments are now as fresh as when we
put them on first in Afric, at the marriage of
the king's fair daughter Claribel to the King of Tunis."

Adrian:

"Tunis was never graced before with such a paragon to
their queen."

Gonzalo:

"Not since widow Dido's time."
(*The Tempest, II.1*)

When Adrian questions Gonzalo's analogy between Tunis and Carthage, Gonzalo insists that:

"This Tunis, sir, was Carthage."
(*The Tempest, II.1*)

By having Gonzalo emphasize the equivalence of Tunis and Carthage, Shakespeare points out that the process illustrated in "The Tempest" relates to events associated with the foundation of Rome. Shakespeare's reference to Dido is an indication that "The Tempest" describes a similar evolutionary stage but on a higher turn of the evolutionary spiral. In this context it is interesting to look at the sequence of events presented in "The Tempest". This sequence is summarized by Gonzalo's final comment:

"In one voyage
Did Claribel her husband find at Tunis,
And Ferdinand, her brother, found a wife
Where he himself was lost, Prospero his dukedom
In a poor isle and all of us ourselves
When no man was his own."
(*The Tempest, V.1*)

Gonzalo's comment about "one voyage" is a reference to this as well as to the previous journey. The previous journey led Aeneas from corrupted Troy via Carthage to the founding of Rome, a new world of ancient times. Aeneas' journey was directed by corrupted demigods. It ended up with the fiasco of the Roman cycle. Some 2,500 years later, Aeneas' journey is repeated by Ferdinand. This later episode is directed by Prospero, a man developed within the modern Italian evolutionary branch.

Ferdinand's journey takes him from corrupted Naples via Tunis ("This Tunis, sir, was Carthage") to the founding of a New World. On the same journey Claribel is brought to Tunis. Tunis represents an intermediary state of the transmission chain. For Ferdinand's journey to be successful, he has to pass through Tunis; Claribel has to stay there with her husband. In this way Claribel replays the role of Dido. Adrian's comment "Tunis was never graced before with such a paragon to their queen" emphasizes the constructive role of the current Tunisian King. Previously, Aeneas failed to discharge this role correctly. In "The Winter's Tale", Florizel foretold this journey when he introduced Perdita as an African Princess. The important thing is to note that Ferdinand's journey is better prepared and is executed effectively.

The Island in "The Tempest" is a modern replica of the situation in the past. Shakespeare indicates that 17th century man was faced with a similar challenge. However, there was a noteworthy difference. Unlike the ancient demigods, 17th century man partially assimilated an impulse of unitive energy. Shakespeare points out that the Island could only be "discovered" after the completion of the journey along the route of the heart within the Italian branch. Such a discovery was predicted in "Two Gentlemen of Verona" by Proteus' uncle:

"Some to the wars, to try their fortune there;
Some to discover islands far away."
(*Two Gentlemen of Verona*, *I.1*)

Prospero's voyage represents an ascending transition from an ordinary state into a higher state. We may notice that the descending/ascending loop has some hysteresis, i.e., the ascending and descending paths are not overlapped. Because of imperfections in the inner structures formed within the ordinary state, the ascending states contain some impurities inherited from the past. This is why the Island is not entirely "new". On the Island there are inhabitants from the "old" world. Shakespeare quite precisely indicates the origin of the islanders. Prior to the arrival of Prospero, the only mortal inhabitants on the Island were Sycorax and her son Caliban. Sycorax, "this blue-eyed hag", was a witch:

"His mother was a witch, and one so strong
That could control the moon, make flows and ebbs."
(*The Tempest, V.1*)

She was banished from Algiers and "was left by the sailors" on the Island a long time before the beginning of the play. Caliban, "not honour'd with a human shape", illustrates an aspect of a degenerated self faculty that was further deformed by being raised in an environment that was disconnected from the transmission chain. In his conversation with Ariel, Prospero indicates that, although Sycorax was banished from Algiers, she was not born there. Shakespeare left a hint that helps identify Sycorax' origin:

"This damn'd witch Sycorax,
For mischiefs manifold and sorceries terrible
To enter human hearing, from Argier,
Thou know'st, was banish'd; for one thing she did
They would not take her life."
(*The Tempest, I.2*)

Despite her terrible sorceries and misdeeds, Sycorax could not be killed. For some reason she was protected. There is only one villain in Shakespeare's narrative who managed to secure such protection. It was Aaron the Moor in "Titus Andronicus", the last play of the Roman cycle. At the end of "Titus Andronicus", Tamora, the Queen of the Goths and Aaron's lover, gave birth to their illegitimate child. Aaron pretended that the baby was a boy. At one moment, however, when he was alone with the child, he complained that the baby was "half me and half thy dam":

"Peace, tawny slave, half me and half thy dam!
Did not thy hue bewray whose brat thou art,
Had nature lent thee but thy mother's look,
Villain, thou mightst have been an emperor:
But where the bull and cow are both milk-white,
They never do beget a coal-black calf."
(*Titus Andronicus, V.1*)

The child had the Moor's complexion ("half me") but Tamora's sex ("and half thy dam!"). In other words, the child was a black girl. Now we may realize that Sycorax, Caliban's mother, was the daughter of Aaron. Sycorax was born in the 4th century Roman Empire at the time of the termination of the Roman cycle (at that time Algiers was part of the Western Roman Empire). She could not be killed because of Lucius' oath. Instead, she was banished from Algiers and transferred onto the Island. Sycorax and Caliban represent spiritual impurities inherited from the terminated Roman branch. Sycorax was transferred to the Island some 12 symbolic "years" (centuries) before Prospero's arrival. We may note that Ferdinand followed the same route as Sycorax, i.e., from the Italian Peninsula via North Africa to the Island.

Ariel represents a certain ability associated with a purified aspect of the intellect faculty. It was this sort of ability that ordinary man was disconnected from as a result of the Fall. Such a disconnection is symbolically illustrated in "The Tempest" as Ariel being imprisoned by Sycorax in a cloven pine. Ariel represents forces that may help man rise up to higher spheres of functioning. It is interesting to note that this is the first time in Shakespeare's narrative that such a spirit appears as a servant to a mortal man. Previously, such spirits were under the control of corrupted forces. It is also important to realize that Ariel, although too gentle to follow Sycorax' commands, is still of a moody and mischievous nature. This is why, occasionally, Prospero has to threaten him in order to secure his services. This behaviour of Ariel is a mark of certain weaknesses in Prospero.

Prospero's situation on the Island corresponds to that of mankind after the Fall. Prospero has been provided with access to developmental techniques. He is sent onto the Island where he may practice and implement his "art". This is symbolically illustrated as Prospero being able to free Ariel. At this moment a link to the Realm is established. In Shakespeare's plays the activation of such a link is marked by the appearance of the "music of the spheres". Prior to Prospero's arrival, the Island was filled with Ariel's groans that:

> "Did make wolves howl and penetrate the breasts
> Of ever angry bears."
> (*The Tempest, I.2*)

Now, however, the Island is "full of noises, sounds and sweet airs, that give delight". Even Caliban is affected by this music:

> "Sometimes a thousand twangling instruments
> Will hum about mine ears, and sometime voices
> That, if I then had waked after long sleep,
> Will make me sleep again: and then, in dreaming,
> The clouds methought would open and show riches
> Ready to drop upon me that, when I waked,
> I cried to dream again."
> (*The Tempest, III.2*)

By freeing Ariel, Prospero gains access to further powers that allow him to control the natural forces. The important thing to remember is that Prospero can exercise his powers only in the presence of the "music". It is this music that empowers him and guides him. It is this music that allows him to exercise the same powers as the mythical demigods. As a matter of fact, Prospero has been given access to more potent powers. For example, Ariel points out that he is able to surpass the speed of Jove's lightings and shake up Neptune's trident:

"Jove's lightings, the precursors
O' the dreadful thunder-claps, more momentary
And sight-outrunning were not; the fire and cracks
Of sulphurous roaring the most mighty Neptune
Seem to besiege and make his bold waves tremble,
Yea, his dread trident shake."
(*The Tempest*, I.2)

Caliban also admits that Prospero is more powerful than Setebos, Sycorax' demigod. Prospero, however, is not a music master. This means that there is someone else who is a music master on the Island. This music master's power surpasses that of the ancient gods. Let's recall that, previously, Neptune and Jupiter were directing Pericles' and Posthumus' adventures. Now it is this invisible guide who monitors and oversees Prospero's actions.

Shakespeare describes the effect of such music in other plays. For example, when Pericles reached Pentapolis, he became a "music's master". In "The Winter's Tale", music enabled the resurrection of Hermione of Sicily. Othello was assisted by "music that may not be heard" when he raised a tempest that completely destroyed the Turkish fleet. Similarly, assisted by the harmony of "immortal souls" in "The Merchant of Venice", Portia of Belmont was able to destroy and then miraculously recover Antonio's ships. In other words, the "music of the spheres" indicates the presence of supracognitive energy, which is the highest evolutionary energy available in the galaxy.

A similar ability was developed by mankind in antiquity. But it was at the point of accessing these extraordinary powers that mankind failed. By abusing these powers, ancient men pulled out a veil that disconnected them from the "music of the spheres". These ancient men started to act as demigods and demigoddesses. These various demigods focussed their activities on pursuing inferior objectives. Ancient mysteries and similar occult practices are fragmented records of this misapplication of developmental techniques.

***

To revitalize the Kingdom of Naples, Prospero needs to bring the King, his son, and his courtiers onto the Island. The play opens as Prospero divines that Alonso, King of Naples, is on a ship passing by the Island. The ship is returning from the nuptials of Alonso's daughter Claribel with the King of Tunis. Also onboard are Prospero's brother Antonio, Alonso's brother Sebastian, Alonso's son Ferdinand, Alonso's royal advisor Gonzalo, lords Adrian and Francisco, Alonso's servants Stephano and Trinculo. With the help of Ariel, Prospero raises a tempest, which causes the ship to run aground on the Island. He separates the Neapolitans survivors of the wreck into three groups. Each group represents one of the ordinary faculties. Then each of the faculties is exposed to different experiences. Various aspects of the intellect faculty are represented by King Alonso, Sebastian, Antonio, Gonzalo, Adrian, and Francisco. The heart faculty is represented by Ferdinand, Alonso's son. Alonso's servants Trinculo and Stephano are aspects of the self faculty.

With the help of Ariel, Prospero exposes Alonso and his companions to some solemn music. This music puts all but Alonso, Sebastian and Antonio to sleep. A moment later, Alonso also falls asleep. The most corrupted aspects, i.e., Sebastian and Antonio ("this muddy vesture of decay"), are immune to the music:

Sebastian:

"What a strange drowsiness possesses them!"

Antonio:

"It is the quality o' the climate."

Sebastian:

"Why
Doth it not then our eyelids sink? I find not
Myself disposed to sleep."

Antonio:

"Nor I; my spirits are nimble.
They fell together all, as by consent;
They dropp'd, as by a thunder-stroke."
(*The Tempest, II.1*)

As soon as the others are put in a state of "sleep", the corrupted aspects manifest themselves in greater prominence. This is illustrated by Sebastian's and Antonio's attempt to kill their sleeping companions. In other words, this experience allows for the identification and sorting out of the most destructive aspects. Ariel prevents the murder. In the next step of the process, the destructive aspects of the intellect will be exposed to a reforming rebuke.

Prospero also uses music when working on Ferdinand. In this case, the music allows Ferdinand to arrive at a state where love is perceived as the supreme priority, i.e., over emotional attachments such as sorrow, fury, and passion. The following comment by Ferdinand is a precise account of the working of the music on the heart faculty:

"Sitting on a bank,
Weeping again the king my father's wreck,
This music crept by me upon the waters,
Allaying both their fury and my passion
With its sweet air: thence I have follow'd it,
Or it hath drawn me rather. But 'tis gone.
No, it begins again."
(*The Tempest, I.2*)

Ferdinand follows the music and ends up meeting Miranda. Ferdinand and Miranda fall in love with each other. According to the initial plan, Mamillius of Sicily, Ferdinand's predecessor, was marked for this particular experience.

Prospero implements a slightly different approach when dealing with the various aspects of the self faculty. In this case, Stephano and Trinculo are separated from the others and put together with Caliban. This encourages them to show off their most destructive behaviour. Caliban represents a degenerated self faculty inherited from Rome. Caliban asks Stephano to be his god:

"I'll show thee every fertile inch o' th' island;
And I will kiss thy foot: I prithee, be my god."
(*The Tempest, II.2*)

Stephano happily accepts the role of Caliban's god. Caliban encourages Stephano to kill Prospero and become the king of the Island. But some music played by Ariel leads the conspirators to a filthy-mantled pool:

"so I charm'd their ears
That calf-like they my lowing follow'd through
Tooth'd briers, sharp furzes, pricking goss and thorns,
Which entered their frail shins: at last I left them
I' the filthy-mantled pool beyond your cell,
There dancing up to the chins, that the foul lake
O'erstunk their feet
(*The Tempest, IV.1*)

All of this is a preparation for the rebuke in the final scene, when Prospero and Ariel set upon them spirits in the shape of hunting dogs. At the end of this experience, they realize what their true position is with respect to the others. The overall effect is summarized by a surprisingly remorseful Caliban:

"I'll be wise hereafter
And seek for grace. What a thrice-double ass
Was I, to take this drunkard for a god
And worship this dull fool!"
(*The Tempest, V.1*)

At the end of the play all three faculties are re-united. They form a new partially purified and reformed being of Naples.

Prospero's main challenge is to use his power in the right way. Such powers have been made available to him in order to perform specific tasks. These powers should not be used for personal advantages or egotistic purposes. Prospero faces the same challenge as the ancient men did: he should not abuse his powers.

At one point Prospero asks Ariel to call forth some spirits to perform a masque for Ferdinand and Miranda:

"Thou and thy meaner fellows your last service
Did worthily perform; and I must use you
In such another trick. Go bring the rabble,
O'er whom I give thee power, here to this place."
(*The Tempest, IV.1*)

The spirits assume the shapes of the three goddesses Juno, Ceres, and Iris. Let's notice that Prospero refers to the goddesses as Ariel's "meaner fellows" and "the rabble, o'er whom I give thee power". This reconfirms a new hierarchy within the invisible world. Namely, Prospero has been granted temporary power over Ariel; Ariel can rule over the ancient goddesses.

The appearance of Juno is another reference to Dido's story and illustrates the evolutionary progress achieved as a result of the implementation of the modern evolutionary branches. The demigoddesses are the remaining accomplices of the Boar from "Venus and Adonis". The goddesses perform a short masque celebrating the rites of marriage and the bounty of the earth. The masque is a demonstration of Prospero's powers. By asking Ariel to bring Juno, Ceres, and Iris he demonstrates that he can control them. The masque, however, is not part of the process. Shakespeare points out that Prospero has arranged the masque simply to show off his powers in front of Ferdinand and Miranda. The masque marks Prospero's weakness. We should keep in mind that all the spirits, including the demigoddesses, hate Prospero. Here is Caliban's comment about it:

> "they all do hate him
> As rootedly as I."
> (*The Tempest*, III.2)

This is why Juno is trying to take advantage of Prospero's weakness. Now we may recognize in Juno a maculated Black Lady. Juno sends Iris to call upon the spirits called Naiads. The appearance of the Naiads is dangerous, because they can distract one's attention by their mystifying beauty. The Naiads arrive and dance together with some harvesters. Prospero is further pleased, admiring the "harvest" and mistaking it for his own achievement. At this moment, Prospero does not remember that the seed for this particular harvest was prepared a long time ago, and its cultivation was not his doing. He also forgets that this thanksgiving harvest is a reference to some future time. This evolutionary "oasis" is not ready for harvest yet. In other words, at this very moment, Prospero is driven by "some vanity" and "fancies". Despite his relatively high developmental state and access to extraordinary powers, Prospero is not entirely free from egotistic desires. Because of this, he nearly loses his entire enterprise, just as the ancient men did. Caliban is about to succeed in destroying the seed of the next evolutionary cell. At the last moment, Prospero receives a warning in the form of:

"a strange, hollow, and confused noise"
(*The Tempest, IV.1, stage directions*)

Prospero awakes from his fancies and manages to avoid making an error that could turn his project into a complete fiasco. Ferdinand and Miranda are surprised by Prospero's aggravation caused by the fact that he realizes that he nearly made the same error as the ancient men.

The episode with the masque is a further indication that Prospero's journey and his experiences are directed; his dealing with supernatural forces is carefully monitored. In other words, Prospero is guided. But Prospero's guide remains invisible to the audience. This guide is identified in "A Midsummer Night's Dream", i.e., the concluding play of Shakespeare's narrative.

In the final act of the play, Shakespeare inserted a scene showing Ferdinand and Miranda playing chess. This scene is a reference to the situation described in "Othello". Miranda represents the same impulse of unitive energy as Desdemona. Like Othello and Desdemona, Ferdinand and Miranda cannot consummate their marriage before this particular phase of the process is completed. However, Ferdinand does not follow Othello's way and does not require Miranda to go through the painful experiences that Desdemona was faced with. This is why Miranda is worried that Ferdinand does not play a fair game with her:

"Sweet lord, you play me false."

When Ferdinand protests:

"No, my dear'st love,
I would not for the world."

Miranda, like Viola in the final scene of "Twelfth Night", demonstrates her spiritual maturity by expressing her readiness to accept whatever is needed to achieve their spiritual goal:

> "Yes, for a score of kingdoms you should wrangle,
> And I would call it, fair play."
> (*The Tempest, V.1*)

Miranda does not have to go through such challenging experiences, because Desdemona cleared the way to the higher state. Miranda is already in the higher state, which corresponds to Desdemona's Mauritania.

After their adventures on the Island, Ferdinand and his companions will return to Naples. Their experiences on the Island will become for them merely a magical dream. It will be this dream that will drive them towards their return to this "oasis" of the New World.

Prospero needs to return to Milan to work on his next assignment. Before leaving the Island, Prospero breaks his staff and throws away his book. These instruments of "rough magic" have a limited application. They are only effective when dealing with ordinary, i.e., underdeveloped men. By breaking his staff and drowning his book, Prospero indicates that he has completed his current task:

> "But this rough magic
> I here abjure, and, when I have required
> Some heavenly music, which even now I do,
> To work mine end upon their senses that
> This airy charm is for, I'll break my staff,
> Bury it certain fathoms in the earth,
> And deeper than did ever plummet sound
> I'll drown my book."
> (*The Tempest, V.1*)

Prospero clearly underlines the significance of "some heavenly music". The "heavenly music" provides the guidance: those who are able to hear it and follow do not need any magical kit.

At the end of the play, in the epilogue, Shakespeare offers a test by which the audience may experience a tiny fragment of Prospero's challenges. The function of the test is the same as that of the masque, i.e., to outmaneuver the audience by offering them illusionary powers:

> "Now my charms are all o'erthrown,
> And what strength I have 's mine own,
> Which is most faint: now, 'tis true,
> I must be here confined by you,
> Or sent to Naples. Let me not,
> Since I have my dukedom got
> And pardon'd the deceiver, dwell
> In this bare island by your spell;
> But release me from my bands
> With the help of your good hands:
> Gentle breath of yours my sails
> Must fill, or else my project fails,
> Which was to please. Now I want
> Spirits to enforce, art to enchant,
> And my ending is despair,
> Unless I be relieved by prayer,
> Which pierces so that it assaults
> Mercy itself and frees all faults.
> As you from crimes would pardon'd be,
> Let your indulgence set me free."
> (*The Tempest, Epilogue*)

The audience has seemingly been empowered to either release Prospero from the Island or keep him there. This indulgence offered to the audience is similar to that intended by the goddesses during the masque: to keep them asleep by pleasing them with illusory powers. If the audience accepts such fantasy and believes in it, they will fail the test. They will remain asleep.

English evolutionary branch

According to Shakespeare's presentation, the English branch was chosen as a venue for the appearance of a spiritual guide who would direct the process in 17th century Europe. The plan called for a reigning king to acquire such a guiding capacity. A visible and recognizable guide would provide the conditions for the most effective implementation of the next phases of the evolutionary process.

The preparations for the appearance of such a guide were initiated after the events described in "Macbeth", i.e., after the termination of the Celtic branch. In the 12th century, Geoffrey the Fair, Duke of Anjou, came into contact with a genuine source of developmental activities. He adopted as his family emblem the broom plant (*planta genista*), hence the Plantagenets. In the symbolic language, the broom indicates a "forceful occasion", i.e., recognition of the "right time, right people, and right place" for the activation of a specific phase of the evolutionary process. Geoffrey, by displaying a broom plant, signalled that he was capable of recognizing such an occasion and knew how to use it for developmental purposes. It was at that time that the English evolutionary branch was activated. The whole Plantagenet dynasty was deeply involved in activities that were responsible, among other things, for the creation of chivalric orders in Europe.

The English branch was activated with the purpose of developing an adequate inner structure that would be capable of assimilating the full evolutionary charge. But then something went wrong. As a result of the break with Navarre, England was cut off from the Cyprian link. This was similar to the situation that occurred in Italy when Bohemia was severed from Sicily at the time of "The Winter's Tale". The evolutionary impulses designated for the English branch could not be transmitted. As described in the discussion of "As You Like It", these impulses were preserved in the Forest of Arden, i.e., within the French branch. Several attempts were made to unite the English and the French branches, but without success. Historically, these attempts were manifested as the Hundred Years' War, i.e., a series of conflicts waged between England and France in the 14th and 15th centuries.

As a result of the break, the English branch could not be provided with creative and unitive energies. Without these energies it was not possible to implement the advanced methodology. Instead, the English branch had to be developed by using impulses of conscious energy, i.e., an earlier mode of the evolutionary spectrum. Because the royal channel became sterile, the conscious energy had to be invested outside of "the royal blood". Symbolically, this is illustrated as impulses of conscious energy represented by young women who do not belong to the royal families. The kings of the History Plays, however, are marrying Spanish, French, and English princesses. This is why there is no "falling in love" in the History Plays. The arrangement of the marriages is driven entirely by ordinary political and strategic motives.

Without the presence of higher modes of energies, the overall development within the English branch had to follow the traditional approach. The traditional approach is limited to the correct alignment of the ordinary faculties. This correct alignment provides an inner structure, which is capable of containing the higher impulses. There was still a possibility that the overall situation could be changed and the higher impulses could be made available later on.

The efforts that aimed at sustaining the evolutionary potential of England are illustrated by Shakespeare in his History Plays. "King John" describes the first stage of the English evolutionary branch.

King John

As a result of its initial contact with a developmental centre, the English branch acquired a new aspect within itself. This aspect was related to conscious energy. At the beginning of the process this aspect could be described as an alien or as a bastard if one would like to draw a parallel to social or family structure. Such a bastardized aspect would be recognized and accepted only by the more balanced elements of the being. At the initial stage, however, the overall environment would not be ready to allow a bastard to play a leading role. Therefore, this aspect would operate in the background, discreetly monitoring the process.

The Bastard, a character from "King John", plays such a role in the first play of the English branch. The action of the play is set at the beginning of the 13th century, i.e., at the same time as "All's Well That Ends Well". The Bastard represents a link to the original source of evolutionary activities. Shakespeare points out that the Bastard is related to the historical figure of Richard Plantagenet:

> "King Richard Coeur-de-lion was thy father."
> (*King John, I.1*)

Richard Plantagenet, King of England and Lord of Cyprus, was the famous Coeur-de-lion (Lionheart). This name contains the initiatory words "heart" and "lion". The "heart" refers to the spiritual heart faculty. The "lion" means a "man of the way", that is an aspirant on the path to higher development. Richard's nickname is thus an announcement, to those who understand, that he has been initiated.

The Bastard becomes the most compelling character in the play. He is unswervingly loyal to the king. At the same time he is not afraid to point out mistakes made by the king. For example, he denounces deals made between King John and the King of France, and between King John and the Pope. He criticizes the royal desire for riches and self-interest. In other words, the Bastard discreetly guides the being of England.

At the end of the play King John dies. The Bastard and the lords swear allegiance to John's son, Prince Henry, over his father's dead body. Henry becomes King Henry III. The Bastard makes the final speech of the play in which he cheers on the unconquerable force of England:

> "This England never did, nor never shall,
> Lie at the proud foot of a conqueror,
> But when it first did help to wound itself."
> (*King John, V.7*)

The Bastard confirms England's potential for development, but he indicates that this being has to be reformed first before it will be ready to fulfil its evolutionary function.

Richard II

After the transmission break with Navarre, an extra effort was needed to try to re-connect the English branch to its original source. To achieve this, a group of dedicated members would need to be formed. Such a group would attempt to carry on its developmental work. It would adopt certain colours as its symbols to indicate their developmental objectives. For example, if its prime objective was spiritual reformation, then most probably for its colour symbols it would adopt gold and blue. These colours symbolize the golden sun in the blue sky. The clear unclouded blue sky symbolizes a balanced mind, within which it is possible to start to see "gold", the first sign of the operation of a reformed heart. This particular colour code was the origin of the "blue blooded nobility", the term that indicated the existence of spiritually developed men among ordinary humanity. The basic unit of such a group would be called a circle that could be symbolized, for example, by a garter.

There is a historical record of such a group. The group has been known as the Order of the Garter. The Order of the Garter was created in 1348. It was inspired by King Edward III. The members of the Order of the Garter were divided into two garters of thirteen each, one under Edward III and the other under his eldest son, the Black Prince. Its colours were blue and gold. Its aims were overtly chivalric. Its patron saint was St. George, a Syrian. They chose as their slogan a salutation to the cupbearer, i.e., their spiritual guide. This salutation, in its original language, sounded very similar to the French "*Honi soit qui mal y pense*". Later on this sound was adopted as its literary English translation, i.e., "Dishonored be he who thinks evil of it".

The first task of such a group would be to identify the limitations of worldly ambitions and wants. Signs of such recognition are indicated by King Richard II in his soliloquy:

> "I'll give my jewels for a set of beads,
> My gorgeous palace for a hermitage,
> My gay apparel for an almsman's gown,
> My figured goblets for a dish of wood,
> My sceptre for a palmer's walking staff,
> My subjects for a pair of carved saints
> And my large kingdom for a little grave,
> A little little grave, an obscure grave."
> (*Richard II, III.3*)

Richard is the main character of the second play of the History Plays. The play is set nearly two centuries later than "King John". It should be noted that King Richard II was the first among the kings of England who was initiated into the Order of the Garter. Another main historical character of this play is John of Gaunt who was also a Knight of the Order of the Garter.

Richard, who ascended to the throne as a young man, is a regal and stately figure, but he is wasteful in his spending habits, unwise in his choice of counsellors and detached from his country and its people. He spends too much of his time pursuing the latest fashions, spending money, and raising taxes to fund his pet wars in Ireland and elsewhere. When he begins to rent out parcels of English land to certain wealthy noblemen in order to raise funds for one of his wars, and when he seizes the lands and money of a recently deceased and much respected uncle to help fill his coffers, both the noblemen and the commoners decide that Richard has gone too far.

Richard has a cousin, named Henry Bolingbroke, who is a great favourite among the English commoners. Henry is the son of John of Gaunt, Richard's uncle. Henry is far more pragmatic and capable than Richard.

Early in the play, Richard exiles Henry from England for six years due to an unresolved dispute over an earlier political murder. The dead uncle whose lands Richard seizes was John of Gaunt. When Henry learns that Richard has stolen what should have been his inheritance, he assembles an army and invades England. The commoners, fond of Henry and angry at Richard's mismanagement of the country, welcome his invasion and join his forces. One by one, Richard's allies desert him and defect to Henry's side. There is never an actual battle; instead, Henry peacefully takes Richard prisoner. Richard is imprisoned in a remote castle. Henry is crowned as King Henry IV. Later on, an assassin, who follows Henry's ambivalent wish, murders Richard.

The king, members of his family and his courtiers represent various aspects of the ordinary faculties of the being of England. Since its initiation, there is always one aspect that provides a link to the initial evolutionary impulse. Such aspects form an internal transmission chain within the English branch. At the same time, there are a few individuals among those representing the various aspects of the intellectual faculty who are aware of the higher purpose of this being. However, such awareness takes the form of brief moments that appear only infrequently. Very often these flashes of realization seem to be confusing and imprecise. These happen in situations when the king's actions are questionable or go against ordinary moral, religious, or social norms. It seems that there is awareness, at least among some of the courtiers, of the concept of the "King", his role and his function. Although at this stage of development, they do not have the capacity, as yet, to recognize the righteous "King". They assume that the reigning king represents the supreme being. Therefore, they are confused because they are using artificial means to determine who the king is or who should be recognized as the king. At this stage of development, England has not yet experienced the taste of perfected states. Therefore, the understanding and behaviour of the various aspects of this being are still driven by theoretical and conceptual beliefs.

For example, John of Gaunt refuses to take action against King Richard. His reasoning is based on his conceptual belief that God divinely appoints the king of the nation. He refuses to attack the murderers of his brother, because the person who is most to blame for the murder is King Richard himself. Gaunt refuses to raise arms against King Richard, not out of loyalty to him as a relative, nor out of fear for the power of the king, but rather because he believes, as do many of the play's other characters, that the king of a nation was appointed by Heaven, and that an act of rebellion against the king would therefore be blasphemous. If Richard has caused Gaunt's brother's death, then Heaven must revenge it; because Richard is the Lord's substitute, and, as Gaunt says:

"I may never lift
An angry arm against His minister."
(*Richard II, I.2*)

It is the gap between the concept of "King" and the person wearing the crown that drives the plots of the History Plays. Shakespeare used the term "the hollow crown" to convey the difference between the "King" and a king. Here is King Richard's comment about it:

> "for within the hollow crown
> That rounds the mortal temples of a king
> Keeps Death his court and there the antic sits,
> Scoffing his state and grinning at his pomp."
> (*Richard II, III.2*)

The crown is "hollow" or "empty" because the state of "King" does not correspond to the person wearing it. According to Shakespeare's presentation, the true status of "King" is not determined by the crown, but by the inner being of a person. Richard's crown was "hollow" because he had not arrived yet at the state of true King. The History Plays are an illustration of the process that gradually leads to the development of true "Kinghood".

At this stage of development, Richard starts to realize that he, like all underdeveloped persons, has a multiple and changing personality. This is quite remarkably illustrated in his soliloquy while he is in prison. Richard indicates to the audience that his own thoughts could be represented as various people:

> "My brain I'll prove the female to my soul,
> My soul the father; and these two beget
> A generation of still-breeding thoughts,
> And these same thoughts people this little world."
> (*Richard II, V.5*)

Richard's language may seem obscure unless the readers realize that Shakespeare describes a certain degree of spiritual realization.

Henry IV

Awareness of one's multiple and changing personalities induces a constructive mental action that may lead to the reformation of some of the leading aspects of the being. Shakespeare illustrates this stage of the process in "Henry IV".

The play is set in the first years of the 15th century. At that time England is in the middle of a civil war. Powerful rebels have assembled against King Henry IV in an attempt to overthrow him. King Henry has recently become ill because of his worry over the war, his implication in the death of King Richard, and the misbehaviour of his eldest son, Prince Harry. In the meantime, the rebel leaders gather their army to battle the king.

Throughout the play Henry retains his tight hold on the throne and never loses his majesty. Henry remains stern and resolute, but he is no longer the force of nature he appears to be in "Richard II". At the same time, however, he becomes reflective about his role and his responsibilities. His gradual awakening is marked by his meditation on sleep:

"How many thousand of my poorest subjects
Are at this hour asleep! O sleep, O gentle sleep,
Nature's soft nurse, how have I frighted thee,
That thou no more wilt weigh my eyelids down
And steep my senses in forgetfulness?
Why rather, sleep, liest thou in smoky cribs,
Upon uneasy pallets stretching thee
And hush'd with buzzing night-flies to thy slumber,
Than in the perfumed chambers of the great,
Under the canopies of costly state,
And lull'd with sound of sweetest melody?
O thou dull god, why liest thou with the vile
In loathsome beds, and leavest the kingly couch
A watch-case or a common 'larum-bell?

Wilt thou upon the high and giddy mast
Seal up the ship-boy's eyes, and rock his brains
In cradle of the rude imperious surge
And in the visitation of the winds,
Who take the ruffian billows by the top,
Curling their monstrous heads and hanging them
With deafening clamour in the slippery clouds,
That, with the hurly, death itself awakes?"
(*Henry IV, part 2, III.1*)

Shakespeare uses the characters of Henry IV and his eldest son, Prince Harry, to illustrate the difference between innate capacity and acquired experience. Prince Harry, who first appears in "Henry IV", spends most of his youth in taverns, hanging around with a bunch of vagrants. King Henry IV is gravely concerned over his son's misbehaviour. It is important to note that King Henry's understanding of his son's behaviour is not based on inner perception and knowledge. King Henry's evaluation of Prince Harry's actions is a result of his and others' opinions and his own previous experiences. King Henry IV rebukes his son for not behaving correctly. He tells him that he has almost completely alienated himself from the whole court and the other members of the royal family. The hopes and expectations that he had of him have vanished. Every man secretly predicts Harry's downfall. King Henry says that if he himself had appeared so often in public, so overly familiar to people, so freely accessible, so cheap and available to the common hordes, then public opinion, which helped him get the crown, would have stayed loyal to King Richard II, the previous king. Henry would have stayed a banished man, with no reputation and no promise of success. But because he was so rarely seen in public, when he did appear they looked at him with amazement, as if he was a comet. Men would tell their children, 'That's him!' Others would ask, 'Where? Which one's Henry?' Then he assumed a courtly manner. He made himself look so humble that he won the loyalty of men's hearts. They even treated him as a royal in the presence of the crowned King Richard. He was like a ceremonial robe that is admired because it is so rarely seen. Meanwhile, frivolous King Richard kept company with shallow and superficial companions. King Richard was quick with a joke but quickly out of jokes. He degraded his dignity, mixed his royalty with capering fools, had his great name disgraced with their scorn, and ruined his authority by laughing at the jokes of foolish boys. He spent his time in common places, surrendering himself to the pursuit of popularity. They saw him every day and it was like overdosing on honey: a little too much is as bad as far too much. So, when he wanted to appear as King, he was like a cuckoo in June, heard but not noted. Seen, but by eyes so used to seeing, that they took him for granted. They were stuffed, gorged, and full with his presence. And that is exactly, says King Henry, the way Prince Harry stands now. He has lost his princely dignity by associating with vile criminals. Everybody is sick of seeing him all the time.

Prince Harry, however, is driven by his inner perception. He does not rely on the opinion of his father or other courtiers. He is following his inner voice. He knows that he has to play an important role. He has to use a very different approach if he is to succeed. His approach follows that symbolized by the colours gold and blue of the Order of the Garter. Right at the beginning he says that he knows what his vile associates are like. For a while, therefore, he will tolerate his lazy and rowdy companions. But in doing this he will be like the golden sun, that allows the clouds to temporarily hide its beauty from the world. When the sun wants to be itself again, it breaks through the mists and fog. Then it is more loved through its previous absence. And because people have missed the sun so much, they are that much more impressed when it finally appears. If every day of the year was a holiday, playing would be as dull as working. But when it's rare, it's looked forward to. Nothing is as precious as an unexpected occurrence. So when he will put a stop to his wild behaviour and accept the responsibilities of being the king, he will look better and attract more people. Like bright metal on a dark background, his reformation will shine even more brilliantly when it's set against his wicked past. For now, therefore, he will continue to be so wild as to make wildness his art. But he will redeem himself when the world least expects it.

King Henry IV's complains about his son are quite ironic, because Harry's approach follows the same strategy as his father's. The only difference is that Harry has to play both roles, i.e., his father and King Richard. This is why, at the beginning, Harry mimics Richard II's behaviour in order to establish a reference pattern for his future reformation. Here is how perceptive Warwick explains Harry's behaviour:

> "My gracious lord, you look beyond him quite:
> The prince but studies his companions
> Like a strange tongue, wherein, to gain the language,
> 'Tis needful that the most immodest word
> Be look'd upon and learn'd; which once attain'd,
> Your highness knows, comes to no further use
> But to be known and hated. So, like gross terms,
> The prince will in the perfectness of time
> Cast off his followers; and their memory
> Shall as a pattern or a measure live,
> By which his grace must mete the lives of others,
> Turning past evils to advantages."
> (*Henry IV, part 2, IV.4*)

Warwick's explanation is an accurate description of Prince Harry's approach. When time was ripe, Harry went through quite a remarkable reformation. This reformation may be compared to the appearance of a new flower, or a new tree that has taken root in the garden and is showing its first buds. Shakespeare has quite precisely described it as the change that was observed in Harry at the moment of his father's death:

"The breath no sooner left his father's body,
But that his wildness, mortified in him,
Seem'd to die too; yea, at that very moment
Consideration, like an angel, came
And whipp'd the offending Adam out of him,
Leaving his body as a paradise,
To envelop and contain celestial spirits.
Never was such a sudden scholar made;
Never came reformation in a flood,
With such a heady currance, scouring faults
Nor never Hydra-headed wilfulness
So soon did lose his seat and all at once
As in this king."
(*Henry V*, *I.1*)

It should be emphasized that it was the Bastard in "King John" who provided the seed of this new tree.

In his descriptions of the behaviour of Richard II, Henry IV and Prince Harry, Shakespeare describes three consecutive stages of the process leading to true "Kinghood". The first stage is represented by Richard II. Richard II has neither royal quality nor wit to pretend that he does. Henry IV is witty enough to skilfully pretend that he is worthy. Prince Harry is perceptive enough to implement a more effective strategy.

Henry V

The reformation of young Prince Harry affected his knowledge of theological matters, domestic policy, war strategy, and political topics. His rebirth was a puzzle to many, because the young Prince used to spend a lot of time drinking with uneducated, crude and superficial companions. He used to get drunk, seeking out entertainment, seemingly with no interest at all in learning or contemplation.

However, this reformation requires that Harry, after becoming King Henry V, leave behind his former companions, including Sir John Falstaff. Harry has to leave his former companions behind because they have not been able to perceive and understand the transformation that has taken place. Therefore, they were not able to harmonize themselves with this new phase of Henry V's function and his mission.

Henry V's mission is symbolically described as the Battle for France. It may help to comprehend the described process if we remember that Henry V's goal is to re-establish a link to the source. The link may be established by acquiring access to the evolutionary impulses. As indicated in the discussion of the French plays, these impulses have been stored in France.

Henry V lays claim to certain parts of France based on his distant roots in the French royal family and on a very technical interpretation of ancient laws. When the Prince of France sends an insulting message in response to these claims, Henry V decides to invade France. Supported by the English noblemen and clergy, Henry V gathers his troops for war. The climax of the war comes at the famous Battle of Agincourt, at which the English are outnumbered by the French five to one. When Henry V gives his famous St. Crispin's Day speech about honour, he talks about evolutionary energies. Evolutionary energies exist as a positive commodity; they can be accumulated and stored. When the time is ripe, they can be released into the world. Henry portrays the evolutionary energies as a fixed amount of "honour" that will be divided among all the victors. This is why there is no room for unfit soldiers. Henry V therefore gives his soldiers freedom to make the choice to fight with him or go home. Those who choose to stay and fight with him will be granted nobility, they will become brothers, and they will be elevated to a higher level of being:

> "We few, we happy few, we band of brothers;
> For he to-day that sheds his blood with me
> Shall be my brother; be he ne'er so vile,
> This day shall gentle his condition:
> And gentlemen in England now a-bed
> Shall think themselves accursed they were not here,
> And hold their manhoods cheap whiles any speaks
> That fought with us upon Saint Crispin's day."
> (*Henry V*, *IV.3*)

The Battle of Agincourt is used by Shakespeare to describe an example of the manifestation of a forceful occasion. It helps to comprehend the outcome of the battle to note that a spiritual octagonal union had been activated within the French branch at the time of "As You Like It". A wave of "glory" generated by this octagon reaches Agincourt. Henry V and his remaining soldiers are able to absorb this wave of glory. The English rout the French despite the fact that they are outnumbered. Henry realizes that his victory is not a result of his doing:

> "Praised be God, and not our strength, for it!"
> (*Henry V*, *IV.7*)

Yet, in the final scene, Henry V requests a reward for himself. His reward is Katharine, the French Princess, whom Henry demands should become his wife:

> "Yet leave our cousin Katharine here with us:
> She is our capital demand, comprised
> Within the fore-rank of our articles."
> (*Henry V*, *V.2*)

Henry V marries Katharine, the daughter of the French King. The marriage reinforces the peace agreement between England and France.

This marriage may seem to be the needed outcome for the current situation. However, from the perspective of the evolutionary process, it was not the optimal solution. It looks as if Henry followed the original plan. According to that plan, the evolutionary charge was supposed to be invested into the French royal family. Therefore, his marriage with the French Princess was part of "within the fore-rank of our articles". Because of the break with Navarre, the impulse of unitive energy designated for the intellect faculty within the English branch remained in the Forest of Arden. It was represented by Phoebe, a shepherdess. It seems that Henry was not aware of the change. Henry would have had to abandon the royal court and go to the Forest of Arden to meet Phoebe there. Otherwise, according to Touchstone, Henry, like William, remained "damned like a roasted egg: all on one side".

Henry, in his youth, perceived that he needed to abandon the court. And he did. Instead of going to Arden, however, he spent his time in the taverns and brothels of London. At that time he met Nell, Poins' sister. Harry may have been attracted to Nell. It may be presumed that Nell represented the impulse of conscious energy that was available within the English branch. Therefore, marrying Nell would have been the second best option. But marrying a woman from the lower class was not on Prince Harry's list. This is indicated in an episode inserted in "Henry IV". It is the episode where Prince Harry has just received a letter from Falstaff, in which Falstaff accuses Poins of spreading rumours about Harry marrying Nell:

Prince Harry:

"Must I marry your sister?"

Poins:

"God send the wench no worse fortune! But I never said so."
(*Henry IV, Part 2, II.2*)

But even this option was impossible for Harry. Like Hamlet, Harry was not able to recognize his highest priority. He was "of too high a region" to consider marrying someone from the lower class. He was not ready to give up his "hollow crown".

It was at this point that the Bohemian intervention was commenced in the Balkans as illustrated in "Twelfth Night". One of the objectives of the Bohemian intervention was to develop rapidly a highly developed intellect as a substitute for Prince Harry. This aspect of the intellect would be needed for the formation of the English octagon.

Henry VI

The Battle of Agincourt marks the high tide of the evolutionary wave. This high tide is induced by the event taking place in the Forest of Arden. However, England is not capable, as yet, of fully benefiting from it. Therefore, this being has to go through a period of recess before the next crest arrives. The play "Henry VI" illustrates a period when previously dormant destructive aspects start to mar the being. The presence of these destructive aspects is referred to by Chorus in "Henry V":

"O England! model to thy inward greatness,
Like little body with a mighty heart,
What mightst thou do, that honour would thee do,
Were all thy children kind and natural!"
(*Henry V, II. Prologue*)

The disunity between various aspects of England is described as a quarrel between the Duke of York and the Duke of Somerset. The

English lords select red or white roses to indicate whose claim they believe to be correct. Then, they all watch King Henry VI to see whose side he is going to support. Henry says it shouldn't matter what rose he wears, since he loves both his lords, yet even as he says this, he picks Somerset's red rose. Henry, by aligning himself with Somerset, is setting in motion the Wars of the Roses.

There are two attractions placed in the nature of man. One of these attractions is to lift a man to his higher spheres of functioning. Another attraction is to stoop him down to a kind of low, bestial life. Therefore, two forms of external agencies are needed to bring these attractions into operation. The external agency that brings the attraction to the higher forms of living is often called an angel, and the one which leads man astray is called a demon. In human life, however, there are many combinations of these two extremes that lead to the existence among the agents of many mixes, grades and shades. These various attractions are very often described in traditional myths as fairies, spirits, and ghosts. Therefore, when man enters on a spiritual journey, he encounters a sort of dichotomous situation. On one side, he is provided with new forms of protection, safety, and guidance. On the other, he is exposed to new distracting challenges.

The presence of the invisible attractions is marked in "Henry VI" by the appearance of Joan of Arc and Talbot. They together signify the disunited roses.

Joan of Arc is a shepherd's daughter. Joan relates that one day, when she was tending her sheep, a vision appeared to her and told her to free her country from calamity. This figure showed itself in all its glory; the divine rays brought Joan her beauty. The appearance of Joan is an echo of the event in the Forest of Arden. Her appearance is a side effect of the activation of the French octagon. She has accidentally intercepted the wave generated by the octagon. It is the same wave that led Henry V to his glory in the

Battle of Agincourt. Joan realizes that she may exercise her extraordinary power. She assumes that, after the death of Henry V, it is her turn to dominate the world. She compares her role to that of Cleopatra's:

"With Henry's death the English circle ends;
Dispersed are the glories it included.
Now am I like that proud insulting ship
Which Caesar and his fortune bare at once."
(*Henry VI, part 1, I.2*)

Joan represents that aspect of the intellect that has been uplifted by contact with the evolutionary wave. As a result, she has been granted certain insights into current and future events. For example, she tells the Dauphin of France that she will lead the French troops in breaking the Britons' siege on Orléans. Her words prove to be true. Because of that, the Dauphin of France is very impressed.

Joan's appearance is only an indication of the potential of the evolutionary forces. But Joan's self-centredness leads her away from the optimal and constructive fulfilment of that potential. First, she misunderstands her role; secondly, driven by her egotistic motives, she misuses her capacity. In other words, she represents a partially purified aspect of the intellect faculty; she is a manifestation of a maculate white rose. She ignores the chivalric code of conduct in her methods of fighting. Her actions serve to increase the war's viciousness. For a short time she exercises her destructive influence.

Joan's appearance is bound together with the personage of Talbot. Talbot illustrates a partially purified aspect of the heart faculty. He is a manifestation of a red rose. Talbot is aware of Joan's origin and capacity. This is how Talbot describes her:

"Here, here she comes. I'll have a bout with thee;
Devil or devil's dam, I'll conjure thee:
Blood will I draw on thee, thou art a witch,
And straightway give thy soul to him thou servest."
(*Henry VI, part 1, I.5*)

Talbot fights for the honour of king and his country. His behaviour and his methods of military leadership are based on the noble conduct of chivalry. He displays extraordinary physical powers. He is so feared by the French that, when he is captured, they have archers guard him even while he sleeps. After being released, he conquers many towns and fortifications in France, until he encounters Joan. Talbot gets trapped on the battlefield at Bordeaux. He is killed in that battle.

After the downfall of Talbot, Joan cannot last much longer. At a critical moment, Joan calls for the help of her invisible agents. Previously, Joan described them as the carriers of glorious rays. At this moment, however, her own corrupted state is such that she sees them as demons. The "demons" refuse to speak to her. She reminds them that she has always offered her blood to them in exchange for their help. Yet the "demons" show no interest in her offerings. Joan, without the support of the invisible agents, has to go down. She is captured and burned at the stake.

Talbot and Joan represent an example of two opposite forces that work together towards the same goal. They symbolically illustrate the above-mentioned dichotomous situation. The fate of Joan and Talbot indicate the limited value of the experiences associated with the premature awakening of intuitive knowledge and extraordinary powers. Joan was linked to the invisible forces. However, her still selfish nature did not allow her to use this experience in a constructive way. On the other hand, Talbot's intention was correctly aligned with the overall course of the process. He also had access to extraordinary powers. However, he was lacking perceptive insight into the events. Therefore, he was not able to effectively use his powers. These abilities, as represented by Joan and Talbot, are manifested as mutually destructive. The intellect and the heart faculties are disunited and fogged by dormant negative elements. This being has to overcome these limitations to continue its progress.

The disappearance of Joan and Talbot allows the corrupted self faculty to dominate the being for a brief time. This is illustrated by the revolt of the commoners. Cade is the leader of the commoners' revolt. His violence is aimed at those who can read or write and he kills those who support schools. His reign of terror erases any rights of women and makes them fair game for rape. In other words, he attacks those who symbolically represent the intellect and the heart faculties.

Cade's troops enjoy the pleasures of mob rule more than any promise of progress or freedom. Their violence shows the dangers of popular rule: it represents a being that is driven by the "universal wolf", i.e., the corrupted self faculty. This revolt represents a situation in which the self faculty is coming back into prominence and takes control over the intellect and the heart faculties.

Richard III

The play "Richard III" describes a stage where the previously unearthed destructive aspects are gradually diminished.

The destructive aspects are not confronted directly. Instead, a negative aspect is either implanted or selected from those already present there. This aspect is allowed to manifest itself in its fullest strength. Following the rule "like attracts like", all destructive aspects agglomerate around it. Then, all these agglomerated destructive aspects are isolated from the others. This leads to a situation where the negative aspects cannot help but turn against their own weaker members. When they are weakened by this self-induced destruction, they can be diminished more effectively. In a parallel operation, the constructive aspects get support from the invisible agencies. In other words, seemingly unfortunate events may in reality be part of a certain cleansing mechanism. Such a corrective mechanism is quite precisely described, step-by-step, in "Richard III".

After a long civil war between the royal families of York and Lancaster, England enjoys a short period of peace under King Edward IV. But Edward's younger brother, Richard, resents Edward's power and the happiness of those around him. Richard is malicious, power-hungry, and bitter about his physical deformity. Richard begins to aspire secretly to the crown. He declares outright that he intends to stop at nothing to achieve his wicked goals:

"Why, I can smile, and murder whiles I smile,
And cry 'Content' to that which grieves my heart,
And wet my cheeks with artificial tears,
And frame my face to all occasions.
I'll drown more sailors than the mermaid shall;
I'll slay more gazers than the basilisk;
I'll play the orator as well as Nestor,
Deceive more slily than Ulysses could,
And, like a Sinon, take another Troy.
I can add colours to the chameleon,
Change shapes with Proteus for advantages,
And set the murderous Machiavel to school.
Can I do this, and cannot get a crown?
Tut, were it farther off, I'll pluck it down."
(*Henry VI, part 3, III.2*)

There are many people between him and the crown. Richard decides to kill anyone who stands in his way and he manages to become the king of England.

Richard is a compelling symbol of the intellect faculty in its degenerated form. Despite his open allegiance to evil, he is a charismatic and fascinating figure. Because of this, some well-intentioned but weak characters cannot help but sympathize with him, or even be attracted to him. For example, Lady Anne, who has an explicit knowledge of his wickedness, allows herself to be seduced by his brilliant wordplay. She agrees to marry him.

Richard's reign of terror causes the common people of England to fear and loathe him. At the same time, he gradually alienates nearly all the noblemen of the court. When rumours begin to spread around about a challenger to the throne who is gathering forces in France, most of the noblemen defect to join his forces. The challenger is the Earl of Richmond, a descendant of a secondary branch of the Lancaster family. In the meantime, Richard tries to consolidate his power. He has his wife Anne murdered so that he can marry his niece. Such a marriage would further enhance his grasp of the throne. At this point, however, Richard starts to lose his control over the situation.

Richmond invades England. The night before the decisive battle, as both leaders sleep, they begin to dream. This scene illustrates an example of a situation in which the invisible agencies get involved in the process. A parade of the ghosts of all those whom Richard has murdered comes across the stage. First, each ghost stops to speak to Richard. Each condemns him bitterly for his or her death, tells him that he will be killed in battle the next morning. Then each ghost moves away and speaks to the sleeping Richmond, telling him that they are on his side and that Richmond will rule England and father a race of kings. In a similar manner, eleven ghosts move across the stage. Richard wakes out of his sleep sweating and gasping. For the first time Richard is terrified.

Afterwards, Richard speaks brusquely to his remaining supporters. At that moment he is essentially isolated from his courtiers and his family members. As a result of his malicious nature, he has killed anyone who was close to him; his brothers, nephews, and even his own wife are all dead at his hand; his mother has cursed and abandoned him; and Buckingham, who was once his closest friend, has been sent to execution. Richard has gradually destroyed all his close relationships. Now he is still in power, but he is alone. In his battle speech Richard mocks the enemy soldiers, calling them "a scum of Bretons and base lackey peasants". His troops outnumber Richmond's by three to one. Therefore, Richard is sure that might makes right, and that:

> "Conscience is but a word that cowards use,
> Devised at first to keep the strong in awe:
> Our strong arms be our conscience, swords our law."
> (*Richard III, V.3*)

In contrast, Richmond, very much Richard's opposite, claims to fight for honour. He is gracious and friendly to both his noblemen and his soldiers. Richmond asks his men to remember the beauty of the land that they are saving from a tyrant, and the wives and children whom they will be making free. He reminds his men that he himself will die in battle if he cannot win, and if he does succeed then all his soldiers will be rewarded. Richmond brings back the chivalry, the code of proper conduct.

Richard is killed in the battle. Richmond is crowned King Henry VII. Promising a new era of peace for England, the new king is betrothed to young princess Elizabeth in order to unite the warring houses of Lancaster and York. The red and the white roses are reunited.

Henry VIII

The play "Henry VIII" describes the last stage of the English branch. Once the destructive aspects have been diminished, it is possible to form a balanced and united being. At this stage, all major aspects of the being are becoming conscious of the overall purpose.

The play "Henry VIII" describes a significant moment in English history, namely England's break from Rome and the Catholic Church. In 1531, King Henry VIII disappointed that his wife Katherine had borne him no male heir, decided to divorce her. His advisors argued that the marriage was invalid, but the Pope ruled against the divorce. Nevertheless, Henry divorced Katherine and married Anne Boleyn, a knight's daughter.

It is obvious that the character of Henry VIII is fully aware of the rule "right people, right place, and right time". Henry does not interfere with the flow of events. He only acts when a forceful occasion requires his intervention. For example, he does not intervene when Buckingham, his wife Katherine, or his right-hand man Wolsey are in trouble. However, he gets actively involved when the courtiers plot against Cranmer, his trusted adviser. It is the first time that we see him as an active king. Never before has Henry seemed to pay attention to the plots churning behind the scenes that placed people in and out of his favour. However, Henry is prompted to save Cranmer. Why does Henry protect Cranmer? The answer to this question provides the key to the understanding of the entire series of Shakespeare's History Plays. Namely, Cranmer has to play a critical role in the final stage of the process. All characters that were previously eliminated had to go because their presence was blocking the circumstances leading to the ultimate outcome of the process: the birth of Elizabeth. Buckingham had to go because he believed that he had a claim to the throne; Katherine had to go because she did not give birth to the right heir; and Wolsey had to go because he opposed Henry's marriage to Anne.

It is important to notice that Anne, although from a noble family, is not of royal blood. Here is Wolsey's comment about it:

> "The late queen's gentlewoman,
> a knight's daughter,
> To be her mistress' mistress! the queen's queen!"
> (*Henry VIII, III.2*)

This indicates that Anne represents the currently available impulse of conscious energy. At the time of "Henry IV", this impulse was represented by Nell, Poins' sister. It was this impulse that Prince Harry was supposed to assimilate earlier on. This means that this "marriage" was delayed by some 100 years or so. Cranmer is aware of the importance of the marriage. Cranmer helps to arrange the circumstances that make it possible for Henry to marry Anne. It may be presumed that Cranmer represents the aspect that provides a link to the evolutionary transmission chain. This particular link was grafted onto England some 400 years before. It is the same link that was provided by the Bastard in "King John". We may notice that, at this stage of the process, all major characters are becoming conscious of the overall purpose. Regardless of their own individual fate, they all accept graciously the chain of events, even if this means their own fall or death. For example, in his last words just before he is executed, Buckingham offers prayers and blessings to the King:

> "my vows and prayers
> Yet are the king's; and, till my soul forsake,
> Shall cry for blessings on him: may he live
> Longer than I have time to tell his years!"
> (*Henry VIII, II.1*)

After being cast away from the court, Wolsey admits his errors and expresses his gratitude to the King:

> "The king has cured me,
> I humbly thank his grace; and from these shoulders,
> These ruin'd pillars, out of pity, taken
> A load would sink a navy, too much honour!"
> (*Henry VIII, III.2*)

When Katherine hears of Wolsey's death, she is able to forgive his bad treatment of her. Then Katherine stresses her own humility to the King. Humility and forgiveness come to all those cast off by the King.

Cranmer has to be present at the birth and baptize the king's newborn child. Cranmer is capable of recognizing that the new born Elizabeth has inherited the "benediction" of King Edward the Confessor. As pointed out in the analysis of "Macbeth", Anne Boleyn, the mother of Elizabeth, inherited King Edward's crown:

> "Edward Confessor's crown,
> The rod, and bird of peace, and all such emblems
> Laid nobly on her."
> (*Henry VIII, IV.1*)

In the last scene Cranmer baptizes Elizabeth and announces her future greatness:

> "This royal infant -heaven still move about her!-
> Though in her cradle, yet now promises
> Upon this land a thousand thousand blessings,
> Which time shall bring to ripeness: she shall be -
> But few now living can behold that goodness -
> A pattern to all princes living with her,
> And all that shall succeed: Saba was never
> More covetous of wisdom and fair virtue

Than this pure soul shall be: all princely graces,
That mould up such a mighty piece as this is,
With all the virtues that attend the good,
Shall still be doubled on her: truth shall nurse her,
Holy and heavenly thoughts still counsel her:
She shall be loved and fear'd: her own shall bless her;
Her foes shake like a field of beaten corn,
And hang their heads with sorrow: good grows with her:
In her days every man shall eat in safety,
Under his own vine, what he plants; and sing
The merry songs of peace to all his neighbours:
God shall be truly known; and those about her
From her shall read the perfect ways of honour,
And by those claim their greatness, not by blood.
Nor shall this peace sleep with her: but as when
The bird of wonder dies, the maiden phoenix,
Her ashes new create another heir,
As great in admiration as herself;
So shall she leave her blessedness to one,
When heaven shall call her from this cloud of darkness,
Who from the sacred ashes of her honour
Shall star-like rise, as great in fame as she was,
And so stand fix'd: peace, plenty, love, truth, terror,
That were the servants to this chosen infant,
Shall then be his, and like a vine grow to him:
Wherever the bright sun of heaven shall shine,
His honour and the greatness of his name
Shall be, and make new nations: he shall flourish,
And, like a mountain cedar, reach his branches
To all the plains about him: our children's children
Shall see this, and bless heaven."
(*Henry VIII*, *V.5*)

Cranmer says that the infant holds great promises for England, and
few now can imagine the great things she will accomplish. She will

know truth, she will be loved and feared, and she will be a great ruler. In other words, Cranmer announces the actualization of the "unconquerable force of England" and the "inner greatness" that was predicted by the Bastard in "King John" and by Chorus in "Henry V". Cranmer says that when she dies, she will be reborn like a phoenix in her heir, "as great in admiration as herself".

Cranmer's description of Elizabeth's heir is consistent with the witches' prophesy in "Macbeth". Cranmer adds that Elizabeth's heir "from the sacred ashes of her honour shall star-like rise". The circumstances that led to the appearance of this "heir" are described in "The Merry Wives of Windsor".

The Merry Wives of Windsor

A new evolutionary cell that sprouted from the English branch is presented in "The Merry Wives of Windsor". This new cell marks the initiation of the next evolutionary cycle.

The initial stage of a new cycle is determined by the current projection of the cosmic matrix and the evolutionary gains achieved during the previous phases of the process. Ideally, the first stage of a new cycle would be the continuation of the last stage of the previous cycle. However, because of human imperfections and errors, there can be delays and interruptions in the process. This is why the first stage of a new cycle might be overlapped with certain intermediate stages of the previous cycle. Such an overlap would indicate that a particular being must be exposed several times to the same evolutionary template before it is able to assimilate it effectively. In other words, multiple exposures serve as multi-layered "coatings" that may be required for the completion of the process.

"The Merry Wives of Windsor" is the only play that describes life in Elizabethan England. Yet, Shakespeare brings to Windsor Sir John Falstaff together with his page Robin, Pistol, Nym, Bardolph, Shallow, and Mistress Quickly. These characters appeared previously in "Henry IV" and "Henry V", plays set up some 200 years earlier. This anachronistic reappearance of Falstaff and his company is an indication that the first stage of the new evolutionary cycle initiated in Elizabethan England is overlapped with the third and fourth stages of the previous cycle illustrated in the History Plays.

In accordance with the initial plan, the evolutionary gains achieved within the French branch were to be transferred to England. Because of the break with Navarre, the impulses designated for England could not be transferred at the time of "Henry V". Instead, an effort was made to use the French evolutionary charge to revitalize the royal court of Navarre. As illustrated in "Love's Labour's Lost", this undertaking did not succeed. In the meantime, a container capable of holding the advanced evolutionary charge was made available within the English branch. It was symbolically marked by the birth of Elizabeth at the conclusion of "Henry VIII". Now, therefore, it is possible to transfer the evolutionary charge from France to England. The presence of the French evolutionary charge in England is symbolically indicated in an episode with Caius, a French doctor. Let's recall that the French charge included four impulses, i.e., *red, yellow, black*, and *white*. When united, these four impulses are transmuted into *green*, "the colour of lovers". Doctor Caius is in possession of a green box ("un boitier vert"). He intends to deliver this green container to the English royal court ("Je m'en vais a la cour"):

"Pray you,
go and vetch me in my closet un boitier vert, a box,
a green-a box: do intend vat I speak? a green-a box."

"Je m'en vais a la cour - la grande affaire."
(*The Merry Wives of Windsor*, I.4)

This "green-a box" is a symbolic indication that a container that is capable of containing the octagonal union was transferred from France to England. Doctor Caius refers to this fact as "la grande affaire". This is a confirmation that Shakespeare uses Elizabeth I as a symbolic container capable of carrying the entire evolutionary charge that was invested in England at that time. In this symbolic presentation, Elizabeth I is the eighth king who appeared in the witches' prophesy in "Macbeth".

The French octagon was formed in "As You Like It", the play that takes place at the same historical time as "Henry V". At that time, however, it was not possible to transfer the evolutionary charge to England. Prince Harry was incapable of making a journey to the Forest of Arden. Now, however, it is possible to fulfil the originally intended function of the English branch. But this requires overlapping "The Merry Wives of Windsor" not only with "Henry IV" and "Henry V", but also with "As You Like It". We may expect, therefore, to meet in Windsor some characters who appeared previously in the Forest of Arden.

Despite its capacity to hold the entire evolutionary charge, the English royal channel became sterile. In Shakespeare's symbolic language such a situation is referred to as a period of chastity when, for instance, a woman becomes a votaress of Diana. Oberon, in his comment to Puck in "A Midsummer Night's Dream", clearly indicates that "Elizabeth" ("a fair vestal throned by the west") became such a votaress:

"Flying between the cold moon and the earth,
Cupid all arm'd: a certain aim he took
At a fair vestal throned by the west,
And loosed his love-shaft smartly from his bow,
As it should pierce a hundred thousand hearts;

But I might see young Cupid's fiery shaft
Quench'd in the chaste beams of the watery moon,
And the imperial votaress passed on,
In maiden meditation, fancy-free."
(*A Midsummer Night's Dream, II.1*)

The fact that "Elizabeth" was immune to Cupid's arrow symbolically points out her inner perfection. However, as long as she remained a "virgin", she could not discharge her evolutionary function. Because of the sterility of "Elizabeth", the evolutionary charge had to be transferred into another milieu within the English branch. This is why, at that time, it was necessary to shift the transmission of "nobility" to another channel. This shift was also indicated in the witches' procession of the kings:

"And yet the eighth appears, who bears a glass
Which shows me many more; and some I see
That two-fold balls and treble scepters carry"
(*Macbeth, IV.1*)

There is a break in the procession of the kings. Namely, the followers of the eighth king appear in another milieu, i.e., they are reflections in a mirror that is held by Elizabeth. In his description of Elizabeth, Cranmer also alluded to the transmission "not by blood" but through another milieu:

"those about her
From her shall read the perfect ways of honour,
And by those claim their greatness, not by blood."
(*Henry VIII, V.5*)

Let's take a look at the main features of Windsor as presented in "The Merry Wives of Windsor". This will allow us to identify in what form and where the evolutionary charge has been transferred.

The two leading characters of the play are Mrs. Page and Mrs. Ford, i.e., the merry wives of Windsor. Their husbands, Mr. Page and Mr. Ford, are two aspects of the heart. This means that the merry wives represent two impulses that have been assimilated by the heart faculty. Mistress Page (*red*) and Mistress Ford (*yellow*) are in control of the being of Windsor. Previously, these two impulses appeared in the Forest of Arden as Rosalind and Celia, and like Rosalind and Celia who were described as "thou and I am one", the merry wives are inseparable. Here is Mr. Ford's comment about it:

> "I think, if your husbands were dead,
> you two would marry."
> (*The Merry Wives of Windsor*, III.2)

It is important to underline two new features of the being of England as compared to the one presented in the History Plays. Namely, it is the first time that the heart faculty is the leading faculty of this being. Secondly, the leading aspects are within the English middle class represented by the families of Mr. Page and Mr. Ford. At one point, Falstaff even addresses Mr. Ford as a "mechanical", that is, a person of the working class:

> "Hang him, mechanical salt-butter rogue!"
> (*The Merry Wives of Windsor*, II.2)

Previously, the members of the royal family served as the protectors of the evolutionary process. This would indicate that at the time of "The Merry Wives of Windsor" a new transmission channel was needed in order to secure the process. The shift from the royals towards the middle class allowed for the formation of a much stronger heart faculty. It is not a coincidence that the new stage is overlapped with the one described in "Henry V". In his St. Crispin's Day speech, King Henry alluded to a transition of "nobility". King Henry said that ordinary men, who chose to stay and fight with him, would "gentle" their conditions; they would be granted nobility. In this context "nobility" indicates an ability to participate actively in the evolutionary process.

Mrs. Page, Mrs. Ford and their husbands represent the quad of the heart that was transferred from the Forest of Arden into the English branch. At that time, the other two impulses were represented by Phoebe (*black*) and Audrey (*white*). If the current state of Windsor is a result of an overlap with the Forest of Arden, then these two other impulses should also be present in Windsor. Let's recall that, from the time of the activation of the Cyprian link, these two impulses were designated for the English branch.

Anne Page, the daughter of Mrs. Page, represents the third impulse. Shakespeare helps the audience to identify her evolutionary function. In the final scene, two contenders to Anne's hand, Master Slender and Doctor Caius, are incapable of recognizing Anne's true "colour". Anne is disguised as one of the fairies who appear in the masque staged in Windsor Park. The fairies are of various colours, i.e., "black, grey, green, and white". Slender runs away with "a boy in white" and Doctor Caius ends up marrying "a boy in green". Therefore, the particular impulse that is represented by Anne is neither *white* nor *green*. It is coloured in *black*. In other words, this is an impulse of unitive energy designated for an aspect of the intellect faculty. Anne of Windsor is neither scornful nor sarcastic. It looks like the balanced environment of Windsor enabled the cleansing of this impulse from its ancient impurities. Previously this particular energy was represented by Phoebe, a shepherdess of the Forest of Arden. At that time, Prince Harry was incapable of meeting her. "The Merry Wives of Windsor" is a repeat of that previous situation. But Prince Harry is visibly absent in Windsor. There is, however, another royal prince who is capable of fulfilling this evolutionary function.

Master Fenton is one of the suitors of Anne Page. But Fenton is an outsider in Windsor. This is one of the reasons why Mr. Page does not accept Fenton as an appropriate suitor. According to Mr. Page, Fenton "is of too high a region" to be a suitable candidate for Anne's husband:

"The gentleman is of no having:
he kept company with the wild prince
and Poins; he is of too high a region; he knows too
much."
(*The Merry Wives of Windsor*, III.2)

Mr. Page accuses Fenton of keeping company with "the wild prince and Poins". This quote is a reference to Prince Harry and Poins who appeared in "Henry IV". But there are no traces of Harry and Poins in Windsor. It seems that Fenton comes from a very different world. Therefore, the above quote serves rather as a comparison than a direct description of Fenton's origin. Namely, Mr. Page means that Fenton is like Harry. This refers to the episode in which Harry and Poins were talking about Nell, Poins' sister. Mr. Page indicates that Master Fenton is like Harry "of too high a region" to be trusted. Fenton's affection for Anne cannot be sincere. Mr. Page thinks that Fenton is after Anne's dowry.

Fenton's origin is disclosed during his conversation with Mistress Quickly. In this conversation Shakespeare draws the audience's attention to Fenton's "wart":

Mistress Quickly:

"Master Fenton, I'll be sworn on a
book, she loves you. Have not your worship a wart
above your eye?"

Fenton:

"Yes, marry, have I; what of that?"

Mistress Quickly:

"Well, thereby hangs a tale: good faith, it is such another Nan; but, I detest, an honest maid as ever broke bread: we had an hour's talk of that wart."

"and I will tell your
worship more of the wart the next time we have confidence; and of other wooers."
(*The Merry Wives of Windsor*, I.4)

Shakespeare uses a wart or a mole as a mark or a "natural stamp" of certain estranged members of royal families. In this way Shakespeare points out Fenton's royal origin ("thereby hangs a tale"). Let's recall Viola's and Sebastian's reunion at the conclusion of "Twelfth Night":

Viola:

"My father had a mole upon his brow."

Sebastian:

"And so had mine."
(*Twelfth Night*, V.1)

Viola's and Sebastian's father was the spiritual "King" of Messaline. In this way Shakespeare indicates that Fenton is linked to the spiritual "royals" of the Bohemian branch. At the time of "Hamlet", this particular aspect of the intellect was represented by the Danish Prince. In the final scene, Hamlet passed his mandate to Fortinbras, a young Norwegian Prince. Afterwards, Fortinbras made a sea journey to England. In this way, the Bohemian experience was brought to England. At the time of "The Merry Wives of Windsor", Fortinbras appears as Master Fenton. He is a Norwegian Prince and, at the same time, provides a link to the spiritual royals of the evolutionary transmission chain. Unlike Prince Harry, Fortinbras was able to give up his Norwegian "hollow" crown. He abandoned the royal court, crossed the sea and arrived in Windsor where he met and fell in love with Anne, the Black Lady of Windsor. But now "the gentleman is of no having".

The arrival of Fenton in Windsor marks the fulfilment of the third objective of the Bohemian intervention, i.e., the development of a leading aspect of the intellect for the English branch. Fenton encompasses the experiences of Duke Orsino, Duke Vincentio of Vienna, Hamlet, and Fortinbras. During these previous experiences, this particular aspect was exposed to several manifestations of the Black Lady, i.e., Viola, Isabella, and Ophelia. Therefore, he has been properly prepared for meeting Anne. This confirms that Windsor is at the point where the evolutionary waves generated by the Viennese and the French octagons have been superimposed.

Windsor is quite balanced and harmonious. Such a harmonious being is capable of dealing with the interferences caused by the presence of a few impurities. Falstaff represents such impurities. Falstaff's attempt at seducing Mrs. Ford and Mrs. Page is a mark of interference with the process. The merry wives design and execute a protection plan as soon as they detect Falstaff's attempt to disturb Windsor's balance. As they cleanse Windsor from its impurities, the merry wives prepare the conditions for the activation of an octagonal inner structure within English society. Mrs. Page directs this part of the process. In her previous appearance as Rosalind, Mrs. Page has gained experience with the formation of such an octagonal structure. From the very beginning she knows who Fenton is and what his potential is: he is the intended husband for her daughter. However, Mrs. Page faces two challenges. First, she does not want to directly confront her husband, who intends to marry Anne to Master Slender. Secondly, Mrs. Page wants to make sure that the young couple is ready for their marriage. Mrs. Page refers to these challenges in her remarks to Fenton:

"Come, trouble not yourself. Good Master Fenton,
I will not be your friend nor enemy:
My daughter will I question how she loves you,
And as I find her, so am I affected.
Till then farewell, sir: she must needs go in;
Her father will be angry."
(*The Merry Wives of Windsor, III.4*)

This is why Mrs. Page has arranged a set of obstacles for the young couple. If Anne and Fenton are really in love, they will be able to overcome these obstacles.

Anne Page knew the schemes that were prepared by her parents. Therefore, it was up to her to make the final decision. Mistress Anne's stratagem is implemented during the Fairy Queen masque in Windsor Park. It should be no surprise that, at the end of the play, Mrs. Page accepts the marriage of Anne and Fenton without any objection:

"Well, I will muse no further. Master Fenton,
Heaven give you many, many merry days!
Good husband, let us every one go home,
And laugh this sport o'er by a country fire;
Sir John and all."
(*The Merry Wives of Windsor, V.5*)

Anne and Fenton were able to understand their situation and demonstrate their readiness and maturity.

The completion of the process is realized during the Queen Fairy masque. Again, it is Mrs. Page who has proposed and designed the event. She has used the old tale of "Herne the hunter" as the pretext for its implementation.

The Queen Fairy masque may seem to be a rather silly and irrelevant folk ceremony. In reality, the masque that takes place in

Windsor Park is an illustration of quite an advanced spiritual event. All of the tasks of this particular developmental stage are accomplished during the masque. First, Windsor is cleansed from its spiritual impurities, i.e., Falstaff's mischievous nature is exposed and neutralized; Mr. Ford is cured of his jealousies; Doctor Caius and Slender prove that they are unworthy of marrying Anne because they are incapable of recognizing her true "colour". Secondly, the cleansing enables the formation of an octagonal union.

The masque is performed in Windsor Park. The event starts with an invocation delivered by Mistress Quickly:

"Fairies, black, grey, green, and white,
You moonshine revellers and shades of night,
You orphan heirs of fixed destiny,
Attend your office and your quality."
(*The Merry Wives of Windsor*, *V.5*)

Then Pistol announces the specific tasks that are to be performed:

"Elves, list your names; silence, you airy toys.
Cricket, to Windsor chimneys shalt thou leap:
Where fires thou find'st unraked and hearths unswept,
There pinch the maids as blue as bilberry:
Our radiant queen hates sluts and sluttery."
(*The Merry Wives of Windsor*, *V.5*)

Although the phrase "Our radiant queen" may be read as a reference to Queen Elizabeth I, its inner meaning applies to the Fairy Queen, represented by Anne Page. The entire event in Windsor Park is a preparation for Anne's marriage. We may recognize that fires "unraked" and hearths "unswept" are symbolic references to the presence of "impurities" within the previous channel of the evolutionary transmission. The cleansing process is the preparation for the octagonal union.

The masque contains direct references to the Order of the Garter. The following quote describes the chamber where the Knights of the Order of the Garter gather during their annual reunions:

> "Search Windsor Castle, elves, within and out:
> Strew good luck, ouphes, on every sacred room:
> That it may stand till the perpetual doom,
> In state as wholesome as in state 'tis fit,
> Worthy the owner, and the owner it.
> The several chairs of order look you scour
> With juice of balm and every precious flower:
> Each fair instalment, coat, and several crest,
> With loyal blazon, evermore be blest!"
> (*The Merry Wives of Windsor*, V.5)

"The several chairs of order" refer to the individual stalls assigned to the members of the Order in St. George's Chapel at Windsor Castle, the Knights' traditional meeting place. In the following quote Mistress Quickly, who is disguised as a fairy, gives instructions to the other fairies. The readers might recognize that Mistress Quickly's instructions contain elements of a ceremonial meeting of the Order:

> "And nightly, meadow-fairies, look you sing,
> Like to the Garter's compass, in a ring:
> The expressure that it bears, green let it be,
> More fertile-fresh than all the field to see;
> And 'Honi soit qui mal y pense' write
> In emerald tufts, flowers purple, blue and white;
> Let sapphire, pearl and rich embroidery,
> Buckled below fair knighthood's bending knee:
> Fairies use flowers for their charactery."
> (*The Merry Wives of Windsor*, V.5)

The fairies are asked to use "emerald tufts" and flowers to express the Order's motto "Honi soit qui mal y pense". As pointed out in the analysis of "Richard II", "Honi soit qui mal y pense" is a salutation to the "cupbearer", i.e., the Order's spiritual guide. The event is performed in a ring (a "garter") formed by the participants. Such a "garter" is a reference to the basic unit of a group of initiates. The above quote refers to purple, blue, and white, i.e., the colours used by the Order of the Garter in the 17th century.

One important thing, however, is the fact that it is not the Knights but the "fairies" who execute the event. Secondly, the participants of the event are members of the middle and working classes. Among the fairies are Mistress Quickly, Sir Hugh Evans, and Pistol. The effect of the event on the participants is indicated by the changes induced in Mistress Quickly, Hugh Evans, and Pistol. Previously Mistress Quickly and Sir Hugh Evans could not understand each other because of their linguistic deficiencies. Now, however, Sir Hugh Evans has "miraculously" been healed from his speaking idiosyncrasies. Mistress Quickly, who previously mixed the meaning of words, impeccably delivers her poetic message that also includes a phrase in French. In this way, Shakespeare indicates that Mistress Quickly represents the fourth (*white*) impulse of the evolutionary charge. At the time of "As You Like It" this particular impulse was represented by Audrey, a shepherdess. Mistress Quickly and Pistol form the fourth couple of the octagon. Shakespeare inserted a brief episode to show how an ordinary person may get into contact with a developmental activity. It is the episode when Pistol meets Mistress Quickly, and immediately recognizes that there is something special about her:

"This punk is one of Cupid's carriers:
Clap on more sails; pursue; up with your fights:
Give fire: she is my prize, or ocean whelm them all!"
(*The Merry Wives of Windsor*, II.2)

At the end of the play Pistol is a different person. His characteristically garbled way of speaking has also been miraculously improved. During the masque Pistol speaks flawlessly and fluently. Let's recall that Pistol fought in the Battle of Agincourt. As indicated by King Henry V in his St. Crispin's Day speech, it was this experience that did "gentle his condition".

During the Queen Fairy masque, the evolutionary charge carried by "Elizabeth" was transferred into the middle and lower classes of 17th century England. Mrs. Page, Mrs. Ford, Anne Page, and Mistress Quickly represent the current manifestations of the evolutionary charge invested in Windsor. Unlike the octagons formed previously in the Forest of Arden and Vienna, the octagon activated in Windsor is fully balanced. There was no need for patches. This is why the colour green appears ("green let it be"). The sterile green box of Doctor Caius is now replaced by an active structure. As indicated earlier, the appearance of the colour green marks the formation of the enneagon: a ninth point appears within the octagonal inner structure. This will permit the addition of an extra dimension to this new structure, i.e., to expand it into the higher state.

William Page

It is important to notice that the colour *green* was not among the colours of the Order of the Garter. The colours used by the Order of the Garter are related to the previous phases of the process. Now, however, *green* appears within the English society. The colour *green* is a sign that the conditions were correctly prepared for the appearance of a spiritual king. It was this king that was foretold by the witches in "Macbeth".

So, who is this king?

Robin is a page serving Falstaff. Previously, he was serving the Royal Prince. At one point, Mrs. Page demands that Falstaff give Robin to her as a token of his love. Falstaff agrees. Here is Mrs. Page conversation with Robin:

Mrs. Page:

"Nay, keep your way, little gallant; you were wont to be a follower, but now you are a leader. Whether had you rather lead mine eyes, or eye your master's heels?"

Robin:

"I had rather, forsooth, go before you like a man than follow him like a dwarf."

Mrs. Page:

"O, you are a flattering boy: now I see you'll be a courtier."
(*The Merry Wives of Windsor*, III.2)

...

"Thou'rt a good boy: this secrecy of thine shall be a tailor to thee and shall make thee a new doublet and hose."
(*The Merry Wives of Windsor*, III.3)

Mr. and Mrs. Page adopted Robin as their son. Robin's name is changed to William Page. William appears in the next episode where Mrs. Page is asking Sir Hugh Evans to examine her son, so she may see how much he has learned from being in grammar school:

"Sir Hugh, my husband says my son profits nothing in the world at his book. I pray you, ask him some questions in his accidence."

After the examination, Mrs. Page concludes:

"He is a better scholar than I thought he was."
(*The Merry Wives of Windsor, IV.1*)

As has been pointed out in the discussion of "As You Like It", Shakespeare used the character of "William" to describe some of his own experiences.

It is said that it would take an ordinary man a thousand years to experience what a wise man experiences in one lifetime. Shakespeare incorporated this relationship in the plays and the sonnets, respectively. The plays encompass the evolutionary progress of western civilization realized over several historical millennia, while the sonnets illustrate Shakespeare's personal progress which he achieved in his lifetime. In order to calibrate these two types of experiences, Shakespeare had to include himself in the plays. Namely, Shakespeare's disclosed details about himself and his background by choosing "William Page" as a character that represents him. But even these few details about the author were encoded in quite an intricate form. In this way Shakespeare indicates that he had to remain anonymous in order to maximize the impact of his writings. This is in accordance with the rule which says that the true artist is him whose work is anonymous, for in that way nobody stands between the learner and that which is to be learned.

Shakespeare inserted a few episodes from his own life into several plays. In order to be consisted with his narrative, "William" appears only in those plays, which are overlapped with "The Merry Wives of Windsor", i.e., "Henry IV", "Henry V", and "As You Like It". As indicated earlier, William appeared in "As You Like It". Now it is clear why Touchstone did not allow William to marry Audrey; marrying Audrey was not William's role. William was to fulfil a different function. At that time, however, neither William of Arden nor the overall situation within the French branch was ready for fulfilling this function.

An earlier stage of William Page's life is illustrated in "Henry IV". He appears there as the page of Prince Harry. At one point, Prince Harry gave the boy to Falstaff:

> "And the boy that I gave Falstaff: He had him from
> me Christian; and look, if the fat villain have not
> transformed him ape."
> (*Henry IV, part 2, II.2*)

The above words were spoken by Prince Harry in the same episode where he was talking with Poins about Nell, Poins' sister. The boy was privy to this conversation. In other words, he witnessed the cause of the sterility of the English branch.

During the war in France at the time of "Henry V", the boy was a servant to Pistol. The boy realized that Pistol and his two companions, Nym and Bardolph, were just thieves and liars. According to the boy, these three would steal anything and call it a trophy. Instead of fighting, they would keep themselves busy stealing. The boy complained that they would like him to join them in their misdeeds. He refused, because for him taking something from someone's pocket and putting it into his own would be just plain stealing. Such villainies nauseated him:

> "As young as I am, I have observed these three
> swashers. I am boy to them all three: but all they
> three, though they would serve me, could not be man
> to me; for indeed three such antics do not amount to
> a man. [...] I must leave them, and seek some better service:
> their villany goes against my weak stomach, and
> therefore I must cast it up."
> (*Henry V, III.2*)

Later on the boy ended up together with Pistol in the Battle of Agincourt. The boy was fluent in French. He acted as a translator for Pistol when Pistol captured Monsieur le Fer:

Pistol:

"Come hither, boy: ask me this slave in French
What is his name."

Boy:

Ecoutez: comment etes-vous appele?
(*Henry V, IV.4*)

The boy could not fulfil his function while in the company of the
Royal Prince. Prince Harry did not recognize what the boy's
potential was. Nonchalantly, Harry gave the boy to Falstaff. The
boy had to wait until the overall situation was correctly aligned.
Afterwards the boy reappeared as Robin in Windsor at the time of
"The Merry Wives of Windsor". We may notice that among those
present in Windsor, the boy and Pistol are the only two characters
who experienced the Battle of Agincourt. In other words, the boy
had also gained "nobility" in Agincourt.

The boy's fluency in French indicates that he was born or grew up
in a noble family of French origin. We may presume that, in
accordance with the custom, at the age of seven years he was sent
to a court to be a pageboy. It looks like William ended up at the
royal court. As a pageboy, he would receive training in horseback
riding, hunting, hawking, combat, singing, playing chess, etc., etc.
Shakespeare inserted into his plays several episodes with pageboys.
The pageboys are one of the most respected among Shakespeare's
characters. When Rosalind disguises herself as a boy, she changes
her name to Ganymede, i.e., Jupiter's page:

"I'll have no worse a name than Jove's own page;
And therefore look you call me Ganymede."
(*As You Like It, III.1*)

In other words, a Shakespeare's *page* serves as a messenger from the
Realm. Consequently, Shakespeare's pageboys are actively involved
in serving the evolutionary process. For example, in "Timon of

Athens" a Page delivers instructions from Marina to Timon. Moth, the Page of Don Adriano in "Love's Labour's Lost", explains the meaning of the colour code used in the symbolic illustration of evolutionary impulses.

William has been trained in Windsor Park, which is an equivalent to the Forest of Arden. He took part in the masque when the Windsor octagon was activated. Afterwards he is ready for the second part of his training. According to Mrs. Page, William is going to be a courtier. In other words, William will be "roasted" on both sides: he will be trained in the "forest" and at "court". It is then that William will meet the Indian Prince. The Prince will prepare him for the assimilation of the full evolutionary charge that was activated in Windsor Park. The full details of William's spiritual training and his experiences are described in the sonnets. Finally, he will appear as a guide in "A Midsummer Night's Dream", i.e., the concluding play of Shakespeare's narrative.

William has been trained to become the future spiritual king who is to direct the next stage of the evolutionary process. He was raised in a family of custodians. Through Mrs. Page of Windsor, Rosalind of Arden, and Helena of Rousillon, he is a spiritual heir of Gerard de Narbon, the last Troubadour. For many generations, this family has been actively involved in the preservation of the evolutionary process, initially within the French and then within the English branches. The members of this "family" were the custodians of the evolutionary charge invested in "Elizabeth I".

William absorbed the spiritual charge from "Elizabeth" by assimilating the Windsor octagon. Cranmer, at the conclusion of "Henry VIII", indicated the appearance of this spiritual king who would be reborn "from the sacred ashes of her honour":

"but as when
The bird of wonder dies, the maiden phoenix,
Her ashes new create another heir,

As great in admiration as herself;
So shall she leave her blessedness to one,
When heaven shall call her from this cloud of darkness,
Who from the sacred ashes of her honour
Shall star-like rise, as great in fame as she was."
(*Henry VIII, V.5*)

In Sonnet 1, the Indian Prince alluded to William's future role in the following way:

"Thou that art now the world's fresh ornament,
And only herald to the gaudy spring"
(*Sonnet 1, 9-10*)

Now it is possible to fully appreciate the progress made between the times of "Henry IV" and "The Merry Wives of Windsor". The spiritual impotency of England at the time of "Henry IV" was symbolically illustrated in the episode with Prince Harry and Poins, where they were talking about Nell, Poins' sister. Now, this arrangement is replaced by Fenton, William, and Anne, William's sister. Fenton marries Anne. William is the future guide. The evolutionary impotency of the medieval royals has been transmuted into the full potency of a member of 17th century English middle class.

"The Merry Wives of Windsor" carries an important message to those who are familiar with the evolutionary process. The nature of the message suggests that the play was intended for a performance during one of the Garter Feasts. It may be presumed that the play served as an announcement of the transfer of the transmission channel from the Knights of the Order of the Garter into a select group among the middle and lower classes. This transfer was needed to increase the effectiveness of the process. The previous transmission channel was exhausted. It had lost its developmental capacity and gradually turned into sterile ceremonies. Elizabeth I, the Virgin Queen, was the last link of the previous transmission channel. The advanced projection required a fresh and fertile transmission medium. It seems that, at that time, certain members of the middle and the working classes were properly fit for discharging such a noble function.

The Second Millennium

According to Shakespeare's presentation, the modern European evolutionary cycle came to its completion at the beginning of the 17th century. It was then that the Sicilian and the Cypriot links converged and formed a new evolutionary cell in Europe. It was then that Jupiter's oracle

"lopped branches, which, being dead many years,
shall after revive, be jointed to the old stock and
freshly grow"
(*Cymbeline*, *V.4*)"

was fulfilled. The new cell was embedded in a certain fraction of the European society. This group of people experienced a taste of human perfection. It was a brief and fleeting experience. It did not last long. Nevertheless, it marked the commencement of the second spiritual millennium of the modern world. Shakespeare described this experience in "A Midsummer Night's Dream". The play is the concluding episode of Shakespeare's narrative.

A Midsummer Night's Dream

Athens as presented in "A Midsummer Night's Dream" encompasses the European experiences of the most recent as well as the previous evolutionary cycles. Let's recall that Shakespeare used Milan as New Athens to describe the evolutionary progress within the Sicilian link. Athens of "A Midsummer Night's Dream" is the site of the concluding episode of the sequence that includes Athens of "Timon of Athens", Milan of "Two Gentlemen of Verona", and Milan of "The Tempest". The inner structure of Athens of "A Midsummer Night's Dream" has been developed within the final stages of the Italian evolutionary branch. The leading aspects of Athens are Theseus, Lysander and Demetrius. Theseus represents Athens' intellect; Lysander and Demetrius are two aspects of the heart.

The young lovers Demetrius and Lysander are the current reflections of Valentine and Proteus from "Two Gentlemen of Verona". They encompass the experiences of the young men of the Italian branch. Similarly, Helena and Hermia are the current projections of the corresponding impulses invested into the Italian branch. The appearance of Helena and Hermia in Athens means that Miranda did not go to Naples. After her encounter with Ferdinand on Prospero's Island, this particular impulse was transferred back to Athens (Milan). While entering the ordinary state of Athens, this impulse was split again into two. Helena, the taller of the two, represents an impulse of unitive energy (*red*); Hermia is an impulse of creative energy (*yellow*). Previously, these two impulses were manifested within the Italian branch by Sylvia and Julia in "Two Gentlemen of Verona", Juliet and Rosaline in "Romeo and Juliet", Bianca and Katharina in "The Taming of the Shrew", Portia and Jessica in "The Merchant of Venice".

The adventures of Demetrius and Lysander clearly demonstrate that they have not been purified from their developmental deficiencies. They are still driven by sensual desires. This is indicated by Demetrius' and Lysander's vulnerability to a magic juice and to an herb called Dian's bud. The magic juice is made from Cupid's flower; Dian's bud is an antidote to the juice:

"Dian's bud o'er Cupid's flower
Hath such force and blessed power."
(*A Midsummer Night's Dream, IV.1*)

In his last two sonnets, Shakespeare explained that only corrupted men are affected by Cupid's flower and Dian's bud. Spiritually developed men and women are immune to "this rough magic".

Demetrius' inconstancy, however, was patched up with Cupid's flower. Similarly, Lysander's love for Hermia was restored with the help of Dian's bud. This means that the union of the heart experienced in the forest near Mantua at the conclusion of "Two Gentlemen of Verona" was not permanent. This brief experience was needed to prepare the impulse of unitive energy for Prospero's project. After their return from the forest to Milan, these two aspects of the Italian heart were separated. Their inner states were reversed to their ordinary ones.

Theseus is the current representation of the Duke of Milan. He encompasses the experiences of Prospero. Theseus is presented as the conqueror of Hippolyta, Queen of the Amazons. According to Shakespeare, the Amazons represented the ordinary senses. (As illustrated in "Timon of Athens", the Amazons were ruled by Cupid). Prospero was prone to Juno's distracting influence. Juno's was a manifestation of a maculate Black Lady. Through this experience, however, Theseus was well prepared to conquer Hippolyta. Hippolyta is the current manifestation of the White Lady.

The Fairyland of Oberon and Titania is much richer than Prospero's "bare island". Now we may realize that Prospero's Island described in "The Tempest" represented only a tiny fragment of the Fairyland that is described in "A Midsummer's Night Dream". This particular higher state was activated prior to Prospero's arrival.

The world of fairies is a symbolic illustration of the higher state that is now attached to Athens. The higher state operates outside of the ordinary limitations of time and space. The fairies represent the various invisible forces operating within the higher state. Through this state it is possible to exercise extraordinary skills and power which control the entire environment. The quality and characteristics of the fairy kingdom are a reflection of the spiritual purity of a particular being. The more advanced the being, the purer and more cooperative are the invisible forces that are attached to and conjugated with it. In "A Midsummer Night's Dream", King Oberon and Queen Titania represent these super corporeal aspects.

The fairies are various manifestations of Ariel, the spirit who served Prospero. At the conclusion of "The Tempest", Ariel was freed from Prospero's command. This is how Ariel described his future freedom:

"Where the bee sucks, there suck I:
In a cowslip's bell I lie;
There I couch when owls do cry.
On the bat's back I do fly
After summer merrily."
(*The Tempest, V.1*)

One of the fairies in "A Midsummer Night's Dream" provides a clue to the sort of freedom which was granted to Ariel. Here is the description of the fairy's current services:

"And I serve the fairy queen,
To dew her orbs upon the green.
The cowslips tall her pensioners be:
In their gold coats spots you see;
Those be rubies, fairy favours,
In those freckles live their savours:
I must go seek some dewdrops here
And hang a pearl in every cowslip's ear."
(*A Midsummer Night's Dream, II.1*)

Ariel's freedom meant his return to the Fairyland. Ariel wanted to be freed from the control of Prospero, a mere mortal being, so he could serve Oberon, the King of the Fairyland. Now Ariel appears as Puck. Here is Puck's comment in which he expresses his feeling towards mortals:

"Lord, what fools these mortals be!"
(*A Midsummer Night's Dream, III.2*)

One of the new features of the Fairyland is the presence of Oberon. Shakespeare adopted the character of Oberon from that of a sorcerer in the legendary history of Gaul of the 5th century. Oberon marks the first appearance of a new line of subdued deities of Western European tradition. He is the current replacement for the Boar, Venus' jealous consort from "Venus and Adonis". Oberon explains to Puck that they themselves are a different sort of spirits:

"But we are spirits of another sort."
(*A Midsummer Night's Dream, III.2*)

Because of the break in the Sicilian link, this higher state is still contaminated by residual impurities inherited from ancient times. Titania represents a demigoddess who, like Juno, is maculated by the experiences from the past. Titania is the current manifestation of a maculate Black Lady (Phoebe, after whom the Black Lady of the Forest of Arden was named, was also one of the mythological Titans). Her impurity is highlighted by the fact that she is prone to the effect of the magic juice. Her deficiency is manifested by her quarrel with Oberon. The quarrel is projected down onto the ordinary state and disturbs Athens. First, it affects Hippolyta. In a couple of instances, Hippolyta shows traces of defiance towards Theseus. Another effect of Titania's transgression is manifested by Demetrius' inexplicable change of heart. He leaves Helena and pursues Hermia. This disturbance is further enhanced by Egeus' animosity towards old Nader, Helena's father. Egeus, Hermia's father, tries to use Demetrius' sudden attraction to Hermia to settle old scores with Helena's father. This animosity between the fathers is an echo of the ancient grudge inherited from Verona.

Despite his advanced state, Theseus is unable to fix the situation. Like Prospero, his ability is partially maculated by the impurities within the Fairyland. To be effective, a corrective action has to be implemented within the Fairyland by an experienced traveller, i.e., a guide is needed to perform such a task. This is why Theseus has to ask for help. Fortunately, there is such a guide in Athens. Theseus' request is answered.

This guiding aspect was developed within the English branch at the conclusion of "The Merry Wives of Windsor". At the end of the Fairy Queen masque, the balanced octagon was activated: the Windsor octagon could be transmuted into an enneagon. This provided the needed conditions for the appearance of a new guide. At that time the guide was identified as William Page. Now William Page appears in Athens as Nick Bottom, a stage-struck weaver. Nick Bottom is the first in the line of the spiritual "kings" who were projected into the middle class of 17ᵗʰ century England. He is the spiritual king who was foretold by the witches in "Macbeth" and by Cranmer at the conclusion of "Henry VIII".

Nick Bottom encompasses the experiences that previously took place within the French, Bohemian, and English branches. His inner state is marked by the colour *green*. Here is a description of Nick Bottom given in the final scene of the play:

> "These lily lips,
> This cherry nose,
> These yellow cowslip cheeks,
> Are gone, are gone:
> Lovers, make moan:
> His eyes were green as leeks."
> (*A Midsummer Night's Dream, V.1*)

The other colours mentioned in this description represent the impulses that are present at Theseus' court during the mechanicals' performance, i.e., *white* (lily), *red* (cherry), and *yellow* (cowslip). They apply to Hippolyta, Helena, and Hermia, respectively. Now we may fully appreciate the economy and efficiency of the Bohemian intervention implemented at the time of "Twelfth Night". The intervention was needed so that 17th century Western Europe could be provided with a guide who would be able to direct the next phase of the evolutionary process.

Nick Bottom resides among the mechanicals and is highly respected by them. He has to communicate with them according to the measure of their understanding. Despite his malapropisms, he is perfectly understood by his fellow mechanicals. According to the mechanicals, Nick Bottom:

> "hath simply the best wit of any handicraft
> man in Athens."

> "Yea and the best person too; and he is a very
> paramour for a sweet voice."
> (*A Midsummer Night's Dream, IV.2*)

By seemingly wanting to assume the parts of Thisbe and the lion, Bottom teaches the mechanicals how to perform these particular roles. The mechanical's rehearsal takes place "at the duke's oak", in the forest near Athens. This is a repeat of the Fairy Queen masque performed at the old oak tree in Windsor Park in "The Merry Wives of Windsor". This particular group was formed as a result of the overlap of the final stages of the French, Bohemian and English branches. It was at that time that the evolutionary function was transferred from the royal channel onto select individuals of the English middle and working classes. In other words, it is now a group of "mechanicals" who provides a link to the transmission chain. Nick Bottom and the mechanicals constitute a cell of the new civilization formed within 17th century European society. Their role is to protect and advance the evolutionary process. This group uses theatre to inject developmental ideas into 17th century Europe. We may recognize in the character of Nick Bottom the author of Shakespeare's plays; the "mechanicals" are the King's Men, Shakespeare's theatre company. Previously the Knights of the Order of the Garter were charged with protecting the evolutionary process. The transfer of this evolutionary function was symbolically indicated by the list of the Principal Actors included in the 1623 First Folio. Like the founding members of the Order of the Garter, the Principal Actors were arranged into two groups or garters; each garter consisting of thirteen members.

Let's recall that the original plan called for a reigning king to acquire such a guiding capacity. This would allow for a recognizable guide to be in charge of the evolutionary process in Europe. A visible and recognizable guide would provide the conditions for the most effective implementation of the next phases of the process. Such an attempt at having a recognizable guide was previously made within the Roman evolutionary cycle, where Julius Caesar was supposed to play such a role. It did not work in Rome. Shakespeare indicates that neither was it possible to install such a function in 17th century Europe. Therefore, the overall approach had to be adjusted accordingly. Instead of a reigning king and his court, the King's Men, i.e., a playwright and his theatre troupe were empowered with such a function. Nick Bottom directs the overall process, but his guiding function remains invisible to a rational mind or a speculative intellect. A spiritual guide who, like Bottom, has to operate in disguise in order to discharge his function, is the main feature of Shakespeare's plays and sonnets. A guide is represented by such characters as Othello, Don Pedro, Petruchio, Feste, Lucio.

Nick Bottom is able to travel to the Fairyland to fix the situation there. There are only two human beings that are capable of accessing the Fairyland, i.e., Nick Bottom and the Indian boy. Now we may recognize the Indian Prince in "a lovely boy, stolen from an Indian king". The visits to the tent with the *elephant*, granted by the Indian Prince to the poet, were actually journeys to the

Fairyland, i.e., to a higher inspirational state. Bottom refers to these journeys as dreams:

"I have had a most rare
vision. I have had a dream, past the wit of man to
say what dream it was: man is but an ass, if he go
about to expound this dream. Methought I was -there
is no man can tell what. Methought I was, -and
methought I had, -but man is but a patched fool, if
he will offer to say what methought I had. The eye
of man hath not heard, the ear of man hath not
seen, man's hand is not able to taste, his tongue
to conceive, nor his heart to report, what my dream was."
(*A Midsummer Night's Dream*, IV.1)

According to Bottom, ordinary man does not have any idea about such "dreams". It was during these visits that the Fairyland was gradually developed. Now this higher state is accessible to Bottom directly from the forest, which represents the currently operating intermediate state. This is why he does not have to pass over stormy seas to get to the fairyland. At one point, it was possible to bring Prospero there. Guided by "a most auspicious star", Prospero was taken away from Milan (i.e., New Athens) and tossed upon the Island. At the time of Prospero's visit, Nick Bottom was trained by the Indian Prince. The Indian Prince was the invisible guide who was monitoring and directing Prospero's adventures illustrated in "The Tempest". It was the Indian Prince who warned Prospero against Juno's plot. Prospero also compared his experiences to "dreams":

"We are such stuff
As dreams are made on, and our little life
Is rounded with a sleep."
(*The Tempest*, IV.1)

Prospero indicated that the purpose of mankind is to serve as a base for developing such dreams, i.e., the higher states of the mind ("we are such stuff as dreams are made on").

In Shakespeare's sonnets there are echoes of Bottom's journeys to the "Fairyland". In Sonnet 50, for example, the poet refers to a *beast* that carried him there. The "beast" is a reference to the *ass* that allows the poet to travel to the Fairyland where he may meet the Indian Prince. The poet's joy remains in the Fairyland; his return to Athens means separation from the Indian Prince, his spiritual guide. In this context, the meaning of the "beast" and the poet's hesitance to move faster become quite obvious. This why such a journey is perceived by him as "heavy":

> How heavy do I journey on the way,
> When what I seek (my weary travel's end)
> Doth teach that ease and that repose to say
> Thus far the miles are measured from thy friend.
> The beast that bears me, tired with my woe,
> Plods dully on, to bear that weight in me,
> As if by some instinct the wretch did know
> His rider lov'd not speed being made from thee:
> The bloody spur cannot provoke him on,
> That some-times anger thrusts into his hide,
> Which heavily he answers with a groan,
> More sharp to me than spurring to his side,
> > For that same groan doth put this in my mind,
> > My grief lies onward and my joy behind.

The poet complains that leaving the higher state and going back to the ordinary state makes him sad and distraught. It is hard for him to separate himself from the Indian Prince's company. The "beast" that carries him moves very slowly. The beast's behaviour is a reflection of the poet's hesitance. The poet implies that the poor beast somehow knows that he does not want to move quickly away from his joy. Even with angry blows, the poet is not able to force his beast to move faster. The beast answers with a groan, which hurts the poet even more, because it reminds him that his challenges and difficulties are ahead of him, and all true joys are left behind.

Nick Bottom's encounters with Titania and "a lovely boy, stolen from an Indian king" were also described by Shakespeare in his sonnets. In the sonnets, the Indian Prince appears as the Fair Youth and Titania as the Black Lady. The poet described his first encounters with the Black Lady in Sonnets 127-128:

"In the old age black was not counted fair,
Or if it were, it bore not beauty's name:
But now is black beauty's successive heir."
(*Sonnet 127, 1-3*)

In these lines the poet emphasizes the fact that the appearance of the Black Lady is a new experience for ordinary man.

Now it is possible to understand the complications of the poet's encounters with the Black Lady of the sonnets. This amorous Black Lady was the wife of Oberon. The poet was not to be united with her. Instead, the poet was trained by his guide in how to deal effectively with this rather difficult experience. This training was needed so he would be able to deliver a rebuke to Titania. In order to discharge his function properly, Bottom has to be immune to Titania's promiscuity. We may note that during his encounter with Titania, Bottom rather ignores her and enjoys chatting with her fairies. Bottom's behaviour annoys Titania. At one point she interrupts Bottom's chatting and asks her fairies to "bring him silently" to her bower:

"Come, wait upon him; lead him to my bower.
Tie up my love's tongue bring him silently."
(*A Midsummer Night's Dream, III.1*)

Bottom's encounter with Titania may be easily misinterpreted by assuming that there was sexual intercourse between Bottom and the Queen of the fairies. This is definitively not so. Titania's temptation of Bottom is equivalent to Juno's attempt at charming Prospero. Bottom's project would be nullified if he allowed himself to be seduced by Titania. Titania's comment clarifies the situation:

"The moon methinks looks with a watery eye;
And when she weeps, weeps every little flower,
Lamenting some enforced chastity."
(*A Midsummer Night's Dream, III.1*)

Titania indicates that at this very moment the watery moon enforces "chastity". As a matter of fact, the "chastity" enforced upon Titania is the most remarkable moment in the entire canon of Shakespeare's plays. It encapsulates the outcome of the modern evolutionary process. It is this enforced chastity that symbolically demonstrates the achieved progress. There are no more corrupted demigods or demigoddesses acting as the prime movers of human destiny. The Boar of "Venus and Adonis" is now replaced by a highly developed man who supervises the process. A sexual encounter between Titania and Bottom would bring the process back to the ancient times when demigods and demigoddesses were interfering in human affairs. Symbolically, it would nullify the evolutionary progress achieved over a period of several spiritual millennia.

The Indian Prince, i.e., the Fair Youth of the sonnets, was the poet's spiritual guide. At this point it is important to notice that Titania's attraction to the Indian Prince was of the same nature as her fascination with Bottom. The following quote describes her fondling the Indian boy:

"Crowns him with flowers and makes him all her joy."
(*A Midsummer Night's Dream, II.1*)

And here is a description of her caressing Bottom:

"For she his hairy temples then had rounded with a coronet
of fresh and fragrant flowers."
(*A Midsummer Night's Dream, IV.1*)

The encounters of the Indian Prince and Bottom with Titania help
us to understand the nature of the poet's experiences with the
Black Lady described in the sonnets. It also helps us to grasp the
symbolic meaning of Shakespeare's presentation to know that, at
that time, the evolutionary process was directed from "the farthest
Steppe of India", i.e., the centre was located in north-western India.
It was directed by the King from India, the father of the Indian
Prince. This is why Oberon also came to Athens from India:

"Why art thou here,
Come from the farthest Steppe of India?
(*A Midsummer Night's Dream, II.1*)

In "A Midsummer Night's Dream" Shakespeare indicates how the
visits to the Fairyland were arranged. Namely, they were scripted
into the mechanicals' rehearsals. Although Peter Quincy brought
the script of "Pyramus and Thisbe", it was Bottom who drafted it
and then adapted it for the performance. Only Bottom would be
able to have Puck playing an active role in the mechanicals'
rehearsal. Puck's entry during the mechanicals' rehearsal is
indicated in the script when Bottom "goes but to see a noise that
he heard, and is to come again":

"But hark, a voice! stay thou but here awhile,
And by and by I will to thee appear."
(*A Midsummer Night's Dream, III.1*)

A moment later when Bottom appears to the mechanicals, his head
is transformed by Puck into that of an ass. Bottom has to be
transformed into an "ass", because this allows him to discharge his

function. Bottom's transformation into "some vile thing" is needed for the magic juice to have the desired impact on Titania. In other words, Bottom's transformation into an ass was included in the original script of "Pyramus and Thisbe". For obvious reasons, this particular episode is not needed when the play is presented at Theseus' court.

Let's recall that previously we met such a character in "Much Ado About Nothing". It was Dogberry, another "ass", who played a similar role. Shakespeare, for no apparent reason, wanted the audience to remember that Dogberry was a special kind of "ass":

"But, masters, remember that I am an ass;
though it be not written down,
yet forget not that I am an ass."
(*Much Ado About Nothing, IV.2*)

This was an indication that this kind of "ass" appears in another play to discharge a similar role.

After his return from the Fairyland, Bottom and his mechanicals stage at Theseus' court their presentation of "Pyramus and Thisbe".

Pyramus and Thisbe

It was Bottom who arranged with Theseus that the mechanicals' performance of "Pyramus and Thisbe" be selected for presentation:

"for the short and the long is, our
play is preferred."
(*A Midsummer Night's Dream, V.1*)

Bottom delivered this message to the mechanicals prior to Theseus' conversation with Philostrate, the Master of the Revels.

During Theseus' wedding dinner, his guests are talking about their adventures from the previous night. They are trying to figure out what happened to them in the forest during that very strange night. It is then that the mechanicals arrive and Peter Quince delivers his prologue:

"If we offend, it is with our good will.
That you should think, we come not to offend,
But with good will. To show our simple skill,
That is the true beginning of our end.
Consider then we come but in despite.
We do not come as minding to contest you,
Our true intent is. All for your delight
We are not here. That you should here repent you,
The actors are at hand and by their show
You shall know all that you are like to know."
(*A Midsummer Night's Dream, V.1*)

At first glance, Quincy's words do not make much sense. Then, the audience notices that, if Quince had read this speech with "proper" punctuation, it would mean:

"If we happen to insult you, we hope you know that we
didn't come here intending to offend you. We come here
with the good intention of showing off our little bit of skill.
That's all we want to do. Please keep in mind that we came
here only to please you. Our true intention is to delight you.
We didn't come here to make you feel sorry."

Such understanding of Quince's prologue is an example of the working of intellectual reflexes. The reflexes kick in and provide a satisfying explanation. Demetrius and Lysander, as well as the audience, are pleased with their own cleverness and are having fun laughing at the seemingly ridiculous performance of the mechanicals. In this way they miss the message that is specially prepared for them. Namely, the mechanicals arrive at Theseus' court to explain what really happened during that previous night. In this context, Quincy's introduction, with its unchanged punctuation, says:

> "Our intention is not to please you, but to tell you 'all that you are like to know'. You, however, may be offended by what you find about yourself. In other words, we do not come here with the intention of making you happy. Our performance will fulfil its purpose by showing you your ignorance, so you may be able to do something about it."

Quincy's introduction applies to all of Shakespeare's plays and to all audiences and readers. Let's keep in mind that Shakespeare's plays may seem to flatter the audience, but only if the audience's self-conceit allows them to do so.

The structure and the content of "Pyramus and Thisbe" is quite complex. With a few symbols and a few seemingly confused words, this play-within-the play summarizes the evolutionary gains achieved in 17th century Europe. This is why Philostrate introduces "Pyramus and Thisbe" as "tedious" and "brief".

The original story of "Pyramus and Thisbe" was set in the ancient city of Babylon. In this way Shakespeare indicates that the causes of the lovers' difficulties were events that occurred in ancient times. It was this "ancient grudge" that led to the collapse of the Hellenic civilization. The ancient world was disconnected from the chain of transmission. The transmission gap occurred in the higher state and its effects were recorded in ancient myths as the interference of the various demigods and demigoddesses into human evolutionary progress.

"Pyramus and Thisbe" contains five episodes. These episodes may be entitled "The Wall", "The Lion", "The Moon", "The Bloody Mantle", and "The Lovers' Death". The titles of the episodes refer to various symbols used by Shakespeare. The episodes are presented in reverse chronological order, i.e., starting with the most recent event. In this respect "Pyramus and Thisbe", or Bottom's "most rare vision", is a continuation of the five stages of Pericles' inspirational vision. "Pericles, Prince of Tyre" summarizes the evolutionary efforts implemented over the time span from antiquity till the initiation of the modern branches in Western Europe. "Pyramus and Thisbe" summarizes the outcome realized through the implementation of the modern branches.

The Lovers' Death

Let's start with the last episode. This episode refers to the beginning of the story. It is set up at the time of "Romeo and Juliet". The fact, that Romeo and Juliet face the same obstacles as their Babylonian predecessors, points out that Italy in the 16th century faced the same evolutionary challenge as ancient Babylon in the 20th century BC. The death of Pyramus and Thisbe in Babylon did not have any effect on the removal of these obstacles.

However, there was a significant difference between the ancient world and the Italy of "Romeo and Juliet". At the time of "Romeo and Juliet" an evolutionary distribution grid was put in place and Italy was linked to it. The original story of "Pyramus and Thisbe" was replayed in "Romeo and Juliet", but within a context that belonged to a higher turn on the evolutionary spiral. It was then that the "wall", symbolically representing the "ancient grudge", came down for the first time. This is why, at the end of his performance, Bottom draws the audience's attention to this important fact:

"No assure you; the wall is down that
parted their fathers."
(*A Midsummer Night's Dream, V.1*)

Bottom points out that this episode does not belong to the original
story from Babylon. This particular episode describes the removal
of the first layer of the wall, which reappeared at the time of
"Romeo and Juliet". It took several thousands of years to arrive at
this point.

It is important to note that the final episode of "Pyramus and
Thisbe" does not take place in the "moonshine":

"Tongue, lose thy light;
Moon take thy flight."
(*A Midsummer Night's Dream, V.1*)

Bottom emphasizes this by sending the Moon away.

The Lion

"Romeo and Juliet" was a preparation for the final stage of the
Italian branch described in "Two Gentlemen of Verona". It was
then that the young lovers could finally be briefly united in the
forest near Mantua. Before they could be united, however, they had
to overcome another obstacle. This obstacle was related to traces
of beastly or sensual attractions. Symbolically this obstacle was
illustrated as the appearance of a "hungry lion". Let's recall that in
"Two Gentlemen of Verona" Silvia alluded to the fact that sensual
attractions reduced Proteus to the beastly state of "a hungry lion":

"Had I been seized by a hungry lion,
I would have been a breakfast to the beast,
Rather than have false Proteus rescue me."
(*Two Gentlemen of Verona, V.4*)

Proteus' attempt to rape Silvia was a symbolic indication of this destructive tendency.

It was also sensual affection ("hungry lion") that led to the premature marriage of Romeo and Juliet. Juliet was not protected by the "beams of the watery moon". This is why Bottom announces in the last episode that his lover was "deflowered":

> "O wherefore, Nature, didst thou lions frame?
> Since lion vile hath here deflower'd my dear:
> Which is -no, no -which was the fairest dame
> That lived, that loved, that liked, that look'd
> with cheer."
> (*A Midsummer Night's Dream, V.1*)

"Since lion vile hath here deflower'd my dear" is not Bottom's malapropism. He states the fact: at her death Juliet was not a virgin.

The Moon

The "beams of the watery moon" may protect against the "hungry lioness". This is the role of the Moon in the next episode. Pyramus points out that this episode takes place in the full Moon:

> "Sweet Moon, I thank thee for thy sunny beams;
> I thank thee, Moon, for shining now so bright."
> (*A Midsummer Night's Dream, V.1*)

The Moon protects Thisbe against the lion. When Starveling recites:

> "This lanthorn doth the horned moon present."

Right away Theseus, who is the only member of the audience who understands the play, explains:

"He is no crescent, and his horns are
invisible within the circumference."
(*A Midsummer Night's Dream, V.1*)

In the episode with the Moon, Thisbe represents Rosaline from "Romeo and Juliet". At that time Rosaline was under Diana's protection against Romeo's sensual desires:

"she'll not be hit
With Cupid's arrow; she hath Dian's wit;
And, in strong proof of chastity well arm'd,
From love's weak childish bow she lives unharm'd."
(*Romeo and Juliet, I.1*)

Rosaline is removed from Verona and reappears as Diana in the French plays at the time of "All's Well That Ends Well". Then she reappears as Aliena in "As You Like It". This is presented as Thisbe running away from the lion and leaving behind a bloody mantle.

The Bloody Mantle

It was the reformation of Aliena's partner, Oliver, that was marked by a "bloody napkin" in "As You Like It". The "bloody napkin" was a symbolic sign indicating that the "hungry lioness" was overcome. Similarly, "a hungry lion" in the forest near Mantua was overcome by Valentine at the conclusion of "Two Gentlemen of Verona". Presently, the environment of the forest near Athens is a reflection of the forest near Mantua. The "hungry lion" was partially overcome by the application of Dian's bud.

The Wall

The first episode of the mechanicals' performance illustrates the current situation of Athens. The young couples face the same challenge as Pyramus and Thisbe. The "ancient grudge" that interferes with the process is again symbolically represented by a "wall", i.e., developmental inadequacies that are present within Athens. These inadequacies form a barrier against evolutionary progress. Remaining pieces of the "wall" have to be removed so Athens can be cleansed of its impurities. In this episode of "Pyramus and Thisbe", the "wall" reflects the animosity between Egeus and old Nedar, the fathers of Hermia and Helena, respectively. This animosity is an echo of the conflict between the Montagues and the Capulets described in "Romeo and Juliet". However, neither Lysander and Hermia nor Demetrius and Helena have to go through such a painful trial as their predecessors, because they have benefited from these previous experiences. At the time of the mechanicals' performance this particular "wall" has already been removed. This is indicated by the exit of Snout, who plays the Wall:

"Thus have I, Wall, my part discharged so;
And, being done, thus Wall away doth go."
(*A Midsummer Night's Dream*, V.1)

Theseus draws the audience's attention to this fact by emphasizing the meaning of Snout's exit:

"Now is the mural down between the two neighbours."
(*A Midsummer Night's Dream*, V.1)

In this way Theseus indicates that the remaining layer of the "wall" has been removed. It was removed at the moment of Titania's awakening. This is why the young lovers could arrive at a happy end.

***

Lysander's and Demetrius' experiences in the forest were needed to diagnose their inner state. As it turned out, their inner states were still somewhat corrupted. The same applies to Titania; she proved to be vulnerable to the effect of the juice. This is why it was necessary to patch them up with magic juice and Dian's bud so an octagonal union could be formed in Athens.

An octagonal union is formed at the end of the play. It consists of four couples, i.e., Theseus and Hippolyta, Oberon and Titania, Demetrius and Helena, Lysander and Hermia. Through the presence of Oberon and Titania, the octagon formed in Athens is an ascending one; it reaches the higher state. It provides a ladder allowing to climb up from the ordinary state of Athens to the Fairyland, i.e., beyond the ordinary limitations of time and space. In this way, a select group of Europeans was exposed to this latest experience of the *elephant*. It gave them a foretaste of a perfected state. However, because of its inner flaws, this octagonal structure could not be sustained. This octagon is inferior to that formed at the conclusion of "Pericles, Prince of Tyre". The higher state represented by the Fairyland is not of the highest quality yet. There is some hysteresis between Pentapolis and the Fairyland. Therefore, a fuller experience has to be delayed for some future time. At that future time, the patches affixed to the heart and the intellect faculties will either removed or replaced. The important thing is that there was a guide who was able to diagnose the situation and administer the needed remedy.

The formation of an octagonal union in the forest near Athens is the concluding episode of Shakespearean canon. It illustrates the outcome of the modern phase of the evolutionary process that was initiated in Western Europe after the completion of Pericles' mission. The formation of the Athenian octagon marked the commencement of the second spiritual millennium of the modern world.

The Two Noble Kinsmen

The inner design of Shakespeare's plays is invisible to a merely rational mind or a speculative intellect. This is why the analysis presented here will be wholly unconvincing to those who claim logic as the highest principle. It will appear to be no more than a proof based on selected instances. It can be easily ridiculed, particularly if taken out of context. Shakespeare illustrated this kind of incomprehension as the reaction of the young lovers who ridiculed the mechanicals' performance of "Pyramus and Thisby". Similarly, irritated Hamlet did not grasp the meaning of "The Murder of Gonzago" and as a result fell into his own mouse-trap. In other words, there is no rational or intellectual means to provide a proof of the interpretation of the plays. Neither is it possible to identify the inner structure of the plays by applying scholarly methods based on aesthetic or linguistic criteria.

It is possible, however, to enhance the visibility of the inner design of Shakespeare's plays. One way to provide such an insight would be to construct a "dumb play", i.e., a play from which the "music that may not be heard" is intentionally removed. Such a play would be based on the plot of one of Shakespeare's plays. It would employ some of Shakespeare's characters and episodes, but would be based on ordinary psychological and moralistic sequences. Its action would follow a linear thinking pattern and psychological realism. It would contain a number of Shakespeare's symbols, but used at random. It would also contain some references to developmental techniques, but applied incorrectly and used for the wrong purposes. Most importantly, the resonating relationship between a guide and his disciple would be removed. In other words, the play would be purposely sterilized by removing its inner content. In order to serve its purpose such a play would have to be written, at least partially, as beautifully as Shakespeare's plays. In this way the sterile content would be packaged in an attractive but meaningless container. Such a container would be decipherable by scholarly or intellectual inquiry: it would be accepted as one of Shakespeare's writings.

It turns out that such a sterilized play was purposely constructed. Its title is "The Two Noble Kinsmen". Its purpose was to demonstrate that the evolutionary progress achieved over the time span of several spiritual millennia belongs to the subtle areas of the human mind and is not detectable by ordinary intellectual, artistic, or scientific methods.

"The Two Noble Kinsmen" is an intentionally sterilized copy of "A Midsummer Night's Dream". It also contains several episodes taken from other Shakespeare plays. It includes Shakespeare's symbols and references to the developmental techniques. All of these are used incorrectly and for the wrong purposes. To further emphasize their misuse, the ways of their application are visibly caricatured. Most importantly, the fairy kingdom of "A Midsummer Night's Dream" is replaced by mythical gods: Mars, Venus, and Diana. Like in ancient myths, these corrupted demigods misuse their power for egotistic purposes. The characters of "The Two Noble Kinsmen" are subjected to their destructive interference. In this way, the play is a representation of a human mind that remains immune to the evolutionary impact of the modern evolutionary cycle.

It is believed that "The Two Noble Kinsmen" was released in 1613 or 1614. The play was first published in 1634 and attributed jointly to John Fletcher and William Shakespeare. The title page had a short note providing a clue to its purpose. Namely, Fletcher and Shakespeare are referred to as:

"the memorable Worthies of their time,"

and we may add, "i.e., Holofernes and Costard, respectively". Holofernes, a schoolmaster, prepared the script for the Nine Worthies' masque in "Love's Labour's Lost"; Costard used the masque to direct the process described in that play. This would indicate that Fletcher, obviously unfamiliar with the overall purpose of the play, wrote the plot. The play was then patched-up and caricatured by Shakespeare. For obvious reasons the play was not included in the 1623 First Folio. The play does not belong to Shakespeare's narrative. However, Shakespeare's name was needed to ensure the play's survival.

Until the 19th century "The Two Noble Kinsmen" was considered to be Fletcher's work. Then, the play's "container" attracted the attention of scholars. Scholars have applied a range of tests and techniques to justify Shakespeare's contributions to the play. Criteria such as metrical characteristics, vocabulary and word-compounding, incidence of certain contractions, kinds and uses of imagery, and characteristic lines of certain types have been used to identify Shakespeare's contributions. Since the 1970s "The Two Noble Kinsmen", i.e., this purposely made un-Shakespearean play, has regularly appeared in collected editions of Shakespeare's plays.

Theatre goers and readers, however, perceive that there is something wrong with "The Two Noble Kinsmen". The play is missing the incandescence and insights of Shakespeare's plays. The most striking feature of the play is the one-dimensionality of its characters: they remain virtually unchanged throughout the entire play. For these reasons, "The Two Noble Kinsmen" is considered to be Shakespeare's most unremarkable play.

In reality, however, "The Two Noble Kinsmen" is quite unique in English literature. It was purposely flawed to help us understand Shakespeare's narrative. However, the play may be fully appreciated only when analyzed in the context of the entire canon of Shakespeare's writings. Then it is possible to see through Shakespeare's message and smile when reading or watching it.

The Lame Man and the Blind Man

Let's recall that the main features of 17th century man were the inconstant aspects of the heart faculty (Lysander and Demetrius) and the highly developed but partially maculated aspect of the intellect faculty (Theseus). In "The Winter's Tale", Shakespeare used the term "lame" to describe a being with an incomplete spiritual heart faculty. In Berowne's meditation on *light*, Shakespeare used the term "blinded" to indicate a partially maculated intellect faculty.

In Sonnet 46 the poet describes his own inner state that corresponds to the situation illustrated in "A Midsummer Night's Dream". It is a state where the inner heart and the inner intellect are not permanent yet. They manifest themselves only occasionally and they are not harmonized. The poet compares this situation to "a mortal war" (another form of the war of the roses) between these two subtle faculties, which fight between themselves for dominance. Shakespeare refers to the inner intellect as "crystal eyes"; the inner heart is described as "the dear heart":

"Mine eye and heart are at a mortal war,
How to divide the conquest of thy sight,
Mine eye, my heart their picture's sight would bar,
My heart, mine eye the freedom of that right,
My heart doth plead that thou in him dost lie,
(A closet never pierced with crystal eyes)
But the defendant doth that plea deny,
And says in him thy fair appearance lies.
To side this title is impannelled
A quest of thoughts, all tenants to the heart,
And by their verdict is determined
The clear eye's moiety, and the dear heart's part.

As thus, mine eye's due is thine outward part,
And my heart's right, thine inward love of heart."

The poet says that his eye does not allow his inner heart to contemplate the guide's essence. The poet's inner heart, on the other hand, disputes whether the eye has the rights to the guide's sight. The inner heart pleads that the essence is stored in him, i.e., a place beyond the eye's reach. But the defending eye denies that claim, and argues that sight is stored in him. To decide whose claim is right, the poet has set-up a panel of jurors. The jurors have declared that the poet's eye has the right to admire the guide's beautiful form, while the inner heart has the duty to immerse itself in the guide's essence.

Despite a lame heart and a partially blind intellect, progress could be made by applying an advanced developmental methodology that was made available at that time. In accordance with this methodology, progress could be achieved by patching up these partially developed faculties and then uniting them, so they could form a temporary octagonal union. Such a union gives a foretaste of a higher state of mind. This experience awakens an inner hunger that has a lasting effect, even for a long time after the disintegration of the union. It is this inner hunger that induces a thirst for some unknown but important knowledge. In this way, man is encouraged to move forward and get closer to the completion of his ultimate evolutionary purpose.

Such a patched up evolutionary state, including a recipe for evolutionary advancement, was prescribed by the King from India, the father of the Indian Prince. This Indian Sage, known as the "Regenerator of the second spiritual millennium", lived at the same time as Shakespeare. He provided the diagnosis and the remedy in his story entitled "The Lame Man and the Blind Man". Like in Shakespeare's writings, the lame man represents an inconstant heart faculty, while the blind man is a partially maculated intellect faculty. None of these faculties on its own is capable of moving forward. The story explains how, despite these deficiencies, progress could be made[7]:

> "A lame man walked into an inn one day, and sat down beside a figure already seated there. 'I shall never be able to reach the king's banquet', he sighed, 'because due to my infirmity, I am unable to move fast enough'.
> The other man raised his head, 'I, too, have been invited', he said, 'but my plight is worse than yours. I am blind, and cannot see the road, although I have also been invited'.
> A third man who heard them talking said: 'But, if you only realized it, you two have between you the means to reach your destination. The blind man can walk, with the lame one on his back. You can use the feet of the blind man and the eyes of the lame to direct you'.
> Thus the two were able to reach the end of the road, where the feast awaited them."

The story encapsulates the entire Shakespearean cannon. The lame man and the blind man are a snapshot of the evolutionary state of a select group of people living in Western Europe in the early 17th century. Such men could move forward, but only if there was a third man, a Friend, whom they would have to recognize and who would explain that there was a difficulty and how this difficulty could be overcome. Shakespeare was such a Friend. In this way, ordinary man has been provided with instructions which allow him to walk out of the darkness and perceive the true essence of the formless *elephant*.

---

[7] This version of the story is included in Idries Shah's "Tales of the Dervishes" (Octagon Press, London, 1967)

REFERENCES

"Tales of the Dervishes", Idries Shah, Octagon Press (1967)

"Shakespeare for the Seeker", Volume 1, W. Jamroz, Troubadour Publications (2012)

"Shakespeare for the Seeker", Volume 2, W. Jamroz, Troubadour Publications (2013)

"Shakespeare for the Seeker", Volume 3, W. Jamroz, Troubadour Publications (2013)

"Shakespeare for the Seeker", Volume 4, W. Jamroz, Troubadour Publications (2013)

"Shakespeare's Sonnets or How heavy do I journey on the way", W. Jamroz, Troubadour Publications (2014)

"Shakespeare's Sequel to Rumi's Teaching", W. Jamroz, Troubadour Publications (2015)